BEYOND PRO-LIFE AND PRO-CHOICE

The Changing Politics of
Abortion in Britain

Fran Amery

First published in Great Britain in 2020 by

Bristol University Press
1-9 Old Park Hill
Bristol
BS2 8BB
UK
t: +44 (0)117 954 5940
www.bristoluniversitypress.co.uk

North America office:
c/o The University of Chicago Press
1427 East 60th Street
Chicago, IL 60637, USA
t: +1 773 702 7700
f: +1 773-702-9756
sales@press.uchicago.edu
www.press.uchicago.edu

© Bristol University Press 2020

British Library Cataloguing in Publication Data
A catalogue record for this book is available from the British Library

Library of Congress Cataloging-in-Publication Data
A catalog record for this book has been requested

ISBN 978-1-5292-0499-5 hardcover
ISBN 978-1-5292-0537-4 paperback
ISBN 978-1-5292-0538-1 ePub
ISBN 978-1-5292-0536-7 ePdf

The right of Fran Amery to be identified as author of this work has been asserted by her in accordance with the Copyright, Designs and Patents Act 1988.

All rights reserved: no part of this publication may be reproduced, stored in a retrieval system, or transmitted in any form or by any means, electronic, mechanical, photocopying, recording, or otherwise without the prior permission of Bristol University Press.

The statements and opinions contained within this publication are solely those of the author and not of the University of Bristol or Bristol University Press. The University of Bristol and Bristol University Press disclaim responsibility for any injury to persons or property resulting from any material published in this publication.

Bristol University Press works to counter discrimination on grounds of gender, race, disability, age and sexuality.

Cover design by blu Inc, Bristol
Front cover image: Stocksy

Contents

List of Tables		iv
List of Abbreviations		v
Acknowledgements		vi
1	Introduction	1
2	Regulating the Female Body	13
3	Passing the Abortion Act 1967	39
4	Feminism Enters the Debate	67
5	Backlash and Appropriation	95
6	Into the 21st Century	123
7	Towards Decriminalization? New Battlegrounds in Abortion Politics	145
8	Conclusion	177
Notes		193
References		197
Index		221

List of Tables

3.1	'Social' concerns in the Silkin and Steel Bills	51
4.1	Abortion Bills, 1969–80	71
5.1	Abortion Bills, 1981–99	96
6.1	Abortion Bills, 2005–12	124
7.1	Abortion Bills, 2013–19	146

List of Abbreviations

ALRA	Abortion Law Reform Association
APPGSRH	All Party Parliamentary Group on Sexual and Reproductive Health
BAME	Black, Asian and minority ethnic
BMA	British Medical Association
BMJ	*British Medical Journal*
BPAS	British Pregnancy Advisory Service
CEDAW	Convention or Committee on the Elimination of all forms of Discrimination Against Women
CQC	Care Quality Commission
D&X	dilation and extraction
DUP	Democratic Unionist Party
EBP	evidence-based policy-making
EVAW	End Violence Against Women
FSRH	Faculty of Sexual and Reproductive Healthcare
HFE Bill/Act	Human Fertilisation and Embryology Bill/Act
HFEA	Human Fertilisation and Embryology Authority
IKWRO	Iranian and Kurdish Women's Rights Organisation
LGBTQ	Lesbian, gay, bisexual, transgender, queer or questioning
MWF	Medical Women's Federation
NAC	National Abortion Campaign
NAPAWF	National Asian Pacific American Women's Forum
NIPT	non-invasive prenatal testing
OAPA	Offences Against the Person Act
PRCH	Physicians for Reproductive Choice and Health
PRH	Physicians for Reproductive Health
RCN	Royal College of Nursing
RCOG	Royal College of Obstetricians and Gynaecologists
RMPA	Royal Medico-Psychological Association
SPUC	Society for the Protection of Unborn Children
TUC	Trades Union Congress

Acknowledgements

I began this research at the University of Birmingham. I am particularly grateful to my supervisors, Stephen Bates and Nicola Smith, for their encouragement, especially in the uncertain first stages of the project, but also for their continued support and advice throughout my career. I would also like to thank Shelley Budgeon, Emma Foster and Laura Jenkins, who provided invaluable feedback at various stages of writing. At Birmingham I was also extremely lucky to be part of a large and welcoming doctoral research community comprised of Linda Åhäll, Laurence Cooley, Drew Futter, Charlotte Galpin, Cherry Miller, Dave Norman, Jonna Nyman, Ken Searle, Liam Stanley, Ben Taylor and many others.

Beyond Birmingham, huge thanks are due Sarah Childs for her feedback and mentorship in the very early stages of my career. I would also like to thank all of the research participants who contributed their time to this project, in particular Abigail Fitzgibbon for her extremely helpful explanations and feedback. A substantial amount of research for the book was conducted in post at the University of Bath, and I am immensely appreciative of all my colleagues in the Department of Politics, Languages and International Studies who provided a warm and supportive environment in which to undertake the project. Special thanks are due Peter Allen, Sophia Hatzisavvidou and David Moon for their feedback on later sections.

This research was funded in part by an Economic and Social Research Council studentship and a British Academy small grant. I am grateful to the funders for making the book possible. Finally, I could not have written this without the lifelong encouragement of my parents and my sister Carolyn (even if I am not a proper doctor). Fran Barer, thanks for being the truest friend anyone could have. Ian Evans and Jenny Heilig, thanks for making me smile always. Sammy Wernick: whatever life throws at us, I would not want to do it without you.

1

Introduction

'Available on demand – an abortion if it's a boy you wanted.' This was the title of a February 2012 *Daily Telegraph* article reporting on a sting operation carried out by the newspaper. *Telegraph* journalists had visited multiple abortion clinics in Britain, posing as women requesting an abortion because of the sex of the foetus. The *Daily Telegraph* reported that its journalists decided to conduct the investigation after (unnamed) 'doctors, academics and pro-life campaigners all alleged that the procedure was being offered at specific organisations' (Watt et al, 2012). The article claimed to have found two doctors working in private practices who were willing to authorize an 'illegal' termination on the grounds of foetal sex alone. The clinics in question were subsequently reported to the police by the Health Secretary, Andrew Lansley.

Although the Crown Prosecution Service ultimately decided not to prosecute either of the accused doctors, sex-selective abortion ballooned into a major political issue. The *Telegraph* article cited a 2007 study that showed a skewed sex ratio among children born to 'Indian-born' women in England and Wales and suggested that this was evidence for sex-selective abortion occurring on a wide scale (Dubuc and Coleman, 2007). Media outlets were quick to raise fears about migrants importing the practice from their country of origin; an article in *The Independent*, for example, claimed that sex-selective abortions were now 'commonplace' among 'some ethnic communities' (Connor, 2014). A particular concern was that women with migrant backgrounds might be forced into having abortions by family members if they were carrying a female foetus. In collaboration with South Asian women's campaign groups Jeena International and Karma Nirvana, the Conservative MP Fiona Bruce launched the Stop Gendercide campaign with the aim of ending the practice.

While the *Daily Telegraph* journalists only managed to secure two appointments in private clinics, and none with major charitable abortion providers such as the British Pregnancy Advisory Service (BPAS) or Marie Stopes, the major providers found themselves dragged into the controversy. The day after its initial story, the *Daily Telegraph* published a further report alleging that a BPAS counsellor had agreed to 'forge paperwork' to allow a woman (accompanied by another undercover reporter) to have an abortion because she wanted a boy instead (Newell, 2012). The appointment was cancelled before the 'patient' had left the premises (and, as discussed in Chapter 7, BPAS dispute the *Daily Telegraph's* version of events). But the case was held up as further evidence that clinics could not be trusted to obey the law. Shortly afterwards, the Health Secretary ordered a wave of surprise inspections on abortion clinics due to allegations that doctors were 'pre-signing' batches of abortion paperwork without seeing the patients first. Former Liberal MP and long-time anti-abortion campaigner Lord Alton opined that abortions had 'become too routine' (Mason, 2013), while during Parliamentary interventions on the issue, MPs heard lurid accounts of 'young Asian girls' being 'marched into clinics' by family members (Dorries in Hansard, 2012: 74–5).

It should be noted here that the legality of sex-selective abortion is contested. The law as it stands makes no mention of sex selection, allowing abortion before 24 weeks' gestation in cases where two doctors have agreed that to continue the pregnancy would involve 'risk, greater than if the pregnancy were terminated, of injury to the physical or mental health of the pregnant woman' (Abortion Act, 1967: s1). In practice, this section of the Abortion Act 1967 is interpreted fairly widely; for example, while age is not an explicit legal ground for abortion, doctors might permit a teenager to have an abortion on the basis that, due to her young age, to carry the pregnancy to term might result in harm to her mental health. Stop Gendercide campaigners argue that sex selection is already illegal, as the sex of the foetus is not named as a legal ground for termination (although they campaign for the law to make this 'explicit'). On the other hand, Ann Furedi, the chief executive of BPAS, suggested that sex selection is legal as long as the legal grounds for abortion are met – if, for example, doctors believe that the woman requesting an abortion could come to harm were her family to discover that she was pregnant with a girl (Furedi, 2013a).

The sex-selection allegations were made in the context of a media climate that is increasingly hostile to migrants, and many of the stories exploit xenophobic fears. Therefore, discussions of sex selection should be cautious and avoid making sweeping claims about any ethnic or national group. This is not to claim that sex selection should not be taken seriously. While recent government reports find no evidence of sex-selective abortion taking place in Britain on a significant enough scale to alter sex ratios at birth among any ethnic group (Department of Health, 2015; 2016), son preference is a real issue facing some South Asian women, and some accounts suggest that sex selection may be taking place on a very small scale (Gupta, 2014). The practice poses clear difficulties for defences for legal abortion based in the rhetoric of 'choice' and 'women's rights'. The selective abortion of female foetuses – where it happens – is a clear case of gender-based discrimination, and campaigners against sex-selective abortion argue that many women undergoing such abortions have not freely chosen them but rather face pressure or coercion from family members.

Interpreting abortion law

The sex-selection debate is just one example of how the terrain of abortion politics has changed in the UK in the 21st century. Recently, disability rights campaigners have sought to abolish the section of the Abortion Act that allows abortion up until birth if 'there is a substantial risk that if the child were born it would suffer from such physical or mental abnormalities as to be seriously handicapped', arguing that it represents discrimination on the grounds of disability. MPs have also introduced Bills attempting to regulate the provision of counselling to women seeking abortion. Some of these would have required women requesting abortion to undergo mandatory counselling, on the basis that women have a 'right to know' that abortion might (according to anti-abortion groups) have negative consequences for their mental health. Others would have prevented clinics from providing counselling in-house, requiring instead that counselling be provided by an independent party. Abortion rights advocates saw this as an attempt to chip away confidence in abortion providers by suggesting they were unable to give objective and professional advice to women seeking their services. What is striking about all of these interventions is their use of the language of rights and equality (in particular gender equality) in ways that are typically associated with the pro-choice movement.

More recently, however, there have been calls for substantial liberalization of abortion law. Most significant of these was a successful cross-party initiative to require the UK government to liberalize abortion in Northern Ireland, where the Abortion Act 1967 never applied, if Northern Ireland's own devolved government did not reconvene by 21 October 2019. This was a huge, game-changing achievement given the predominance of anti-abortion views in Northern Irish politics, and the influence of the anti-abortion Democratic Unionist Party (DUP) over the sitting UK government. The initiative was linked to a broader parliamentary push for the decriminalization of abortion throughout the UK. The Abortion Act 1967 did not abolish criminal sanctions attached to abortion, but rather protects those who have abortions from prosecution if two doctors agree that certain grounds are met. This 'two-doctor rule' has faced challenge for some time on the grounds that it patronizes women and inhibits the efficient delivery of abortion care (Sheldon, 1997; 2016a; 2016b), but more recent campaigns go further in calling for the removal of criminal sanctions entirely. These campaigns originally extended only to England and Wales. Scottish law deals with abortion sanctions differently, while Northern Ireland was originally regarded as 'too difficult' by British politicians. Yet following the 2018 referendum decision to overturn the constitutional ban on abortion in the Republic of Ireland, Northern Ireland was swept into the decriminalization cause.

The current state of the abortion debate therefore cannot be easily characterized in terms of 'pro-life' versus 'pro-choice'. The broader pro-life and pro-choice movements may well inform the actions of prominent figures in the debate, but actors' positions can be complex. For example, many MPs who identify as pro-choice were initially reticent to speak out against the proposed ban on sex-selective abortion. While new battlegrounds have sprung up in the 21st century, the argument of this book is that battles over the legal status of abortion in Britain have *never* split simply along pro-life versus pro-choice fault lines. This is because the Abortion Act itself did not straightforwardly grant a 'right to choose' to have an abortion. Its sections, and the arguments they sparked, exert a substantial influence on abortion debates today.

The idea of a 'right to choose' (or even a 'right to privacy' as in the 1973 *Roe v Wade* decision in the US) was barely part of the language of abortion law reformers in the 1960s. Rather, advocates pointed to the mounting illegitimacy of the existing law in the face of increasing rates of illegal abortion. The cause was helped along by the perception that there was a 'law for the rich', as wealthier women were able to access semi-legal abortions in private medical practices, while poorer women generally had to resort to less safe 'backstreet' methods. The debate also drew public attention to issues of social hardship: the plight of families living in poverty and poor housing, the suffering of women 'overburdened' by too many children, and the fear that some women might be unfit mothers. In short, legal abortion came to be seen by many as a (partial) solution to a host of social problems.

The Abortion Act 1967 did not therefore grant women a 'right to choose'. Rather, it created a coalition between government and medical actors in order to govern women's reproductive decision-making (Sheldon, 1997). The law as it currently stands does not allow 'abortion on demand' – as discussed earlier, there are still criminal sanctions associated with abortion – but rather permits abortion in certain medically controlled circumstances. In most cases this will mean that two doctors have agreed that the pregnancy represents a risk to the pregnant woman's physical or mental health. In other words, the Abortion Act 1967 assigned a paternalistic role to medical professionals in women's reproductive decision-making. Women were to be delivered into the hands of competent doctors, not just because women needed to access safe abortions carried out in hygienic conditions, but also due to the perception that women could not be trusted to make the abortion decision alone – what if women were to seek abortion for 'frivolous' reasons?

Abortion rights campaigners now criticize the Act on the grounds that it is fundamentally patronizing to women. But in the 1960s, in Parliament and among the medical profession, debate raged over the status of the doctor and 'his' relationship to society. Opponents of reform questioned whether 'medical' solutions ought to be sought to 'social' problems, and whether the medical regulation of abortion might transform the identity of the doctor in unacceptable ways. As Chapter 3 shows, this – more than questions of the foetus's 'right to life' or lack of such – was the major stumbling-block to reform. This book demonstrates that abortion debates in the UK still hinge on the identity of doctors, their relationship to women seeking abortions, and their relationship with wider society.

Where we are now

While abortion law has not changed greatly since 1967 – the main alteration being to lower the legal time limit for most abortions from 28 to 24 weeks' gestation – accessing abortion has become much easier in practice. This is due to the expansion across Britain of charitable abortion providers who receive funding from the National Health Service (NHS). However, as this book demonstrates, subsequent debates on abortion have very much been shaped by the original settlement. While the notions of a 'right to life' or the 'rights of the unborn' have remained a constant feature of anti-abortion activism outside of Parliament, it has historically been rare for serious legislative attacks on the Abortion Act 1967 to be framed in such terms. Instead,

Parliamentary opponents of the Act have attempted to portray abortions as harmful to the women having them. Instead of trying to repeal the Act, they have sought to make its terms more restrictive.

Early attempts to amend the Act appealed to the widespread perception of a 'racket' developing in abortion provision, suggesting that doctors in the private sector were neglecting normal standards of care in the pursuit of profit. Such efforts undermined the image of the benevolent, paternalistic physician envisioned by reformists in 1967, instead constructing the 'professional abortionist', a doctor who is irresponsible, profit-hungry and immoral, as a new fear figure. This line of attack on the Abortion Act has been revived in various ways since 1967. Calls for mandatory counselling for women requesting abortions on the basis that clinics cannot be trusted to properly inform women of the health consequences of abortion, or the allegation that some clinics will perform sex-selective abortions 'on demand', are merely its 21st-century incarnations.

'Pro-choice' actors in Parliament have, meanwhile, been forced to defend a regulatory regime that was not created with 'choice' in mind. Even after the language of feminism and women's rights entered popular discourse on abortion, parliamentarians have tended to justify their support for the Act using the old language of women's vulnerability and neediness, frequently appealing to medical authority as legitimating women's reproductive choices. The feeling was that arguments that relied heavily on feminism, rather than on medical opinion, would not resonate within Parliament. While pro-choice campaigners and abortion providers have long called for the removal of criminal sanctions on abortion, their arguments achieved little purchase within Parliament until very recently.

This book argues that this state of affairs is the logical outcome of what was set in motion by the 1967 Act. The Act created a paternalistic relationship between women and their doctors, in which doctors are situated as the gatekeepers of women's reproductive decision-making. This relationship has always been vulnerable to attack. Opponents are able to undermine both the assumption that doctors will always have women's best interests at heart and the assumption that abortion is necessary to protect women's 'health'. Those seeking to undermine the Act have always focused their attention on the relationship between women and doctors that it brought into being, and alleged medical misbehaviour is typically at the heart of the argument that abortion harms women.

But the state of affairs brought into being by the Act is now growing unsustainable on another front. Major medical organizations in the

UK now no longer support the current regime. In June 2017, doctors' representatives within the British Medical Association (BMA) voted in support of the decriminalization of abortion. Three months later, the Council of the Royal College of Obstetricians and Gynaecologists (RCOG) followed suit, stating that 'abortion – for women, doctors and other healthcare professionals – should be treated as a medical, rather than a criminal issue' (RCOG, 2017). The BMA has since 2007 held the policy that the Act's requirement for women seeking abortions to meet specified medical criteria, and for two doctors to sign off on the abortion, should be removed. Similarly, the RCOG has argued since 2008 that the need for two signatures is 'anachronistic' (RCOG, 2008).

What happens when a law rests on the idea that doctor knows best, but doctors themselves begin to disavow this authority? The current settlement for abortion regulation has become unstable. Abortion rights campaigners have seized this moment to press for the removal of criminal sanctions altogether. As mentioned earlier, this has long been an aim of the pro-choice movement in the UK – but it is now, finally, beginning to resonate elsewhere. Significantly, there is now Parliamentary support for decriminalization. Where once pro-choice MPs feared to rock the boat too much, feeling that their priority was to defend a problematic status quo from attack, some MPs are now pushing for further liberalization. Abortion has now been decriminalized in Northern Ireland. But the Labour MP Diana Johnson has also introduced two Bills calling for the decriminalization of abortion in England and Wales. MPs voted in favour of both Bills passing to the next legislative stage. As the Bills were introduced under the Ten Minute Rule,[1] they were never likely to progress, but this is a significant development.

Another critical development is the growing awareness of intersecting inequalities in abortion debates, particularly relating to race and migration and, to a lesser extent in the debates, disability. In the wake of the sex-selection allegations, British pro-choice organizations looked to the US 'reproductive justice' movement for guidance on how to proceed. The concept of reproductive justice was pioneered by networks of grass-roots organizations in the US advocating for the sexual and reproductive rights of black and African American, Asian/Pacific Islander, Middle Eastern/Arab American, Latina, and Native American women. The reproductive justice movement has drawn attention to the ways in which reproduction and maternity intersect with matters of race and class, and, in doing so, has highlighted the marginalization of minority ethnic women within mainstream reproductive rights organizations (Luna, 2009). This book suggests that there are lessons here for UK politics.

Analysing abortion debates

This book is an account of the parliamentary life of the Abortion Act 1967, and its journey towards increasing instability. More specifically, it is an analysis of the shifting *governmentality* of abortion in the UK. According to Nikolas Rose, analyses of governmentality:

> are not studies of the actual organization and operation of systems of rule ... They are studies of a particular 'stratum' of knowing and acting. Of the emergence of particular 'regimes of truth' concerning the conduct of conduct, ways of speaking truth, persons authorized to speak truths, ways of enacting truths and the costs of so doing. Of the invention and assemblage of particular apparatuses and devices for exercising power and intervening upon particular problems. (1999: 19)

The 'apparatuses and devices' for intervening in abortion were developed in Parliament and in negotiations between MPs and various sectors of the medical profession, particularly during the controversy over the 'social clause' of the Abortion Act and the change in doctors' roles it seemed to imply (Amery, 2014). Parliament has remained the main site in which the abortion regime is contested, as evidenced by the 37 Private Members Bills introduced since 1967 that have attempted to amend the Act, plus the various amendments to items of government legislation tabled by backbenchers. Parliamentary debates may not always succeed in persuading MPs to change their stance on an issue, but as 'the symbolic centre of representative democracies' they do 'provide the semantic as well as the symbolic framework within which important social and political questions can be represented' (Bayley, 2004: 12–13). The legislative process is a key site in which negotiations and clashes between different actors are played out, and it is through these struggles that discursive coalitions between different actors (say, abortion reformers, women seeking abortion and the medical profession) are formed.

While Parliament's capacity to initiate legislation is generally limited (Norton, 2005), this is less true in the case of abortion. As abortion is a 'conscience issue', voting on abortion Bills is unwhipped and there is no 'party line'. In addition, the executive does not introduce abortion legislation, although it may help or hinder the progress of a Bill by apportioning time for votes and debates (Marsh and Chambers, 1981). Women's policy agencies, an important focus of much recent feminist analysis, also tend to remain quiet on the issue of abortion (McBride Stetson, 2001a; 2001b; Lovenduski, 2007: 160). Of course, meaning-construction among the medical profession and among women who have abortions is also a crucial aspect of abortion provision, and this has been written about elsewhere (see for example Hoggart, 2012; Beynon-Jones, 2012; 2013).

This book looks primarily, then, at parliamentary debates, bolstered by analysis of relevant documents produced by members of the medical profession and prominent campaigners and interviews with key players. Its scope is restricted to debates in the UK Parliament concerning abortion. This excludes debates about abortion taking place in the Scottish Parliament, the National Assembly for Wales and the Northern Ireland Assembly. However, it does include debates taking place *inside* the Westminster Parliament about Scotland, Wales and Northern Ireland – in particular, the recent debates about decriminalization in the latter. There is a substantial body of research on abortion debates in Northern Ireland's devolved legislature (Side, 2006; Bloomer and Fegan, 2013; Thomson, 2016; 2018a; 2018b; Pierson and Bloomer, 2017; 2018).

Legislative debates do not take place in a bubble but are inextricably linked to socio-political contexts and governmental regimes. In giving an account of the Abortion Act 1967, how it was negotiated and its lasting effects today, this book therefore draws extensively on feminist critique – not just of the Abortion Act itself (of which there is plenty) but also of the role played by reproduction in sexist political and social structures, and thereby of the significance of abortion rights for women's social status. Understanding abortion politics requires a feminist analysis that goes beyond advocating for a legal right to choose. While it has been significant for advocates in helping justify abortion rights to the wider public, the language of 'choice' does not always capture the power relations involved in reproductive decision-making, from the stereotyping of some women as 'unfit' mothers, to individual material circumstances that may render some perfectly legal 'choices' unviable, to political and medical interventions that aim at ensuring that abortions are morally 'justified' or that the 'right' women are having children. The analysis presented here is thereby informed by an account of power, social relations and social movements, with a particular focus on the relationship between feminist and pro-choice actors and the medical profession. It follows the argument of many feminists that the Abortion Act 1967 does not operate as a means of liberating women but rather a means of regulating women's bodies (Fyfe, 1991; Petersen, 1993; Sheldon, 1997).

One final note on terminology: this book talks primarily about 'women' as those targeted by the law. However, women are not the only people directly affected by abortion legislation; transgender men and non-binary people also need access to abortion. LGBTQ activists rightly called for new abortion laws in Ireland to use gender-neutral language, fearing that any law that extends abortion rights only to 'pregnant women' might prevent those who have updated their legal gender markers, and are therefore legally *not* women, from accessing abortion (Braidwood, 2018). Their concerns are well-founded; laws must be drafted in inclusive language. Nonetheless, this book talks about 'women' because the law primarily targets women and it is a specific vision of womanhood – as fragile, irrational, frivolous and in need of protection – that lawmakers had in mind when drafting the Abortion Act 1967. This vision still haunts abortion discourse today and is what this book intends to critique.

Structure of the book

This book explains abortion debates today by placing them in historical context. Chapter 2 discusses the history of abortion law in the UK before the Abortion Act 1967, and sets this in the context of feminist critique, exploring the significance of access to abortion for women's lives and the gendered structure of society. This requires a discussion of feminist writing on pregnancy and motherhood and what these mean for female subjectivity: from Simone de Beauvoir's description of pregnancy as a 'servitude', to Shulamith Firestone's call for reproductive technologies that can separate the process of reproduction from women's bodies, to critiques of how the law has historically handled pregnancy and pregnant women's rights. This chapter also explores the reproductive justice movement, which has emphasized intersectionality in reproductive rights and, in particular, the ways in which the needs of poor, minority ethnic and migrant women may differ from those of white middle-class women: such women often struggle for their right *to* have children, as well as their right to access abortion.

The chapter argues that access to abortion can have radical implications for women's lives, freeing women from compulsory motherhood. Yet celebratory accounts of abortion in the UK must be tempered. Abortion law has always relied heavily on the capacity of the medical profession to regulate women's reproductive choices, displacing control over reproductive decisions from women onto doctors. The Abortion Act 1967 was no exception. Chapter 3 looks at the debates surrounding the passage of the Act and how it operated to extend medical power over abortion. It argues that in order for medicalization to take place, it was necessary to convince doctors that they had a legitimate 'social' as well as 'medical' role. This was achieved in particular through a series of revisions to the controversial 'social clause' of the Act, which provided for abortions for non-medical reasons. Constructions of women seeking abortion as victims or essentially vulnerable – and therefore in need of the authority and paternalistic guidance of the doctor – were central to this process.

Chapter 4 considers the entry of feminist arguments about abortion into parliamentary debates in the 1970s. By the mid-1970s, a contingent of MPs willing to advocate for legal abortion on feminist grounds had developed. However, the wording of the Abortion Act 1967 placed feminist actors in a difficult position; the gendered implications of the Act were troubling, but at the same time it was essential to defend it from attack by opponents of legal abortion. This resulted in some tricky compromises, in which feminist actors would defend a 'right to choose' without examining the failure of the Act to provide exactly that. Yet difficulties were present for anti-abortion actors, who risked being perceived as being 'against' helping vulnerable women. Anti-abortion speeches during this period were ambiguous and confused in how they discussed women, oscillating between portrayals of women seeking abortion as immoral criminals and tragic victims exploited by the medical profession.

Chapter 5 continues this line of analysis into the 1980s and 1990s. By this point, anti-abortion actors were attempting to solve their PR problem by mimicking their opponents' arguments, moving away from a conservative emphasis on morality and vice, and towards an appropriation of the liberal-paternalist and feminist arguments that had been put forward in support of legal abortion. This was done by adopting seemingly feminist language in talking about medical power, exploitation and women's rights. Pro-choice and feminist actors, on the other hand, typically avoided challenging the logics underpinning the Abortion Act 1967. Few alternatives to the current, highly medicalized system of abortion provision were proffered; rather, pro-choice actors were forced into a reactive position defending the Act from anti-abortion attacks.

Chapters 6 and 7 examine abortion debates in the 21st century. Chapter 6 demonstrates how issues such as foetal viability and pre-abortion counselling evolved as a consequence both of past anti-abortion activity *and* how pro-choice feminist actors have made their arguments. The chapter argues that counselling amendments are proposed because they undermine the association between a 'right to choose' and feminist politics and call into question the medical authority on which the Abortion Act 1967 is based. Subsequently, Chapter 7 focuses on the newest battlegrounds in the abortion debate: growing calls for decriminalization and the increasing purchase these are finding inside Parliament, but also new debates about sex-selective abortion and abortion in the cases of severe disability, and the need for the pro-choice movement to organize horizontally to address the needs of all women. It ends with an assessment of the future prospects of both the movement for decriminalization and the movement for more restrictive abortion law.

Chapter 8 first places this discussion in the context of global abortion politics. This entails drawing parallels between, for example, pre-abortion counselling proposals in the UK and similar 'woman-centred' (Cannold, 2002) anti-abortion strategies elsewhere – but also requires situating an intersectional analysis of abortion in the context of the struggle for reproductive justice worldwide, touching on issues of race, ethnicity, migration and nation. There has recently been a twofold shift in the terrain of pro-choice argument in the UK. One the one hand, the pro-choice coalition has shifted from a politics of protection – which emphasizes women's vulnerability and thereby supports a paternalistic, medicalized regime of abortion regulation – to a politics of liberation, which emphasizes women's authority over their own reproductive decisions. On the other hand, there is a growing need to acknowledge intersectional or reproductive justice claims in abortion politics. The coalition has had to wake up to the reality that it has been dominated by middle-class, white and able-bodied women, and adjust its campaigning strategies to incorporate more marginalized groups of women – including those who may well be in very vulnerable positions. The book closes by asking whether the pro-choice movement is being pulled in two different directions, and how it can steer between them.

2

Regulating the Female Body

The aim of this chapter is to think through the significance of motherhood and the reproductive body for women's lives and social status and, in doing so, to demonstrate the radical potential held by access to safe and legal abortion. The classic arguments regarding the 'status of the foetus' (a life or not a life? A person or not a person?) are well-rehearsed and will not be visited in this chapter. Rather, the chapter explores the social significance of reproductive choice. This provides the necessary context for understanding how and why legislators intervene in reproduction, why British abortion regulation has taken the form that it has, and what it means when feminists enter the debate.

This chapter's argument is that access to abortion, alongside access to contraception, is potentially liberatory in that it undoes the association of female embodiment with inevitable motherhood: instead, it presents the possibility that motherhood can be active, engaged, a *choice*. The ability to delay or reject motherhood altogether opens an array of possibilities to women in terms of employment and education. As such, most feminists view legal abortion as a vital step in achieving gender equality. However, these are only *potential* implications of legal abortion. In practice, the liberatory potential of abortion can be constrained in many ways, most pertinently through regulatory systems that reinforce motherhood (Orr, 2017: 108–9) and oblige women to submit to medical authority in the abortion decision and, through racist, classist and ableist social systems that value certain (white, middle-class, able-bodied) women's reproduction while discouraging – or even forcibly preventing – others from reproducing.

These insights are not new, and this chapter draws heavily on excellent work already done by feminist theorists starting with Simone de Beauvoir, as well as the more recent work of feminist legal and policy scholars. However, it argues that a reproductive justice approach that acknowledges intersecting systems such as race and class can add to analysis of UK abortion law and politics. The mainstream reproductive rights movement has extremely valuable insights regarding the sexist basis of British abortion law and the role played by medical authorities in regulating abortion – insights that are now serving it well in the push for full decriminalization. However, it has been worse equipped to deal with some counter-campaigns that have emerged in the last decade, particularly those claiming to address other issues of human rights and equality, such as sex-selective abortion and disability rights.

Pregnancy, motherhood and feminism

Feminists have long argued that lack of control over one's ability to reproduce (or not) is experienced as dehumanizing and alienating. This section begins with Simone de Beauvoir's (2011 [1949]) account of the significance of female embodiment, which has proven controversial among feminists. As a forerunner to later feminist arguments regarding the difference between 'sex' (as biological) and 'gender' (as sociocultural), de Beauvoir resisted any attempt to draw a straight line between 'biological facts' and social outcomes, arguing that biology is not destiny. However, key to her philosophy was the belief that an individual's body is a central aspect of their experience of the world – and of themselves. Pregnancy and reproduction therefore took a central – if somewhat ambivalent – role in de Beauvoir's analysis of women's situation.

Simone de Beauvoir was keen to resist any simplistic identification of women with pregnancy and motherhood, arguing that women's bodies need not be defined by their reproductive capacity. Nonetheless, in her account, this capacity had devastating consequences. The onset of menstruation itself, she averred, seems to inhibit the potential for agency, bringing home to women that their bodies are 'the prey of a stubborn and foreign life', 'alienated and opaque thing[s]' beyond their control (2011 [1949]: 42). This alienation, however, is intensified during pregnancy. She describes pregnancy as a 'servitude' which places women in 'the grip of the species' (2011 [1949]: 43). Reproductive capacity, for de Beauvoir, seemed to eat away at both women's bodies and women's freedom in a way that it cannot for men. She wrote:

> [Woman] is the most deeply alienated of all the female mammals, and she is the one that refuses this alienation most violently; in no other is the subordination of the organism to the reproductive function more imperious nor

accepted with greater difficulty. Crises of puberty and of the menopause, monthly 'curse', long and often troubled pregnancy, illnesses and accidents are characteristic of the human female: her destiny appears more fraught the more she rebels against it by affirming herself as an individual. The male, by comparison, is infinitely more privileged: his genital life does not thwart his personal existence; it unfolds seamlessly, without crises and generally without accident. (2011 [1949]:44)

This overwhelmingly negative take on fertility and pregnancy has drawn substantial criticism. However, the association of pregnancy – in one way or another – with subordination has been a persistent feature of feminist writing following de Beauvoir. It is echoed in, for example, the work of the radical feminist Shulamith Firestone, who argued that feminists should question 'the very organisation of nature' (1971: 2) by harnessing the potential of reproductive technology to detach procreation from women's bodies. Firestone believed that women's 'emancipation' from childbirth would lead to a radical reorganization of family structures, resulting in the full integration of women into society, as equals. The implication of both authors is that the female reproductive body is *necessarily* oppressive; liberation therefore comes from uncoupling reproduction from female anatomy.

Arguments such as these have been contentious. Many feminists objected to this portrayal of the female reproductive function and preferred to locate the origins of women's oppression elsewhere, for example in men's envy of women's reproductive capacity, rather than in that capacity itself (Donchin, 1986). Others note the contradictions in de Beauvoir's account of the female body. Despite arguing that biological facts 'do not carry their meaning in themselves' (2011 [1949]: 47), de Beauvoir seems to say that pregnancy must necessarily, on some level, be an alienating experience that 'enslaves' women to the species. Catriona Mackenzie (1986) argues that de Beauvoir vacillates between an account of the female body as socially constructed and an account of the female body as inherently oppressive. Women's lack of freedom, for de Beauvoir, is a result of patriarchal oppression and does not follow necessarily from 'biological facts' – yet the female reproductive body also somehow in itself inhibits women's quest for subjectivity (Mackenzie, 1986: 147). According to Mackenzie, de Beauvoir meant that reproduction is not the *only* meaning of the female body but that, in order to achieve full subjecthood, women must find ways of escaping their reproductive capacity. Unsurprisingly, de Beauvoir was a prominent advocate of contraception and abortion rights.

Simone de Beauvoir may also be read in ways that do not cast the female reproductive function as essentially oppressive. Passages in de Beauvoir concerning reproduction can be read as phenomenological portrayals of women's experiences of reproduction in a patriarchal social system, even if it is not always clear that this is her original meaning. Sara Heinämaa (1997) argues that the passages on reproduction in *The Second Sex* are best understood as phenomenological, rather than ideological, accounts; in other words, de Beauvoir is describing how actually existing women living in oppressive circumstances experience their bodies, not how *all* hypothetical women, past, present and future, will *always* experience their bodies. When read in this way, this account of maternity is extremely powerful – having, as Linda Zerilli (1992) argues, the ability to subvert the view of reproduction as women's destiny, to be accepted passively and calmly. Instead, it speaks to the reality of women's lived experiences of subordination and suggests reasons for women to resist this subordination.

Read in this way, de Beauvoir and Firestone's accounts chime with later feminist discussions of pregnancy and motherhood. One important example is Adrienne Rich's *Of Woman Born* (1986), in which she chronicled the loss of subjectivity she experienced bearing and bringing up her three sons. Pregnancy itself she experienced as a loss of control and fostering of dependency. Towards the end of her first pregnancy and hospitalization two days prior to giving birth, she felt entirely reliant upon her obstetrician (1986: 26); her third and final pregnancy taught her 'that my body was not under my control' (1986: 28). Once born, her children seemed to make unfair and unreasonable demands on her time and independence yet, at the same time, she felt great guilt at being unable to love them unconditionally. The experience radicalized her: *Of Woman Born* is not a critique of the activity of mothering, but of the (patriarchal) institution of mother*hood* that 'has withheld over one-half of the human species from the decisions affecting their lives' (1986: 13). Echoing de Beauvoir, Rich argued that motherhood as an institution 'has alienated women from our bodies by incarcerating us in them' (1986: 13).

Rich's account moves away from an essentialist account of pregnancy and motherhood as universally negative and towards a critique of the *institution* of motherhood in the context of a sexist society. It locates the causes of women's subordination not in women's bodies but in social structures. This insight has been taken up in analyses of liberal legal and political systems. In an influential account, Susan Bordo

(2003) discusses the status of women as subjects in the culture and legal tradition of the US. She demonstrates that the liberal legal tradition that claims to establish equal individual rights in fact fails to treat women as full subjects, instead treating women 'as mere bodies despite an official rhetoric that vehemently forswears such treatment of human beings' (2003: 72). Bodily integrity, under this system, is normally legally inviolable, even when to violate this right would save the life of another.[1] However, in practice this dictum has not always applied to pregnant women. As evidence, Bordo cites the 1987 Washington DC court decision to force a woman to undergo caesarean section. At 25 weeks' gestation, Angela Carder was diagnosed with a lung tumour, which she opted to treat with chemotherapy and radiation (surgery being ruled out). At this stage of pregnancy, any baby would be unlikely to survive long after birth; nonetheless, when Carder's condition rapidly deteriorated, the hospital administration – alarmed by the decision not to attempt delivery – requested that a court intervene on the foetus's behalf. The court ordered that Carder undergo caesarean section, despite the low likelihood of her survival and her own protests. The baby lived for only two hours following the operation. Carder died two days later (2003: 76–7).

As Bordo points out, 'a woman whom *no court in the country would force to undergo a blood transfusion for a dying relative* had come to be legally regarded, when pregnant, as a mere life-support system for a fetus' (2003: 77; emphasis in original). The case emphasizes the inconsistency and the gendered nature of legal and cultural understandings of subjectivity – pregnant women, it seems, are not considered embodied subjects. Rather, the subjectivity of the foetus seems to detract from the pregnant woman's, resulting in a culture where

> pregnant women are not subjects at all (neither under the law nor in the *zeitgeist*) while foetuses are *super*-subjects. It is as though the subjectivity of the pregnant body were siphoned from it and emptied into foetal life.
> (Bordo, 2003: 88)

Lealle Ruhl locates the problem in the liberal conception of the individual, which she argues cannot accommodate pregnancy, 'either on a philosophical level or on the level of lived reality' (2002: 38). This is because conception and pregnancy lie 'outside the realm of self-willed activities' (2002: 38) – particularly when reliable contraception is not widely available – and because the pregnant subject is 'bifurcated'. Ruhl notes that in court decisions in the US and Canada, the foetus is accorded a status beyond normal subjectivity, entitled to demand sacrifices from its parent that no other liberal subject could. In this sense, the liberal subject with rights and obligations is split in two. The foetus has rights, while the pregnant woman has obligations; woman and foetus are 'not two liberal subjects in one body, but rather *one* liberal subject in two bodies' (2002: 39). This description of legal understandings of pregnancy has obvious resonance with Bordo's observation that pregnant women's subjectivity is 'siphoned off and emptied' into the foetus.

Bordo and Ruhl's observations concern case law but, as Ruhl notes, legal tradition is rooted in a cultural and philosophical tradition with a certain conception of subjectivity – a conception that seems to exclude pregnant subjects. At the heart of this is the notion that pregnancy is not 'self-willed'. Classical liberal theory conceptualizes the individual as rational and as exercising rational control over his[2] body (which is thought of as property, subordinate to the mind). Pregnancy seems to lie outside the scope of this rational management of the body, hence the insistence of classical liberal thinkers such as John Locke that women could not be full citizens (Ruhl, 2002: 38).

These observations do not necessarily mean that pregnancy must preclude full subjectivity. Iris Marion Young has, for example, questioned the assumption that the 'splitting' of subjectivity experienced during pregnancy must automatically entail alienation from the pregnant body (1984: 48–9; see also Tyler, 2000; Lundquist, 2008; Oliver, 2010). In a similar fashion, Rich draws attention to the possibility of seeing pregnancy and childbirth 'as one way of knowing and coming to terms with our bodies, of discovering our physical and psychic resources' (1986: 157). However, the feminist accounts discussed here all converge on one point: that *in the context of a sexist society*, maternity as a social, cultural and legal institution is often experienced by women as oppressive.

Contextualized accounts of motherhood are not complete if they only take gender-based power structures into consideration. The importance of the combined systems of race, class and gender to black women's lives has long been established in black feminist theory (Davis, 1981; Crenshaw, 1989; 1991; Collins, 1990). Famously, Kimberlé Crenshaw coined the term 'intersectionality' to describe this effect, arguing that 'any analysis that does not take intersectionality into account cannot sufficiently address the particular manner in which Black women are subordinated' (1989: 140). Intersecting systems of oppression bear heavily on women's experiences of pregnancy and motherhood (Collins, 2007). Control of reproduction is a central aspect of racial power structures as well as gendered ones. It was vital to the operation of slavery, as slave women's children were needed to replenish the slave labour force; black women were systematically forced to bear children, only to often later be forcibly separated from them (Roberts, 2017: 33–6). In contemporary US politics, black fertility is often regarded as a social problem and targeted by birth control policy (Roberts, 2017). Control of black and minority women's reproduction often takes on a more punitive character, up to and including coerced sterilization practices. In another case of the 'emptying' of women's subjecthood into the foetus, women – usually poor black women – in the US have faced prosecution and heavy sentencing for using drugs during pregnancy, often without evidence that the foetus was harmed (Flavin and Paltrow, 2010; Roberts, 2017: 150–201). Some women have been forced to choose between prison and a contraceptive implant. As Dorothy Roberts contends:

> When a pregnant woman is arrested for harming the fetus by smoking crack, her crime hinges on her decision to have a baby. She can avoid prosecution if she has an abortion. If she chooses instead to give birth, she risks going to prison. Similarly, when a judge gives a defendant the choice between [the contraceptive implant] Norplant or jail, incarceration becomes the penalty for the defendant's decision to remain fertile. If she violates probation by becoming pregnant, she will be sent to prison. Prosecutors and judges see poor Black women as suitable subjects for these reproductive penalties because society does not view these women as suitable mothers in the first place. (2017: 152)

The situation for marginalized women is in significant ways better in the UK than in the US. The provision of reproductive and maternal healthcare through the NHS means that women can more easily choose (or choose not) to become mothers (Lonergan, 2012: 32). However, minority women in the UK still have a greatly increased risk of dying during pregnancy compared to white women, especially if they are black (Nair et al, 2014), in part due to difficulty accessing care and the likelihood of receiving suboptimal care (Ameh and van den Broek, 2008). There are many historical examples of poor, black and minority ethnic women being dissuaded from having children by medical professionals and government policy, and media narratives often portray such women as bad mothers, to be discouraged from reproducing (Lonergan, 2012; 2015). These narratives often dovetail with anti-immigration rhetoric, exploiting fears about 'overly fertile', irresponsible immigrants 'flooding' into Britain and 'scrounging off' the welfare state (Jones, 2013: 52).

To sum up, while feminist writers disagree on the precise nature of the relationship between women and the female reproductive function – is it fundamentally oppressive or not? – there is general agreement that legally and socially, pregnant women have been treated as objects. The needs of the foetus have been consistently prioritized over those of the pregnant woman – even when there is no or limited evidence that sacrificing the woman will save the foetus. Struggles over abortion and other reproductive rights always take place in the context of this history. However, one should not assume that all woman are situated in the same way relative to their capacity to become pregnant: 'liberal' legal and social traditions also have a long history of valuing white motherhood and devaluing all else, as a result discouraging or even penalizing pregnancy among certain groups.

Abortion and women's status

As an intervention into the workings of the female reproductive body, abortion is deeply entwined with questions of women's liberation: this much was intuited by early feminist activists. Margaret Sanger, a prominent American sex educator and birth control activist in the early 20th century, wrote at length on reproductive rights and responsibilities in the essays in her book *Woman and the New Race* (1920). In an essay titled 'Contraceptives or abortion?' she asserted that while abortion is just as 'abhorrent' as child abandonment or infanticide, it is merely symptomatic of women's lack of freedom. Abortion, she argued, occurs when the 'feminine spirit' – women's natural desire to be free – is constrained by social circumstances and unwanted pregnancy; women will always be driven to desperate measures when preferable alternatives such as birth control and sex education are lacking. Elements of this analysis echo throughout more recent feminist writing; compare Sanger's assessment of abortion as symptomatic of a lack of freedom with Catharine MacKinnon's assertion that abortion 'provides a moment of power in a life otherwise led under unequal conditions that preclude choice in ways [women] cannot control ... a window of relief in an unequal situation from which there is no exit' (2005: 141).

However, abortion can have wider-ranging effects than those identified by Sanger and MacKinnon. If the capacity for pregnancy renders women vulnerable to exploitation – not *necessarily* 'emptying' women of subjectivity, but making such an emptying possible – legal, safe and accessible[3] abortion has radical implications both for how women relate to their own bodies and for the structuring of society. Female subjectivity is 'siphoned off' in situations where pregnancy cannot be rejected; hence, the female body is coded as passive and as inevitably becoming pregnant. The capacity to deny the reproductive body thus destabilizes dominant ideas about gender and narratives of women's life course. Simone de Beauvoir depicted abortion as traumatic, not because she saw it as a form of violence to the female body, but because it represented a rupture of feminine values:

> from childhood woman is repeatedly told she is made to bear children, and the praises of motherhood are sung; the disadvantages of her condition – periods, illness, and such – the boredom of household tasks, all this is justified by this marvellous privilege she holds, that of bringing children into the world ... Even consenting to and wanting an abortion, woman feels her femininity sacrificed.
> (2011 [1949]: 545)

Abortion, as a rejection of the childbearing capacity, calls feminine values into question – right down to the meaning of the female body. In the media, motherhood is portrayed as a passive, biological process. This is evident in headlines calling a woman kept on life support for the sake of the gestating foetus a 'brain-dead mother', a usage of the word 'mother' that would not be intelligible were motherhood primarily considered an active, social role (Hartouni, 1991). Gestation, moreover, has been considered 'the natural fact of female bodies' – the female body is a 'natural-familial-maternal body' (1991: 33), a body that passively, inevitably becomes pregnant. Abortion thus fundamentally disturbs how female bodies are understood, indicating that pregnancy and motherhood can be a conscious and active choice rather than an inevitable consequence of engaging in sexual activity while having a female reproductive system.

This understanding of the female body can be disrupted if the reproductive function can be denied. If motherhood does not emerge passively as a natural condition of female embodiment, it must instead be figured as an active and social role and as a *choice* (Hartouni, 1991). The implications of this are broad. The series of interviews conducted with both pro-life and pro-choice women activists in the US by Kristin Luker (1984) seem to confirm that abortion has broad implications for what it means to be a woman. Luker argues that, while the debate between the 'pro-life' and 'pro-choice' movements is, on the surface, about the 'status' of the unborn – incorporating questions about whether, how and when a foetus can be considered a 'person' or a 'human life' – on a deeper level it is also about the status of women. The debate is 'about women's contrasting obligations to themselves and others' and is subsequently '*a referendum on the place and meaning of motherhood*' (1984: 193; emphasis in original).

Through her interviews, Luker identifies the differing 'social worlds' and worldviews of female pro-choice and pro-life activists. The latter, she finds, were unlikely to work in the paid labour force, especially after marriage. They were generally housewives or, if they did work, were in traditionally female occupations such as social work and nursing. Pro-choice women, on the other hand, were generally more highly educated, working women, often with large salaries (1984: 195). To Luker, the activists' views on abortion result from these differences, and stem from vested interests in the legal and cultural status of abortion. The pro-life women interviewed were heavily invested in traditional gender roles and family structure, which were 'satisfying, rewarding, and meaningful' (1984: 201) for them. In contrast, pro-choice women, who generally made use of the traditionally 'male' resources of paid employment and participation in the public sphere, typically experienced an unplanned pregnancy as highly disruptive, threatening their access to these resources.

The normative implications of abortion's connection to gender roles and women's participation in the labour force are significant. The historian Linda Gordon points out that if childbearing and childrearing are no longer imperatives, the 'basic organization of society' is called into question. She identifies this as the source of New Right opposition to reproductive rights:

> Our opposition sometimes appears to know better than we do how radical are the implications of reproductive rights for women. We are talking about undoing the basic gender organization of society, traditional 'femininity' as we have known it, the particular and inevitable attachment of women to domesticity and child raising ... We are talking about reconstructing not only femininity but masculinity, and in the process, altering the bases of our culture. (1986: 25)

Most feminists argue accordingly that that the right to abortion is a fundamental women's right. Early 20th-century socialist feminist Stella Browne, for example, saw free access to abortion as an imperative, freedom of choice being essential for 'the full right of free motherhood' (Riley, 1981: 191–2). While most do not go as far to argue, as Firestone did, that the reproductive body must be denied altogether if liberation is to be achieved, feminists have asserted that women's right to control their ability to conceive is paramount (Nossiff, 2007). Key is that the ability to choose whether or not to be pregnant has cultural consequences, disturbing as it does the construction of the female body as fundamentally a reproductive body and therefore disrupting the link between female embodiment and the social institution of motherhood. Access to abortion, along with access to contraception, makes a host of activities and social arrangements more thinkable and achievable for women than they would otherwise be: sex outside marriage, sex without procreative intent, and uninterrupted participation in the workforce, to name a few.

The significance of abortion will clearly not be experienced in the same way by every woman, or by every body with the capacity to become pregnant. An obvious objection is that some women are unable to become pregnant, or less likely to do so by accident – trans, lesbian, post-menopausal or infertile women, for example. Women's experiences are diverse. However, all women find themselves positioned relative to social and cultural narratives regarding the meanings of womanhood, motherhood and female gender roles. This means that whether an individual woman may become pregnant or not, she will still find herself 'assigned a subject-position linked to a body that has perceived potentialities for birth' (Battersby, 1998: 16). She may, for example, face discrimination in education or in the workplace due to the assumption that she will have children. If women's bodies are regarded as inevitably, passively becoming pregnant, this has implications for *all* women, regardless of their individual fertility status.

It also must be stated that, while legal and accessible abortion is *potentially* liberatory, not all women will experience it in this way. Abortion can take on different meanings in different social contexts. As the following chapter establishes, 1960s reformists did not envision legal abortion as liberating women from the reproductive imperative. Rather, most saw abortion as a class issue, providing partial melioration of the suffering of poor and overburdened women already struggling with large families. If a woman is compelled by poverty to terminate an otherwise wanted pregnancy, it is difficult to regard this as a liberation or a reclamation of the body. Therefore, for many, the ability to choose *not* to have a child is not the most pressing reproductive rights concern. This much is evident from Roberts's account of how black American women have been coerced into having abortions or having contraceptive implants fitted (2017). It is also evident from the history of coerced sterilization of minority ethnic women, women with disabilities, and trans and intersex people around the world (Silliman et al, 2004; West, 2009; Tilley et al, 2012; Rowlands and Amy, 2018). Women who are not coerced into having an abortion may still find that it is heavily encouraged. As Rosalind Petchesky observed in her classic text on abortion in the US: 'For a Native American woman on welfare, who every time she appears in the clinic for prenatal care is asked whether she would not like an abortion, 'the right to choose an abortion' may appear dubious if not offensive' (1986: 8).

The drive for reproductive rights has historically been interwoven with racist and ableist ideologies. Early birth control advocates utilized the language of eugenics in order to legitimize the movement, arguing that unrestrained reproduction would result in 'racial decay'. Contraception was figured as a way to prevent the 'unfit' from breeding (McCann, 1994: 99–134). Margaret Sanger herself gradually shifted away from her initial feminist defence of contraception towards advocacy of contraception as a means to control poor, minority, disabled and immigrant populations (Davis, 1981: 202–71; Roberts, 2017: 56–103). Similarly, the British contraception campaigner Marie Stopes espoused an outright eugenicist position, advocating against the right to reproduce of the 'feeble minded' and 'racially negligent', among others. Such moves by contraception advocates lent legitimacy to the forced sterilization campaigns imposed on minority women. Angela Davis suggests that black women have been wary of the mainstream reproductive rights movement for this reason (1981: 202–3), and similar claims are made by many disability rights activists (Kallianes and Rubenfeld, 1997).

This chequered history has sometimes been used cynically by opponents of legal abortion in their attempts to recruit members of marginalized groups to their cause (take, for example, the use of billboards proclaiming that 'black children are an endangered species' by anti-abortion groups in Atlanta, Georgia [Dewan, 2010]). However, this should not prevent reproductive rights advocates from taking seriously the potential for abortion and contraception to be used in this way. This chapter has suggested that access to abortion has potentially radical implications for women's status. Nonetheless, the coercive use of abortion and other means of reproductive control against marginalized populations suggests that these radical potentials do not follow automatically from legalization. A broader set of social, legal and political arrangements need to be in place for them to occur. As the following sections suggest, these arrangements have never fully been in place in the UK.

The history of abortion law

Before the early 19th century, intent to procure an abortion was only illegal after 'quickening', the point at which a pregnant woman starts to feel foetal movement. Abortion before quickening was criminalized in an 1803 Act, although the distinction between pre- and post-quickening was maintained for the purpose of administering punishment. In 1828, abortion was brought under the banner of 'offences against the person', along with a number of other statutes dealing with crimes such as murder, rape and assault. The next Offences against the Person Act, in 1837, removed the distinction between pre- and post-quickening from the statute book entirely, along with the term itself – now, any 'intent' to procure abortion was simply illegal. The Offences against the Person Act 1861 included pregnant women themselves in the crime of 'intent' to procure an abortion, separate from those found to be 'aiding and abetting' them, who were subject to a lesser punishment (Fyfe, 1991: 162). The Act is still on the statute book today in England and Wales, although the Abortion Act 1967 provides exemptions from criminal sanctions in certain circumstances.

The Infant Life (Preservation) Act 1929 introduced the notion of foetal viability – the length of gestation at which a foetus is assumed to be 'capable of being born alive' – and set this at 28 weeks. For the first time, abortion post-viability came to be legally regarded as murder. However, abortions after 28 weeks were legalized where they were necessary in order to save the life of the pregnant woman (Fyfe, 1991: 163). Nonetheless, this barely changed the situation in practice until the *Bourne* case of 1938 (Hindell and Simms, 1971: 13). In 1938, a 14-year-old girl was raped by a group of off-duty soldiers. After a hospital refused to terminate her pregnancy, the case was taken up by a campaign group, the Abortion Law Reform Association (ALRA), who wrote to Aleck Bourne (at the time, Consultant Obstetrician at St Mary's hospital) and asked him to terminate (Hindell and Simms, 1971: 69–70).

Bourne agreed to carry out the termination after noting the girl's severe distress, later writing that 'in her there was nothing of the cold indifference of the prostitute' (cited in Hindell and Simms, 1971: 70). The notion that access to abortion should be conditional on the perceived distress and virtue of the woman or girl requesting it would go on to feature heavily in debates over legal abortion. In order to force a court ruling that would clarify the legal situation, Bourne informed the police and was charged with a criminal offence. However, Bourne was acquitted on the grounds that it was impossible to distinguish between a woman's life being in danger and her health being in danger. As Justice Macnaghten told the jury: 'Life depends on health, and it may be that if health is gravely impaired, death results' (cited in Hindell and Simms, 1971: 71). If the pregnancy was likely to turn the woman into a 'physical or mental wreck', he added, the doctor who carried out the termination might well be viewed as acting to save the life of the woman. In establishing *health* as a legal ground for abortion, this ruling was extremely liberalizing.

By the mid-1960s, however, it had become clear that existing restrictions on abortion were not functioning to contain it. Illegal abortions were on the rise as women became increasingly determined to flout the law to obtain abortions (Hindell and Simms, 1971: 32–3; Petchesky, 1986: 115). Abortion, in other words, was becoming unmanageable as the law became increasingly ineffective. Women with access to the right resources could have 'discreetly legal' abortions in the private sector, and only women poor enough to consult untrained abortionists using dangerous methods felt the full force of the law (Hindell and Simms, 1971: 39–41). As well as drawing public outrage over the existence of a so-called 'law for the rich', this situation rendered the law unenforceable – it 'was obvious to anyone who examined the problem that both illegal and quasi-legal operations were being carried out on so large a scale that the law had little public support' (1971: 42).

As this chapter has explained, authors have described abortion as at once a signifier, cause and consequence of social change and upheaval, thoroughly linked to gender relations and women's life courses and potentially disrupting the prevailing social order. Rosalind Petchesky (1986: 116–7) has argued that states intervene in reproduction for a number of reasons: for population control, in order to regulate sexual behaviour and norms, and also in order to maintain the social order and its own legitimacy. The legalization of abortion in the US under *Roe v Wade* parallels the UK case in that it was a response to social changes that meant existing abortion laws no longer had credibility. Critical to these changes was women's increasing labour force participation: 'the capitalist economy required reliable means of fertility control to support a growing demand for female labor power' (1986: 115). Women themselves were determined to defy the law, having abortions no matter what, and abortion was slowly becoming accepted as an element of family planning. The government, in order to maintain legitimacy, was forced to respond by changing the law.

The UK state's response to mounting illegitimacy came in 1967 in the form of the Abortion Act. The Act started life as a Bill introduced by the then Liberal backbencher David Steel, although it was supported in its progression through Parliament by the Labour government. It never applied to Northern Ireland, as Home Rule was still in place in 1967. The Act did not 'legalize' abortions for women who sought them so much as decriminalize the doctors who carried them out. It stipulated that abortion could legally be carried out by a registered medical practitioner before the 28th week of pregnancy (later reduced to the 24th week), if two doctors agreed that the pregnancy posed 'a risk, greater than if the pregnancy were terminated, of injury to the physical or mental health of the pregnant woman' or there was 'a substantial risk that if the child were born it would suffer from such physical or mental abnormalities as to be seriously handicapped' (Abortion Act 1967, s1(1)(a)–(d)). Rather than granting women a right to abortion on demand, the Act gave doctors the final say over whether an abortion could be carried out. While different countries have dealt with the abortion 'problem' in different ways, this 'medicalization' of abortion is hardly unique to the UK. The medical profession forms one corner of an 'abortion policy triad' in abortion debates globally, along with women and governments (McBride Stetson 1996: 97). The interests of the medical profession have always been taken into account when constructing abortion policy.

In the UK, however, the law continues to be contested. In the 1970s, several anti-abortion Bills were introduced – most notably by James White (Labour), William Benyon (Conservative) and John Corrie (Conservative) – aimed at curtailing apparent 'abuses' of the Abortion Act 1967 by circumscribing the circumstances in which abortions could legally be carried out. The debate reignited in 1988 with the introduction of the Alton Bill, which aimed to lower the upper time limit for legal abortion to 18 weeks' gestation. While the Alton Bill did not complete its passage through Parliament, it inspired several attempts to amend the Human Fertilisation and Embryology (HFE) Act 1990. The HFE Act eventually lowered the time limit to 24 weeks (a limit that had already been achieved in clinical practice), and more restrictive amendments were defeated.

Since then, attempts to introduce more restrictive legislation have been unsuccessful. However, the issue has not abated. The 2008 update to the HFE Act renewed the debate on abortion law and more (unsuccessful) attempts were made to reduce the upper time limit.

In 2011, Conservative MP Nadine Dorries, along with her Labour co-sponsor Frank Field, sponsored an amendment to the coalition government's Health and Social Care Bill which would have stripped abortion providers of their right to provide independent counselling, instead requiring that this counselling be provided by independent organizations. This amendment was widely regarded as an attempt to slowly erode access to legal abortion (Henebury, undated). This was followed in 2012 by the controversy surrounding the sex-selective abortion allegations, as well as a wave of unannounced inspections on abortion clinics following claims that doctors were 'pre-signing' abortion paperwork without seeing patients. Attempts to reform the law have, however, not all been restrictive. In 2011, for example, the British Pregnancy Advisory Service (BPAS) made a bid to allow women to undergo early medical abortions in their own home. This was unsuccessful, but home abortion became permitted in Scotland in 2017 and in England and Wales in 2018 (see Chapter 7). Since 2017 there has been a renewed push for decriminalization in England and Wales and especially in Northern Ireland, led by female Labour backbenchers such as Diana Johnson and Stella Creasy. This culminated in the passage of a cross-party amendment compelling the UK government to decriminalize abortion in Northern Ireland if the latter's devolved government did not reconvene by 21 October 2019.

This potted history already suggests that the twin poles of 'pro-life' and 'pro-choice' do not capture all that is to be said about the politics of abortion. For starters, we have to contend with the role of the medical profession: how it has defended its interests, and its capacity to determine what can and cannot be included under the banner of 'healthcare'. We also must consider the part gender plays in this, from the stripping of women's traditional power over reproductive healthcare, to the ongoing role played by images of female vice and virtue in abortion debates. Finally, the role of law and policy are complex; it is not simply a case of choosing whether to ban abortion or allow it. Rather, key questions are: who gets to access abortion, for what reasons, and under what conditions? The following section explores ways of making sense of the relationship between gender, the law, the medical profession, and abortion.

Making sense of history

Feminist accounts of this history have tended to depict the Abortion Act 1967 as the outcome of entrenched medical control over female reproduction. Wendy Fyfe (1991) argues that between 1803 and 1967,

UK abortion legislation shifted in focus from religion to medicine, a shift that reflected the increasing ability of the medical profession (and decreasing ability of women) to define and control reproduction. Fyfe connects early Acts concerning abortion with the increasing credibility and legitimacy of the medical profession during this period. By the time of the Infant Life (Preservation) Act 1929, the medical profession had begun to consolidate its expertise in the area of reproduction, and abortion had been increasingly redefined in medical terms. This process involved the gradual displacement of definitions used by women in relation to pregnancy, accompanied by a legal shift towards the criminalization of individual women rather than doctors. From this shift emerged a distinction between legitimate 'medical' abortions (authorized and carried out by medical experts) and criminal abortions (sought outside the clinic and often performed by women) (1991: 163–5). This argument is echoed in the work of Kerry Petersen (1993), who identifies medical control over abortion as an effect of the medical profession's strategy of developing a monopoly over the healthcare system, particularly through the displacement of midwives from their central role in providing reproductive care.

This historical approach allows Fyfe and others to view the Abortion Act 1967 rather differently to popular wisdom: instead of reversing decades of oppressive or misguided legislation, the Act was the culmination of a long process of separation of women from control over reproduction and legitimization of medical expertise in this arena. The Act, after all, did not decriminalize or grant a new 'right' to women seeking abortions. Rather, it 'legalized' abortion by granting protection to doctors carrying out abortions in certain medically controlled circumstances. The common perception of UK abortion law as underpinned by liberal individualism is incorrect; in fact, the 1967 Act was the logical outcome of years of steadily increasing medical control over the sphere of reproduction. The Act succeeded in maintaining the law's legitimacy in the eyes of the public while also ensuring that abortion remained regulated. It dragged abortion from the illegal and invisible 'back streets' and into the visible and regulated sphere of medical practice.

This critique of abortion law is rooted in, and shares some of the failings of, an older critique of medicine. The 'medicalization critique' (Lupton, 1997) has its roots in Marxist perspectives and the social movements that arose in the 1960s and 1970s.[4] Supporters of this critique noted that medicine was amassing power and influence[5] in spite of its apparent lack of effectiveness in treating many conditions. These critics argued that social life was becoming medicalized; in other words, that social problems were increasingly being defined using medical terminology and treated as 'diseases'. Further, they argued that medicalization was a mechanism of social control (Lupton, 1997: 94–5). This charge was taken up by many feminists, who have argued that women in particular have been subject to medical control, especially when it comes to pregnancy and reproductive care (Morgan, 1998; Purdy, 2001).

This is not to say that medicine's 'social' role is new: public health has always aimed to improve sanitation, housing, and other aspects of society, while psychiatry was committed to dealing with and rehabilitating (rather than persecuting or punishing) social 'deviants' (Zola, 1972: 488). Yet it is still possible to identify changes in how sickness and health were perceived alongside the expansion of medicine's role in the mid-20th century. Medicine, at first glance, appears to have lifted moral condemnation from individuals by drawing a distinction between illness and crime: criminals are personally responsible for their actions and therefore can be held accountable, whereas sick people cannot be. Nonetheless, the moral condemnation of sick people was not really lifted but displaced:

> Though [the sick person's] immoral character is not demonstrated in his having a disease, it becomes evident in what he does about it. Without seeming ludicrous, if one listed the traits of people who break appointments, fail to follow treatment regimen, or even delay in seeking medical aid, one finds a long list of 'personal flaws'. Such people seem to be ever ignorant of the consequences of certain diseases, inaccurate as to symptomatology, unable to plan ahead or find time, burdened with shame, guilt, neurotic tendencies, haunted with traumatic medical experiences or members of some lower status minority group – religious, ethnic, racial or socio-economic. In short, they appear to be a sorely troubled if not disreputable group of people. (Zola, 1972: 490–1)

In an explicitly feminist critique of medicalization, Barbara Ehrenreich and Deirdre English's *Complaints & Disorders* (2011 [1973]) explored how medicine worked in particular to control women in the US. For these two authors, through the medicalization of women's lives, medicine became a key contributor to sexist ideology, describing women '*as sick, and as potentially sickening to men*' (2011 [1973]: 32; emphasis in original) and therefore needing to be brought under medical supervision. Moreover, Ehrenreich and English argue that medical practice in the 19th century aimed at controlling or 'taming' women – that it operated as a form of surveillance in which, at the first sign of rebellion, doctors could intervene to 'cure' a 'disease' (2011 [1973]: 82). A great deal of women's 'unruly' behaviour was diagnosed as some sort of 'nervous disorder' and blamed on the female sexual and reproductive organs. Sometimes these 'disorders' were thought to necessitate surgery, involving removal of the clitoris or, more commonly, of the ovaries – the threat of which was 'enough to bring many women into line' (2011 [1973]: 81).

Feminist sociologist Ann Oakley also argues that medicalization has functioned to control women's behaviour. In the UK, the early development of antenatal care occurred at a time when the state's interest in reproduction – along with the legitimacy of state intervention in this area – was being established, towards the end of the 19th century (Oakley, 1984: 34). The notion that public health might be a matter of national interest was established as military men alerted policymakers to the physical 'degeneracy' of army recruits; furthermore, the maladies afflicting the populace were blamed on maternal ignorance (1984: 35–6). Thus, the state and medical profession set about educating women in the proper care of children – and of the pregnant self. Educating mothers was presumably cheaper than providing adequate medical care or housing, 'but the zeal with which it was promoted probably had more to do with perceptions of women's social function' (1984: 38). Moreover, education of new mothers meant education by healthcare professionals, not education by other women with experience of motherhood. Crucially, this education took place as a central part of early antenatal care, only splitting off as a separate activity in the 1960s. Antenatal care was, therefore, to Oakley, about controlling and altering women's behaviour from its inception (1984: 259; see also Oakley, 1980).

For Oakley, this medical control of women's reproductivity is very clearly a *state* mandate: the state has an interest in controlling populations and public health and employs the help of the medical profession to do so (Oakley, 1984: 2). This perception of the state's interest in managing reproductivity has been carried over into feminist critiques of the Abortion Act 1967. Sally Sheldon's pivotal account of UK abortion law (1997) draws upon Foucault in order to make sense of the Act. She understands the medicalization of abortion as a form of biopolitical control – in other words, as 'part of a set of strategies for the administration of bodies and the calculated management of life' (Foucault, 1981: 138–9), involving the supervision and regulation of the domains of health, mortality and reproduction. Biopolitics seeks 'to act upon these domains by reshaping the conduct of those who inhabit them without interdicting their formal freedom to conduct their lives as they see fit' (Rose, 1999: 23). This is Sheldon's understanding of the Abortion Act 1967: it shifted power away from a centralized state and channelled it through a range of institutions and practices, including those of the medical profession.

The Abortion Act 1967, in this sense, did not result in the deregulation of abortion, but rather in a new form of regulation using the capacities of the medical profession to oversee and manage pregnancy instead of the direct intervention of the state. Sheldon stresses the highly gendered nature of this process. The new regulatory role of the medical profession, she argues, was made possible only by appealing to particular constructions of women seeking abortions. Analysing parliamentary debates over Steel's Bill, she observes that women were typically depicted as vulnerable, irresponsible or irrational: as blameless and deserving victims of social circumstance in need of protection, or as undeserving 'feckless girls' (1997: 37) unready for motherhood. Participants also emphasized maternity as a female norm, even when abortions are carried out; abortion was often justified in order to avoid overstraining a woman's 'capacity as a mother' or in terms of the needs of her other children. These accounts of women as unable (whether by nature or circumstance) to take responsibility for their own lives underpinned the decision to transfer power to the medical profession (1997: 32–48). The Abortion Act 1967, according to Sheldon, aimed to 'bring under control women seeking to terminate pregnancies' (1997: 30).

The Act was thus, for feminist critics, a far cry from the liberal measure it is often assumed to be. Rather, it implemented a new form of regulation that utilized the medical profession's capacity for administrative oversight. As Sheldon observes, 'the law clearly aims to protect medical autonomy and discretion rather than to grant substantive rights to the woman' (1997: 27). In political debate as in legislative practice, abortion is recast as a 'health' issue. This means that decision-making power is granted to doctors, rather than to women seeking abortion, ensuring that the final say in abortion is not made by pregnant women themselves. However, for Sheldon, medicalization goes beyond this power shift. In order to open abortion to medical scrutiny and intervention in this way, the image of those seeking abortions as vulnerable, irresponsible and irrational women had to be reemphasized and placed in opposition to the rational, impartial and competent nature of the medical profession. 'Legalization' in this format does not therefore entail women's ability to make decisions about their own reproductive capacities. Rather, 'liberal' abortion legislation is underpinned by, and propagates, the assumption that women are incapable of making such decisions unaided. In this understanding, the medicalization of abortion disempowers women.

Complicating feminist accounts

Accounts of the medicalization of abortion are extremely valuable in that they trouble popular conception of the 1967 Act as a liberalizing measure. However, there is a danger in providing too linear and deterministic an account of how British abortion law has developed. Medicalization is presented as almost inevitable in some feminist analysis, the result of an equally patriarchal state and medical profession conspiring to control women. It seems somewhat defeatist for feminists to envision the state in this way: if outcomes are predetermined and negotiation is foreclosed, why bother to engage in feminist politics at all?

Narratives of abortion legislation can gloss over the fact that regulatory strategies for managing abortion are not entirely coherent; while we see the effect or function of abortion laws, discerning the motivation behind them is much trickier. The process by which abortion legislation is made in the Westminster Parliament is complex: abortion legislation does not often originate in the hands of the executive but rather in Private Members Bills and amendments, and MPs are generally allowed a free vote (Marsh and Chambers, 1981). While the executive does have a role to play, the heightened capacity of MPs to influence abortion law makes it difficult to talk about 'the government' as the central actor in the creation of abortion legislation. This is further complicated by the ad hoc devolution of abortion policy in Scotland, Wales and Northern Ireland, which has resulted in different regimes existing in each of the UK's constituent nations (Moon et al, 2019).

Accounts of the role played by feminists – and in particular feminist MPs – in political debates over abortion further complicate matters. Dorothy McBride Stetson's (2001b) research explores multiple parliamentary debates on abortion: the 1975 White Bill, which would have restricted the grounds for legal abortion and the freedom of abortion clinics, the equally restrictive 1979 Corrie Bill, and the HFE Act 1990, which lowered the time limit for legal abortion from 28 to 24 weeks' gestation. McBride Stetson finds that feminists were consistently successful in achieving their objectives in these debates.

The White and Corrie Bills failed, and while the HFE Act did lower the time limit, this outcome was generally regarded as a success for the pro-choice movement: some exceptions were secured for women who needed later abortions, a potential lowering of the time limit to 18 weeks was avoided, and in any case a limit of 24 weeks was already considered to have been achieved in clinical practice (Hohmeyer, 1995: 42). Moreover, by 1990 the notion, missing from early debates on abortion reform, that abortion is a women's rights issue had been successfully established in policy debates. McBride Stetson asserts that in each debate women were included in the policy process and the outcome was in line with the goals of the women's movement (2001b: 155). How can these findings be resolved with the continued – and definitively antifeminist – medicalization of abortion? This is one of the questions this book asks.

Another problem with critiques of medicalization is that they often posit 'doctors' as a homogenous group. The history of abortion reform suggests that they are anything but. While there certainly has been an observable 'establishment discourse … predominantly concerned with promoting and protecting professional interests' within abortion debates, clinicians have always been prominent voices within reform campaigns (McGuinness and Thomson, 2015: 178). Medical professionals are now some of the biggest advocates of change, with the major British medical organizations calling for reform. Abortion provision has been characterized by 'turf wars' within the medical establishment between providers, and between specialisms, regarding who should be responsible for abortion decision-making and care (McGuinness and Thomson, 2015). The question, then, is not whether the medical profession is 'for' or 'against' abortion, but rather, how different medical professionals have worked with or against women's movements and what the impact of this has been.

A final question is that of how different women have been situated relative to the Abortion Act 1967. The requirements of the Act have certainly placed hurdles in the way of those seeking abortions. In the 1970s, for example, women frequently reported encounters with unsympathetic and patronizing doctors who would not refer them for abortions. Yet in 1977, the feminist magazine *Spare Rib* reported on the case of a black woman who found it easy to access an abortion through her doctor, only to later discover that the same doctor consistently refused abortions and hormonal contraception to white women and was known to want to keep the black population from rising (McGrane and Nicholls, 1977). The ability of individual GPs to block abortion access has now been greatly reduced. However, in the contemporary

UK it is still the case that some women's fertility is encouraged while others' is stigmatized. Feminist analyses must therefore resist the assumption that all women are impacted in the same way by abortion provision and regulation.

This book contends that insights from the reproductive justice movement, which originated in the US, can be fruitfully applied to the UK context. The reproductive justice movement was pioneered by coalitions such as SisterSong and the National Asian Pacific American Women's Forum (NAPAWF) and has sought, alongside the mainstream reproductive rights movement, to defend the *Roe v Wade* ruling that legalized abortion in the US and to maintain access to abortion. However, as 'a movement that is based on a class- and race-conscious feminism' (Gerber Fried 1990: ix), its overall aims are broader. The reproductive justice movement has highlighted issues, neglected by the mainstream reproductive rights movement, that disproportionately affect minority women: for example, HIV/AIDS, access to contraception, forced sterilization, and fibroids (Gerber Fried, 1990; Evans, 2015: 183).

Reproductive justice advocates have also sought to problematize the language of choice typically used by liberal abortion rights advocates. They argue that the latter often conceptualize choice in narrow, legalistic terms, by focusing only on legal and bureaucratic barriers to accessing abortion. This focus can prevent mainstream activism from examining the structural and cultural factors that constrain the free exercise of choice, and from recognizing that for many women, other reproductive choices – to have children, to be fertile – are more pressing concerns than the ability to choose abortion (Gerber Fried, 1990; Kallianes and Rubenfeld, 1997; Luna, 2009; 2011). For this reason, the methods of reproductive justice advocates tend to differ from those of the mainstream pro-choice movement: while not denying that legal rights are important, the former often focus on social and cultural change (Luna, 2011).

The reproductive justice movement has succeeded in shifting the terms of the discourse in the US (Evans, 2015: 183). However, it has not yet made the same strides in the UK. Campaigners suggest that this is due to the less 'extreme' health inequalities in the UK compared to the US (Jackson, 2011; see also Evans, 2015: 183–4) – although, as this chapter has argued, significant inequalities do exist. However, they also indicate the need for a 'broad grassroots movement' (Jackson, 2011) that could incorporate reproductive justice concerns. This book argues that reproductive justice needs to be a central focus of the movement, not just at the grassroots level but also among the major abortion providers and professional advocates. Without a reproductive justice perspective, pro-choice coalitions remain vulnerable to new forms of attack.

The significance of abortion

Feminist theorists disagree regarding the nature of the relationship between women and reproduction. However, across these different perspectives there is broad agreement that if women are shackled to reproduction, and unable to choose how, when and whether they bear children, they cannot be considered free. Feminists working in a variety of different traditions have argued that, in the context of a sexist society, women often experience motherhood as oppressive. Women have found their lives and their needs subordinated, in law and in practice, to those of the developing foetus, even when the foetal life is unviable: sad cases such as those of Angela Carder and, more recently, the needless death of Savita Halappanavar in Ireland demonstrate this. The predominant image of women as inevitably becoming pregnant has negative consequences for women regardless of whether they can or will get pregnant: it mediates access to jobs, to education, and more.

Reproductive choice changes how we think about motherhood, and women's lives outside of it, whether they choose to become mothers or not. When reproductive choice is normalized, the female body can no longer be associated with passive motherhood. Instead, motherhood must be understood as a conscious and active choice. Reproductive choice opens up space to choose things other than motherhood, or to choose to balance motherhood and other pursuits. Abortion in this sense has a radical, liberatory potential, in allowing women to reject, delay, or alter the terms of motherhood. However, this chapter has suggested that this potential is not always fully realized, even when abortion is legal. Abortion can be and has been used against those whose pregnancies are seen as undesirable. It can be a selective tool for ensuring that certain populations do not reproduce overmuch. Any account of reproductive politics must therefore assert that the right *not* to reproduce is not the only reproductive right that matters.

There are other caveats. The specific form taken by abortion regulation in the UK may be interpreted as a way of containing the radical potentialities of legal abortion. The Abortion Act 1967 was always intended to compel women to submit to the judgement of their doctor, vested with the authority to assess whether they 'deserved' an abortion, whether they were 'blameless' in their situation, and whether they would make 'fit' or 'unfit' mothers (as subsequent chapters will suggest, 'fitness' in practice has had racialized, classed and ableist connotations). Reproductive choice was therefore brought under control. In short, the Act worked to de-fuse abortion; instead of signifying the liberated, child-free woman exercising control of her body, abortion came to signify the overburdened mother or frightened 'girl' in need of paternal intervention.

Yet we should also avoid too sweeping an account of how 'doctors' have worked to control abortion. Access to abortion has been substantially liberalized since 1967 – in practice if not in law – thanks in huge part to the expansion of charitable abortion providers, in which clinicians of course play a huge role. The partial unravelling of paternalistic medical control over abortion in practice has caused much consternation among anti-abortion activists. Likewise should we avoid too sweeping an account of the role of legislators in abortion regulation as *either* monolithically sexist and patriarchal, *or* as feminist heroines defending women's rights. Feminist MPs – often working closely with women's sector organizations – played a key part in establishing in public debate the notion that abortion is a women's rights issue. Feminist political analysts have called for acknowledgement of the real feminist contributions that have been made to the abortion debate (McBride Stetson ed., 2001c). However, this book argues that feminist discourse on reproductive rights has sometimes contained gaps and silences and perpetuated injustices. Feminists have not always felt emboldened to challenge the sexist assumptions underpinning the Abortion Act 1976, often finding it less risky to defend the status quo. There have also been significant blind spots around issues of race, class and disability, which are now coming to a head. This book therefore asks: which feminists, acting for which women?

3

Passing the Abortion Act 1967

While health was established as a legitimate ground for abortion in 1938, the Abortion Act 1967 further cemented the medicalization of abortion. As John Keown has observed, the Act more closely resembles the recommendations made at the time by medical bodies than it does the proposals of reform campaigners (Keown, 1988: 85; see also Sheldon, 1997; Fyfe, 1991; Gleeson, 2007; McGuinness and Thomson, 2015). This chapter develops this account. It argues that while medical recommendations did come to dominate the Act, medicalization was not an easy process. Rather, the Act came about as the result of protracted struggle and negotiation – 'horse-trading', as some activists saw it (Munday 2007: 11; Houghton, 2007: 30) – between diverse elements and actors. There was a great deal of resistance to the new regime – among parliamentarians, of course, but, crucially, also among the medical profession, many of whom did not initially accept the 'social' role entailed by performing abortions for reasons other than the pregnant woman's physical health. Establishing the logic of medicalization underpinning abortion regulation therefore required multiple redrafts and negotiations of the so-called 'social clause', which allowed abortions for reasons generally considered 'non-medical'.

David Steel's Medical Termination of Pregnancy Bill, which eventually became the Abortion Act 1967, was not the first attempt to liberalize abortion law. Several such Bills were introduced in the 1950s and 1960s (Marsh and Chambers, 1981: 13; Brookes, 2013: 133–63). However, the most successful of these was the Silkin Bill, which was later passed to Steel. One of the most controversial clauses of this Bill was clause 1(c), nicknamed the 'social clause', which allowed for abortion if 'the health of the patient or the social conditions in which she is living (including the social conditions of her existing children) make her unsuitable to assume the legal or moral responsibility for caring for a child'. Other clauses were also thought by many critics to contain inappropriate 'social' concerns, for example allowing abortion if it was considered that the strain of caring for a child might damage a woman's mental health. The various incarnations of these clauses remained controversial throughout the passage of the Steel Bill. Uncontroversial, however, was the complete absence of any mention of Northern Ireland; the eventual Act simply stated that 'this Act does not extend to Northern Ireland'. According to David Paintin, a professor of obstetrics and gynaecology who advised both Silkin and Steel, the matter of Northern Ireland 'just completely passed to one side' (quoted in Thomson, 2018a: 86).

This chapter explores the debate over the various 'social' clauses inside and outside Parliament. Outside Parliament, the medical profession was split, and indeed a 'turf war' was fought among different branches of the profession over control of abortion decision-making and provision (McGuinness and Thomson, 2015). Some organizations were heavily in favour of reform, claiming that unwanted pregnancies may be harmful to mental health and well-being. Others viewed this as an unacceptable incursion of 'social' demands into the roles and duties of medical professionals. This narrative was taken up by many MPs and peers who opposed Steel's Bill and presented a considerable challenge – far more so than any argument that the foetus had a 'right to life'. This chapter argues that passing the Abortion Act 1967 required relentless redrafting of controversial clauses in such a way as to legalize abortions for a relatively broad range of reasons, while still allowing the medical profession 'ownership' of abortion and of the concept of 'health' more broadly. This was achieved by removing any explicit reference to the 'social conditions' in which a woman requesting abortion might be living while retaining an expansive definition of 'health' encompassing mental health and, implicitly, well-being.

As feminist critics have noted, the success of the Act also relied heavily on the portrayal of women as victims or 'tired housewives' (Sheldon, 1997: 32) in need of paternalistic medical care. This portrayal drew on rhetorics of fear and threat in a way that helped strengthen the grip of medicalization on the parliamentary imagination: medical control over abortion seemed to provide the only escape from a situation in which women were victimized by back-street abortionists using horrifying methods. This way of representing the relationship between doctors and female patients has structured debate about legal abortion in the UK ever since. It has presented a challenge to feminists, who may have misgivings about medical control over abortion, yet have felt compelled to defend the Act from anti-abortion attacks. However, it has also directed the form taken by anti-abortion efforts, which have in many cases not committed wholly to the argument that the foetus is a person with a right to life, but instead sought to undermine the portrayal of healthcare practitioners – in particular, those working in abortion provision – as socially responsible.

The origins of the Abortion Act 1967

Before the 1967 Act came into existence, the regulation of abortion was largely governed by case law. A legal ruling in 1938 allowed abortions to be performed if there was danger to the health, including mental health, of the pregnant women. However, it remained unclear how grave the threat to the woman's health would have to be for an abortion to be performed, and one of the functions of the Abortion Act 1967 was to clarify existing case law (Keown, 1988: 49–83). Contrasting the eventual Act with the Steel Bill as originally drafted, along with its predecessor, the Silkin Bill, highlights the amount of compromise that went into its creation. The history of what came to be known as the 'social clause' is particularly illuminating. The first Bill to receive considerable attention was introduced by the Labour peer Lord Silkin and was heavily based on a draft drawn up by Glanville Williams, a prominent member of the Abortion Law Reform Association (ALRA). Introduced in the House of Lords in November 1965, its first clause caused considerable controversy, and ran as follows:

> 1. It shall be lawful for a registered medical practitioner to terminate pregnancy in good faith –
> a) in the belief that if the pregnancy were allowed to continue there would be grave risk of the patient's death or of serious injury to her physical or mental health resulting from either giving birth to the child or from the strain of caring for it, or
> b) in the belief that if the pregnancy were allowed to continue there would be grave risk of the child being born grossly deformed or with other serious physical or mental abnormality, or
> c) in the belief that the health of the patient or the social conditions in which she is living (including the social conditions of her existing children) make her unsuitable to assume the legal or moral responsibility for caring for a child or another child as the case may be, or
> d) in the belief that the patient became pregnant as the result of intercourse which was an offence under sections

one to eleven inclusive of the Sexual Offences Act 1956 or
that the patient is a person of unsound mind.

Clause 1(b) and its subsequent incarnations have been described by some as 'eugenicist' (Greenwood and Young, 1976: 23–4; Gleeson, 2007: 30–1), and the 21st century has seen attempts to remove clauses relating to disability from abortion law. One would be hard pressed to deny that the language of 'gross deformity' and 'abnormality' used in Silkin's original Bill is stigmatizing and dehumanizing. However, public opinion in the 1960s had turned in favour of abortion for such reasons following tragedies such as the thalidomide scandal and an international outbreak of rubella, both of which had resulted in children being born with severe disabilities (Gleeson, 2007: 30–1; Brookes, 2013: 152; McGuinness, 2013: 222–4). Indeed, some accounts describe the thalidomide tragedy as having reinvigorated the abortion reform movement (Hindell and Simms, 1968). While abortion in cases of severe disability could technically be accessed legally, the law was ambiguous in this area and ALRA identified this as a strong case for reform (Gleeson, 2007: 31). Some members of ALRA, such as the gynaecologist Peter Diggory, were also members of the Eugenics Society (Gleeson, 2007: 30–1, n50).

Clause 1(c) was the first to be labelled 'the social clause'. It was aimed primarily at working-class women who already had several children, and resulted from the growing concern that such women were particularly vulnerable to dying in childbirth or due to an illegal abortion. It also encompassed women living in extreme poverty or addicted to drugs or alcohol, and victims of spousal abuse (Hindell and Simms, 1971: 135). The clause caused a great deal of controversy in the Lords, although many also objected to clause 1(d) and to the provision in clause 1(a) allowing abortions to be performed to avoid injury resulting from the strain of caring for a child. Silkin's opponents felt that sexual offences or social conditions could not in themselves justify abortions. After the Bill was granted a Second Reading, Silkin met with ALRA to discuss revisions. Clause 1(c) was narrowed, becoming a clause focusing on the patient's 'inadequacy as a mother' but not taking account of the social conditions in which she lived (Hindell and Simms, 1971: 136–41). At Committee stage, the Bill was amended to strike out altogether the provision for abortion on the grounds of rape. At this stage, an amendment to strike out the 'social' clause (clause 1(c)) was also moved, but failed. At Report stage the Bill's opponents were better prepared, arguing that the clause called upon doctors to make 'non-medical' judgments that were outside their remit. The clause was struck from the Bill. This was seen as a serious loss by reformists, but nonetheless the Bill received a Third Reading unopposed (Hindell and Simms, 1971: 148–52).

Silkin introduced a similar Bill in the new Parliament in 1966, which was given an unopposed Second Reading. However, by Committee stage Silkin had substantially redrafted the Bill, most notably altering the wording of the 'social' clause to provide for 'capacity as a mother'. This redrafted clause was no longer intended to cover cases where a woman would be 'inadequate' as a mother but simply cases where the pregnant woman herself felt she could not cope with (another) child. This version of the clause was preferred by the Lords and adopted by a four-to-one majority. A further new clause, drafted on the recommendation of the British Medical Association (BMA), required all abortions to be notified to the Ministry of Health (subsequently the Department of Health). However, following Committee stage, the Bill was withdrawn and passed to David Steel, who had drawn third place in the Private Members' ballot[1] and had a good chance of successfully bringing a Bill through the House of Commons (Hindell and Simms, 1971: 136–54).

In redrafting the Bill, Steel took advice from ALRA, which asked that the concept of 'well-being' be inserted, that any doctor regardless of status should be permitted to perform abortions, that rape be reinserted as a ground for abortion, and that the requirement that abortions be notified to the Ministry of Health be dropped. Steel's Bill reinstated the subclause dealing with rape but required that two doctors authorize abortions in all cases except emergencies. While it did not drop the requirement for notification to the Ministry of Health, neither did it allow for notifications to be revealed to police officers. The subclause concerning 'capacity as a mother' was kept in the Bill, but the concept of 'well-being' was not introduced at this time (Hindell and Simms, 1971: 158–60). The new clause 1 ran as follows:

> 1. Subject to the provisions of this section, a person shall not be guilty of an offence under the law relating to abortion when a pregnancy is terminated by a registered medical practitioner if that practitioner and another registered medical practitioner are of the opinion, formed in good faith –
>
> a) that the continuance of the pregnancy would involve serious risk to the life or of grave injury to the health, whether physical or mental, of the pregnant woman whether before, at or after the birth of the child; or

b) that there is a significant risk that if the child were born it would suffer from such physical or mental abnormalities as to be seriously handicapped; or

c) that the pregnant woman's capacity as a mother will be severely overstrained by the care of a child or of another child as the case may be; or

d) that the pregnant woman is a defective or became pregnant while under the age of sixteen or became pregnant as a result of rape.

Despite the changes, these provisions were the source of much controversy within Parliament and among the medical profession and subject to considerable redrafting until the distinct 'social clause' was again eventually removed.

Medical opinion before the Act

Doctors at this time were particularly concerned with preserving clinical freedom and wary of state intervention. The major medical organizations all favoured medicalization, recommending abortion be legal only when certified by registered doctors. What is striking, however, particularly in unofficial commentary, is the level of hostility expressed towards the proposed legalization of 'social' abortions. While some representatives of the medical profession – unsurprisingly, perhaps, the Royal Medico-Psychological Association (RMPA), as well as doctors with ties to the Family Planning Association – stressed the need for abortion on social grounds, this does not seem to have been a widely shared view. Much medical commentary expressed anxiety about a potential pollution or violation of the role of the doctor, brought about by the intrusion of 'social' concerns into the medical realm.

The medical reformists

The BMA's report was relatively neutral. It called for clarification of the law, observing that existing case law did not specify the *extent* to which there must be a threat to the pregnant woman's health for an abortion to be legally justifiable, and recommending that these indications not be defined too closely (1966: 41). However, it did not tackle in any depth the question of abortion on 'social' and/or 'psychiatric' grounds, focusing instead on administrative difficulties. Among these was the question of notification. The report stated that the organization was in favour of notification, but only as a source of health statistics and not for the police to access without a court order. Notifications were to become a crucial issue in the negotiation of a 'socially responsible' identity for doctors.

Other organizations, however, were more outspoken. The medical body by far the most in favour of reform was the RMPA. Its official report on therapeutic abortion held that 'all social circumstances should be taken into account' as criteria for legal abortion (1967 [1966]: 167). This was justified by using a broad definition of 'health' that included both 'direct' and 'remote' effects on well-being; the latter including, for instance, the strain of a large family. The report also argued that in some cases abortions may be conducted for the good of society as a whole: for example, it asserted that mental illness may lead to inadequate parenting, which in turn is likely to produce antisocial children. However, it also stressed that there must be no 'right' to an abortion and no abortions conducted without medical examination: 'In particular, we believe that we should resist attempts to make the termination of pregnancy lawful merely on the grounds that it is inconvenient to either or both parents' (1967: 168). As such, the RMPA constructed the medical profession, including psychiatrists, as the guardians of both health and society.

The Medical Women's Federation (MWF), like the RMPA, utilized a broad definition of 'health' and argued that the 'total environment and circumstances of the pregnant woman should always be carefully considered' (1966: 1512). However, it suggested removal of the 'capacity as a mother' clause, asserting that it would be impossible for doctors to assess this. Overall, its recommendations were, even more so than the reports of other medical organizations, in favour of medicalization, stating not only that abortions should only be legal when certified by two doctors, but also that '[it] is of overriding importance that a climate of opinion should obtain whereby a woman should consult her doctor as soon as she thinks she is pregnant'[2] (1966: 1512).

The medical voices most overwhelmingly in favour of change were, unsurprisingly, found at a conference on legalized abortion held by the Family Planning Association in 1966. Participants frequently argued that the distinction between the medical and the social was false. Sir Dugald Baird, for example, argued that:

> To say that termination of pregnancy is permissible for medical but not for social reasons seems to me quite unjustifiable. This attempted distinction takes no account of the effect of customs, tradition, education, the new status of women in society, and a host of other factors which influence health, happiness, and efficiency. (1966: 16)

Such speakers used the term 'health' to encompass a broad range of factors, as well as aligning themselves with a progressive agenda. In this manner, consultant Rowena Woolf utilized the concept of 'prevention' to similar effect:

> This is the only part of Medicine where prevention is hardly attempted. I know that it is possible to get most women through pregnancy and labour, but what about the rearing of the child? What about the effect of another child on a family already overloaded psychologically and financially? (1966: 71)

This argument brought abortion into line with other medical practices. In this construction, it was not the introduction of legalized abortion that threatened to distort the medical role, but the fact that abortion was currently restricted: doctors were being prevented from carrying out their duty to prevent sickness and disease. This emphasis on threatened identity was repeated in a contribution by the general practitioner Stuart Carne, which argued that the vagueness of case law was making doctors afraid:

> Faced with a lump in the breast which might be malignant, the general practitioner knows what has to be done for his patient and he knows what arrangements he must make to see that the right treatment is provided. Faced with a child with an acute appendicitis, he knows how to arrange emergency surgery – and whom to contact to see it is done. When he is consulted by a woman with a post-menopausal bleed he knows that he must get the opinion of a competent gynaecologist, and he knows exactly how to do that. But will that gynaecologist who is willing to advise on any other gynaecological problem be willing to advise on the indications for a termination – and to carry out the operation if it is indicated? (1966: 75)

Here, abortion is again constructed as an issue of health – a gynaecological problem like 'any other', aside from the legal restrictions. Once again, the law prevents the GP from carrying out 'his' role and duty to the patient. These discursive configurations – of abortion as a 'health' issue, of 'health' as including social concerns, and of the doctor as socially aware and responsible – later became key features of the medicalized regulation of abortion.

The medical purists

The medical reformists were vigorously opposed by others in the profession – perhaps most damagingly by the RCOG. Distinct arguments around medical purity can be discerned in their contributions to the debate. These arguments tended to break down the continuity between psychiatrists, gynaecologists and other doctors, and between physical and psychiatric health, established in the arguments of reformists. Instead, they emphasized a narrow realm of strictly 'medical' practices and complaints, opposed to and threatened by the perceived encroachment of 'social' concerns and the interference of the state.

The RCOG published the most cautious of the reports of the medical organizations (RCOG, 1966). The report favoured a law that simply provided clarification of existing case law, noting that even without clear statute law there was little to prevent a gynaecologist carrying out an abortion 'when he considered it to be indicated on medical grounds' (1966: 850). In opposition to certain proponents of reform who claimed to be struck by the ease of performing abortions given the proper training and equipment (for example, Potts cited in Furedi and Hume, 2007: 40), it stressed that the 'dangers' of inducing abortion could only be weighed up by an expert. In doing so, the report emphasized the difference between obstetricians and gynaecologists and other 'medical men' (in particular psychiatrists), presenting the former as the true guardians of legal abortion. Indeed, this emphasis is made explicit towards the end of the report, where the following is stated:

> The interpretation of any new Abortion Act and its application to medical practice in this country would be largely the responsibility of obstetricians and gynaecologists. It would therefore seem wise that legislators should be reasonably sure of their cooperation before deciding on any alteration of the Law. (RCOG, 1966: 853)

Further, the report downplayed the importance of psychiatric indications, arguing that these may be 'exaggerated' (1966: 850). Psychiatric grounds for abortion were placed in sharp contrast to physical grounds, in a passage underpinned by specific ideas about women's 'maternal instinct':

> Whilst the continuance of pregnancy can have a psychological rather than physical ill-effect, so can induced abortion. There are few women, no matter how desperate they may

> be to find themselves with an unwanted pregnancy, who do not have regrets at losing it. This fundamental reaction, governed by maternal instinct, is mollified if the woman realizes that abortion was essential to her life and health, but if the indication for the termination of pregnancy was flimsy and fleeting she may suffer from a sense of guilt for the rest of her life. (1966: 852)

Thus, the report portrayed women as 'instinctively' maternal and dismissed the possibility that psychiatrists might be appropriate arbiters of when abortion is justified.

Outside of the major medical organizations, the discussion followed a similar pattern. Many doctors were worried that legal reform would somehow pollute the profession with social concerns, and many more were extremely wary of cooperation with the state. These anxieties are exemplified by the arguments of the psychiatrist Myre Sim and the gynaecologist Hugh McLaren, both prominent opponents of 'abortion on social grounds'. In an article published in the *British Medical Journal* (*BMJ*), Sim drew a strict line between medical and social concerns, contending that that members of the profession 'should be doctors of medicine, not socio-economic prophets' (1963: 145) and moreover that under proposed reforms,

> psychiatrists are expected to disregard the clinical facts in order to satisfy a desire for a social reform ... It is essentially a socio-economic problem with the psychiatrist being exploited, for he at present provides the most convenient way around the legal situation. (1963: 148)

McLaren, speaking to the Society for the Protection of Unborn Children (SPUC) and on television, similarly designated abortion 'nothing to do with the art of healing'. Moreover, he suggested that the Steel Bill represented 'state control of doctors', drawing comparisons with Nazi Germany (Catholic Herald, 1967).

While this latter argument is obviously extreme, similar concerns over pollution of the medical role and state interference with medical practice were frequently voiced in the *BMJ*. An article by the medical peer Lord Brain noted approvingly that Lord Silkin had accepted several amendments to his Bill that were suggested by the medical profession and stressed that the idea of 'inadequacy of the mother' was both ill-defined and non-medical (1966: 727–8). Lord Brain also warned that if women felt they were legally entitled to an abortion (as, it was feared, they might if the legal grounds for abortion were too closely defined) 'this may embarrass the doctor–patient relationship' (1966: 729). A little later, a *BMJ* leading article warned that certain provisions of Steel's Bill, 'if taken separately from a consideration of the mother's health, could lead medical men into making decisions on other than their expert knowledge' (*BMJ*, 1966: 1608). In these arguments, it is not restrictive abortion laws that threaten the medical profession, but the encroachment of 'social' concerns and the state.

The *BMJ*'s correspondence pages were little different, with discussion again centring on whether carrying out abortions was an appropriate role for doctors and expressing wariness of the state. Concerning potential pollution of the medical role, letter writers argued, for example, that 'the sanctity of life, whether actual or potential, must be guarded carefully by us all in the medical profession in accordance with our long-established ethical standards and basic training to preserve life' (Pells Cocks, 1966: 539); that 'physicians are fundamentally concerned with making people better when they are ill and with preventing illness whenever possible [and abortion does little to achieve this]' (Clyne, 1966: 1482–3); that abortion on psychiatric grounds would be a case 'of the medical profession bending its scientific backbone in order to accommodate public opinion' (Johnson, 1966: 646); and that once the Act came into law, it would become difficult for doctors to oppose abortion being accepted 'as the remedy for many ... social evils' (Shackleton Bailey, 1967: 352). Concerning medical cooperation with the state, correspondents worried that politicians would 'decide the issue for us' (Pells Cocks, 1966: 539), and proclaimed that the requirement for notification 'smacks of pressure being brought to bear on gynaecologists, of snooping, and of police control, and the thin edge of the wedge would inevitably ultimately affect every branch of the profession, and indirectly the general public' (Theobald, 1966: 978).

There were, of course, opposing voices. For example, one letter to the *BMJ* argued that the medical responsibility 'to relieve human misery' included abortion to alleviate the suffering of women with unwanted pregnancies (MacGillivray, 1965: 1433). Another stressed the validity of abortions for 'social economic, or moral reasons' (de Soldenhoff, 1966: 1168) – albeit while expressing a strong hostility to legal reform and the red tape that would accompany it. The expansion of the notion of health to include social concerns was, however, not widely accepted by *BMJ* correspondents. Overall, the letters challenge the picture of a medical profession in happy alliance with lawmakers; rather, they express a great deal of fear and wariness.

The 'social doctor'

Overcoming these fears required the creation of a narrative establishing the legitimate role of doctors as 'socially responsible' agents of governmental regulation. This was achieved in part through redraft after redraft of the objectionable 'social clause' of the Act, until it was eventually scrapped in favour of a broad clause promoting the concept of 'sociomedicine' (see Table 3.1). In his foreword to Hindell and Simms' *Abortion Law Reformed*, Steel responds to the authors' claim that the loss of the social clause watered down the Abortion Act; 'social conditions,' he argues, 'cannot be and ought not to be separated from medical considerations. I hope that the Abortion Act by its very drafting has encouraged the concept of socio-medical care' (Steel, 1971: 7). However, in Steel's own opinion his strategy for dealing with medical demands was far from slavish, in fact consisting largely of 'playing one body off against the other' (1971: 8). This, he continues, was justified as it would be inappropriate for Parliament to accept the word of the medical bodies as final:

> Parliament is sovereign. Pressure groups and specialist bodies do indeed influence what happens there, and rightly so. But, especially in private members' legislation, Parliament must exercise its judgment amid the tumult of conflicting advice. Its bills are its own property and nobody else's. (1971: 8)

Nonetheless, it is clear that medical objections had a large part to play in the withdrawal of the distinct social clause. In an interview conducted by BPAS decades later, Steel justified the clause's removal by arguing that the Bill's original 'categorisation of abortions as A-B-C-D was wrong ... one should simply have a general approach to the subject which left the judgment in the hands of the medical profession' (in Furedi and Hume eds., 2007: 51). It was the categorization of abortions in this way that was most controversial among doctors, whether due to fears that women would feel they had a right to an abortion in certain defined circumstances, or because it was felt that it was not appropriate for doctors to decide on 'social' issues.

Second Reading

Steel's speech at the Second Reading of the Bill was quite different, and evidently contained some ideas with which he came to disagree. Steel described his original Clause 1(1,a), which would have allowed

Table 3.1: 'Social' concerns in the Silkin and Steel Bills

Bill	Stage	Wording of the social clause(s)
Silkin (first)	Second Reading (Lords)	1. It shall be lawful for a registered medical practitioner to terminate pregnancy in good faith – (a) in the belief that if the pregnancy were allowed to continue there would be grave risk of the patient's death or of serious injury to her physical or mental health resulting from either giving birth to the child or from the strain of caring for it, or … (c) in the belief that the health of the patient or the social conditions in which she is living (including the social conditions of her existing children) make her unsuitable to assume the legal or moral responsibility for caring for a child or another child as the case may be, … *Clause 1(c) was the most controversial of these, although many critics saw the provisions concerning the 'strain of caring for' another child in 1(a) as involving unacceptable 'social' concerns.*
	Committee (Lords)	At Committee stage, reference to the patient's 'social conditions' was removed from clause 1 (c) and replaced by provisions concerning her 'adequacy as a mother'. *Despite cutting the explicit reference to 'social conditions', Silkin made it clear that these would still be covered by the clause. An amendment to strike out clause 1 (c) was moved, but failed.*
	Report (Lords)	Clause 1(c) struck from the Bill by 81 votes to 51.
Silkin (second)	Second Reading (Lords)	This draft of the Bill again made reference to 'adequacy as a mother'.
	Committee (Lords)	The provision concerning 'adequacy as a mother' was changed to one dealing with 'capacity as a mother', meaning it now covered cases where the pregnant woman herself felt she could not cope with a(nother) child. *This version of the clause was preferred by the Lords and adopted by a four-to-one majority. However, the Bill was withdrawn and passed to David Steel.*
Steel	Second Reading (Commons)	1. Subject to the provisions of this section, a person shall not be guilty of an offence under the law relating to abortion when a pregnancy is terminated by a registered medical practitioner if that practitioner and another registered medical practitioner are of the opinion, formed in good faith –

Table 3.1 (cont.)

Bill	Stage	Wording of the social clause(s)
		(a) that the continuance of the pregnancy would involve serious risk to the life or of grave injury to the health, whether physical or mental, of the pregnant woman whether before, at or after the birth of the child; or ... (c) that the pregnant woman's capacity as a mother will be severely overstrained by the care of a child or of another child as the case may be; ... *At this stage, Steel viewed 1 (a) as simply clarifying the existing law, and argued that 1 (c) was essential to liberalisation.*
	Committee (Commons)	Clause 1(a) was substantially widened, now allowing the patient's 'well-being' and 'total environment' to be taken into account. However, clause 1(c) was struck from the Bill (on Steel's suggestion) by an amendment moved by Bernard Braine.
	Report (Commons)	Words concerning the patient's 'well-being' struck from clause 1(a). *Steel argued that the removal of provisions for 'well-being' would not significantly change the Bill, as 'health' included the concept of well-being.*
	Committee (Lords)	An amendment moved by Lord Dilhorne and approved by 87 votes to 86 removed the provisions in clause 1(a) pertaining to the physical or mental health of the pregnant woman's existing children.
	Report (Lords)	The words 'or any existing children of her family' were restored by 86 votes to 69.

Sources: Hansard; Hindell and Simms (1971)

doctors to abort if to continue the pregnancy 'would involve serious risk to the life or of grave injury to health, whether physical or mental, of the pregnant mother, whether before, at or after the birth of the child', as simply 'mak[ing] declaratory and clear[ing] the existing law' (Hansard, 1966: 1073). He went on to argue that in fact, to leave out the social clause would place too great a responsibility on doctors:

> If we in Parliament decide that we want cases of severe social hardship to be considered, we ought to say so. We ought not to demand of the medical profession that they should slip these in under a general Clause relating to physical and mental health. (1966: 1074)

Using a broader definition of health that could include 'social well-being', he elaborated, would be 'possibly slightly dubious' (1966: 1074). While Steel's thoughts concerning the need to distinguish between 'social' and 'health' concerns obviously changed over the course of the debate, the speech constructed a narrative that persisted in the rhetoric of the Bill's supporters throughout its journey through Parliament. In this narrative, doctors, pregnant women and lawmakers all faced a common enemy: the 'back-street' abortionist. As in other speeches, women were depicted overwhelmingly as victims of illegal abortion (among other things). If only, the narrative went, women seeking abortions could be delivered from illegal abortionists into the hands of a properly registered doctor – acting, of course, in accordance with regulations set out by the state – a problem confronting all three could be tackled. For women, this problem was the 'back-street butchery' to which they were vulnerable (Steel in Hansard, 1966: 1079). For doctors, this was the need to assist women critically injured by these abortions, and the inability to prevent 'butchery' by performing safe abortions themselves. And for the state apparatus, of course, this was the mounting illegitimacy of the existing law (but also, in various constructions, the need to 'protect' women and/or doctors). The tying-together of the interests of doctors, women and the state in this way was furthered in the debates that followed, particularly in discussion of, and attempts to amend, the so-called social clause.

A great number of participants in the debates were sceptical of the inclusion of social concerns as grounds for legal abortion. For some, this was due to a genuine mistrust of (some) members of the medical profession, who they felt might abuse this provision. Others, however, were influenced by the scepticism of the major medical organizations themselves – for example, Conservative MP Bernard Braine, who worked closely with these organizations throughout the Bill's passage (Keown, 1988: 99–100). These latter objections provoked considerable redrafting of the clause until its eventual removal; however, in the view of some opponents, the final form the Act took 'smuggled in' social concerns in much the same way as decried by Steel in his opening speech at Second Reading.

In the Second Reading debate, supporters of the Bill persisted with the idea that abortion might be justified on social grounds. Many appealed to 'social problems' such as poverty and overcrowding, but others explicitly expressed the idea that 'health' might include social considerations. Notably, then Labour MP David Owen, himself a qualified doctor, argued that 'the profession must ... accept that society has the right to make certain demands on it ... social and economic background is a vital part of health' (Hansard, 1966: 1114). Like the accounts of pro-reform doctors, these arguments also emphasized threatened identity, depicting restrictive law as preventing doctors from carrying out their duty to help the patient. Proponents described the doctor consulted by a woman seeking an abortion as 'in distress' (Lyons in Hansard, 1966: 1090) and having difficulties providing adequate treatment (Vickers in Hansard, 1109).

Some opponents of the Bill did express concerns about the potential 'destruction' of the 'unborn child' (Hansard, 1966: 1087, 1100, 1131). However, many instead attempted to break down reformists' narratives by attacking the assumption underlying some supporters' arguments that the medical profession could be considered a coherent whole. Their arguments instead divided the medical profession into numerous dissimilar groups. Labour MP William Wells, for example, painted a complex picture, noting that the BMA supported slightly different reforms to those proposed by Steel, that the RCOG was less certain of reform, and that Birmingham gynaecologists were almost uniformly against reform (Hansard 1966: 1082–3). Likewise, Conservative MP Bill Deedes sought to show that medical opinion was complex and divided:

> it is unwise to calculate here too much by consensuses. Certainly, there is a minority of doctors averse to the termination of pregnancies in any circumstances. There must be a minority who strongly support the termination of pregnancies in particular circumstances. There is another minority, a small minority, willing to consider termination of pregnancies without too close regard for circumstances. (Hansard, 1966: 1091)

Such arguments made it more difficult for reformists to claim to represent the demands of 'the medical profession' as a unified whole. In addition, the most popular challenges to the rhetoric of supporters furthered the fear of pollution of doctors' roles and a desire to keep the 'social' and 'medical' realms separate. These arguments stressed that 'social' problems should have 'social' solutions. For example, see Peter Mahon's response to David Owen: 'Does my hon. Friend, in all seriousness, consider that abortion is the remedy for the social evils which he is outlining?' (Hansard, 1966: 1114) and Sir John Hobson's statement that 'I do not think it is right to commit to the hands of doctors decisions on social and economic problems which are to be solved by the termination of prospective life' (Hansard, 1966: 1135). Opponents of reform implied that the Bill would somehow distort the role of the medical practitioner, as in Wells' observation that '[David Steel] was very frank in saying that it was not really a question of health ... One of the fundamental objections to the Clause is that it makes doctors arbiters not of medical questions, but of social ones' (Hansard, 1966: 1085). In a similar vein, Deedes asserted that 'doctors have been treated as subsidiary agents, agents to perform whatever we may consider right or wrong' (Hansard, 1966: 1091), while Kevin McNamara feared that 'the doctor, on the uncorroborated evidence of the patient, is to be placed in the position of judge and jury' (Hansard, 1966: 1130).

Committee stage

Before Committee stage, the pressure of these arguments and those of the medical bodies prompted Steel to amend the social clause. ALRA was strongly in favour of the clause's retention and opposed to the subsumption of social concerns under the banner of 'health', with one member writing that the result would be to 'continue the present practice of making the psychiatrist the scapegoat for such terminations when we all know perfectly well that the mother's mental health isn't the crucial issue' (Diggory cited in Hindell and Simms, 1971: 175). Steel eventually amended clause 1(1)(a) so that doctors could consider risks to the patient's 'well-being' and her 'total environment actual or reasonably foreseeable' (Hindell and Simms 1971: 177), believing that both the BMA and reformers could interpret these provisions to suit themselves. Meanwhile, he proposed to withdraw the clause concerning the woman's 'capacity as a mother' and pregnancy as a result of rape, although some extra words were inserted into subclause (1)(a) allowing 'the health of any existing children of the family' to be taken into account (1971: 185).

During Committee stage, Steel explained that he had dropped the reference to 'capacity as a mother' as it as it appeared to allow 'entirely separate, non-medical grounds for abortion' (Hansard, 1967a: 110). He did not conceal the fact that the new clause 1 still allowed social grounds; however, he argued that these should not be considered separately from medical concerns but as 'part and parcel of a correct medical judgment' (Hansard, 1967a: 110), and stressed that the aim of the Bill was to make life easier for the profession (Hansard, 1967a: 111). Of course, criticisms were raised, particularly concerning the broadness of the concept of 'well-being' (for example, Pannell in Hansard, 1967b: 182; Dalkeith in Hansard, 1967b: 185). Bernard Braine decried 'the appalling difficulty of putting on the shoulders of two medical men the responsibility for making what may be largely social value judgements' (Hansard, 1967a: 115). This was countered by David Owen, who argued that health involved much more than 'illness and complete mental breakdown' (Hansard, 1967a: 145).

Report stage

At Report stage Steel withdrew the language of 'well-being'. This was seen as highly significant by both supporters and opponents of the inclusion of 'social' concerns, but Steel argued that it would not make a dramatic difference to the Bill, as 'health' included the concept of well-being (Hansard, 1967c: 963). Accordingly, debate continued to rage over whether it was appropriate to ask doctors to make 'social' judgments, with participants again arguing that doctors are not 'qualified' to make these judgments (for example, Glover, McNamara in Hansard 1967c: 969, 1029). Some participants suggested that social workers would be better equipped to make these decisions (for example, Jenkin in Hansard, 1967c: 967).

A significant contribution came from Conservative MP Jill Knight, who continued with the theme of 'social solutions to social problems': local authorities could deal with housing, social workers could help overburdened mothers, and the benefits system could help with financial difficulties (Hansard, 1967c: 1033). Interestingly, Knight's speeches frequently employed a progressive rhetoric, underlining, for example, the need to 'have more homes and better facilities and give the parents a rest in caring for [disabled children] or every scrap of help we can, thus sharing the burden... Society is more and more recognising its responsibilities and bearing them' (Hansard, 1967c: 1074–5).

Lords

These lines of argument continued during debates in the House of Lords. Lord Silkin, moving the Bill's Second Reading in the Lords, expressed his disappointment at the removal of the social clause, claiming that 'in the course of its passage through the other place[3] the Bill has been considerably emasculated' (Hansard 1967e: 260). However, others felt that the Bill still allowed abortion on social grounds. Most notably, Viscount Barrington listed the forms the clause had taken in both the Silkin and Steel Bills, from 'inadequacy as a mother', through 'capacity as a mother', to 'well-being' – and finally, 'the health of the mother and/or the existing children of the family'

(Hansard 1967e: 269). This, he continued, was a far more dishonest way of allowing abortion on social grounds than the 'well-being' clause (Hansard 1967e: 270). Accordingly, participants in the Lords debates continued to challenge the inclusion of 'social' concerns – whether these included 'the health of the existing children of the family' or simply a broad interpretation of the health of the pregnant woman.

However, some supporters of the Bill were prepared with a response. Lord Platt, for instance, argued that surely what clause 1(1)(a) refers to

> is in fact a medical indication, because it refers to the physical or mental health [of the mother] ... But, even if this is interpreted as being a social rather than a medical provision, surely doctors for centuries have taken into account the social conditions of their patients before prescribing treatment for them. I know that I have always tried to do this and, what is more, I have always taught my students that they do not understand the full implications of a case unless they have taken into account the social state in which the patient lives. (Hansard, 1967e: 317)

Later, in the Lords Committee stage, Lord Chorley argued that the objectionable words 'refer to the physical and mental health of the children. It is not on purely sociological grounds at all' (Hansard, 1967f: 1004). He continued:

> this is called the social clause, because the social element obviously comes into it; but, basically, it is a medical problem affecting the mental and physical condition of the children. ... Any doctor who tried to decide the thing on purely social grounds, without considering its effect on the mental and physical life of the children, would be going against the law. (Hansard, 1967f: 1011)

In such arguments, Chorley and others like him appear to be becoming frustrated with their opponents' refusal to accept the crucial concept of 'sociomedicine'. The latter part of Chorley's argument involves a lot of rhetorical manoeuvring around the role of 'medicine', as not simply assessing social circumstances, but rather their effect on 'mental and physical life'. It is not clear how the two situations differ. However, in spite of several attempts at amendment – some of which were almost successful – clause 1(1)(a) emerged from the Lords unscathed and incorporating a broad definition of 'health'.

By the later stages of the Bill's passage through Parliament, a distinct logic of medicalization can be discerned in the arguments of Steel and his supporters. This logic breaks down the distinction made by opponents between social and medical concerns, instead articulating a range of concerns – adequate living conditions, good parenting, psychiatric *and* physical well-being – together using a broad definition of 'health'. In this articulation, the role of doctors is not threatened by the need to take all these into account when assessing abortion patients. Rather, it is threatened by the legal situation without the Abortion Act 1967 – as are women and the state.

Women, motherhood and mental health

As Sheldon's classic critique of abortion law demonstrates, the passage of the Bill and, in particular, the social clause relied heavily on specific gendered discourses. The notion that women might have a 'right to choose' seldom cropped up in the parliamentary debates other than dismissively. Rather, women were portrayed overwhelmingly as 'tarts and tired housewives' (Sheldon, 1997: 32) – either as fickle and irresponsible, or as weak and vulnerable victims in need of paternal care (Thomson, 1998: 101–2). Abortion was also frequently justified in terms of motherhood (remember the Silkin and Steel Bills' initial focus on 'capacity' or 'adequacy as a mother') and the family – hence the inclusion of 'the health of any existing children' as a ground for abortion in the eventual Act. These points bear repeating; as the following chapters demonstrate, the gendering of the Act is something that feminist and pro-choice actors engaging with abortion law must still confront.

For anti-abortion participants, women seeking abortion were simply irresponsible, irrational and frivolous 'girls' (Sheldon, 1997: 36–8) who were potentially complicit in the corruption of the medical profession with 'social' concerns. However, the reformists overwhelmingly portrayed women as vulnerable. This chapter has already noted the importance of psychology in validating abortions for reasons other than a strictly physical threat to the pregnant woman's health. Psychiatric discourses of this kind often situate women as particularly vulnerable to blows to their mental health (Flatseth and Madsen, 2013; Gill and Orgad, 2015). David Owen (one of the most outspoken proponents of 'sociomedicine' in the debates) touched on the themes of both vulnerability and motherhood in his speech at Second Reading. Firstly, he observed that 'a woman is susceptible to depression at times of pregnancy' (Hansard, 1966: 1113), before going on to depict 'a woman who ... shares her bed with her husband and two children, with perhaps two other children living and sleeping in the same room' (Hansard, 1966: 1114). Such a woman, if 'precipitated into a depression deep and long lasting' would be 'incapable of looking after those children' (Hansard, 1966: 1115).

The role played by social class in these arguments should be obvious. The 'social' clauses of the Steel and Silkin Bills were always aimed at working-class women, who at the time were subject to high rates of maternal mortality and were also thought to be particularly vulnerable to the strain of caring for an 'overlarge' family. The ways that legal abortion might help address these problems are clear. However, the introduction of methods for limiting the size of working-class families was proposed as the solution to an even broader set of social problems. The closing speech by the Labour MP Renée Short is instructive in this regard:

> We must consider what happens to some of the unfortunate unwanted children born into inadequate homes, disabled children, mentally defective children. They come into the care of the local authority. A research project has been carried out by a Birmingham University social worker, who shows that it is not uncommon for a child of this kind to have up to 10 different homes in five years. The number of foster homes that have broken down has increased during the past few years, and he believes that children coming into care in this way are often more difficult and more disturbed, and that they are the delinquent adolescents. The delinquent adolescents become the parents of more unwanted delinquent adolescent children in the next generation, generating another cycle of cruelty and neglect. (Hansard, 1966: 1162–3)

Abortion is here conjectured as a solution to the specific social problem of 'delinquency' associated, according to MPs, with the working class. Similarly, a speech by the Labour MP Dr John Dunwoody hypothesized that 'problem families' were caused by the breakdown of mothers' ability to '[hold] together the family unit', and that smaller families would restore women to their 'worthwhile function as a mother' (Dunwoody in Hansard, 1966: 1098–9). The supporters of the Bill were therefore able to cast themselves as defenders, not of women's right to choose, but of the institution of motherhood itself.

Working-class women, in the arguments of Steel's supporters, were also extremely vulnerable to exploitation by illegal abortionists. These arguments expose an additional dimension of the logic of medicalization. Medicalization promised a brighter future of happy mothers, happy families, and a harmonious relationship between women and doctors. However, in order to achieve this idealized scenario, legislators had to overcome the threat of back-street abortionists, depicted in evocative language – whether the 'grey-faced woman' with 'Higginson's syringe[4] and a soapy solution' or the more expensive 'hasty medical man whose patient returns to a distant town, there to lie in terror and blood and without medical attention' (Dunwoody in Hansard, 1966: 1089). These arguments are often, again, rounded off with fears for such women's families, such as this from Dame Joan Vickers, quoting a *Lancet* article:

> Countless women undergo the dangers of unprofessional abortion when no pregnancy exists and without having received any medical opinion whatever. Yet it happens that with invalidation or death of these mothers the family disintegrates, for around their health and their capacity to tend the children the whole house revolves and, therefore, these mothers are the very last to be permitted to jeopardise their well-being. (Hansard, 1966: 1109–10)

These images help explain the grip of medicalization on the parliamentary imagination. The language of vulnerability and threat assisted the overall argument that women seeking abortions need to be delivered into the hands of the medical profession, not simply in order to access a clean and safe procedure, but in order to receive paternal 'guidance' whether an abortion eventually takes place or not. As Steel phrased it:

> It may well be that in many cases the effect of introducing the Bill will be that instead of a woman having a back-street abortion, she will discuss the matter with her family doctor, in some way be reassured and feel that she has been offered some guidance, and no abortion will take place at all. (Hansard, 1966: 1076)

Notifications

One aspect of the Bill that seriously worried members of the medical profession was the issue of the notification of abortions to a government authority. This was due to the considerable wariness of the state already noted, and fear of pollution by 'social' concerns. While in favour of notification for research purposes, many doctors were concerned that the police would be able to easily access abortion records – as one doctor said, this might result in 'snooping, and ... police control' (Theobald, 1966: 978). There were also concerns that notification might compromise women's privacy and doctor–patient confidentiality. The medical bodies therefore recommended that notifications should only be disclosed on production of a court order. This request was not conceded, as Steel felt it was sufficient to leave regulations relating to disclosure to the Minister of Health (Keown, 1988: 105).

Critics of the Bill such as Jill Knight and Bernard Braine argued that the medical recommendations on notification should be included in the Bill, but their amendments failed. In response, Steel declared the requirement for notifications to be a 'safeguard against abuse' and racketeering (Hansard, 1967d: 1249). However, as Keown has pointed out, its effectiveness for this purpose is limited: for an abortion to be legal under the Bill and subsequent Act, the doctors involved (presuming they are properly certified) need only to have decided 'in good faith' that the procedure was necessary. The absence of good faith is extremely difficult to prove (Keown, 1988: 131–2). Hence, notifications serve more as a source of statistics and information on abortion – to ensure, in short, that abortion remains *knowable* and hence *governable*:

> A dark mass of female criminality which had been perceived as profoundly threatening to the existing social order (and, in particular, to the family) is thus brought into the open, and isolated in the bodies of individual women where it can be contained, monitored and controlled. The problem of abortion is changed from one of widespread and unquantifiable devi*ance*, to one of isolated, identifiable and treatable devi*ants*. (Sheldon, 1997: 29; emphasis in original)

What the Act also achieved, however, was the constitution of doctors as quasi-state agents in the collection of this information. This, as we have seen, was not an easy prospect for the medical profession to stomach. Keown suggests that the provisions for notification were only accepted by doctors in return for substantial medical freedom, ensuring that the decision to abort remained in their hands (1988: 165).

After the Act

Analysis of medical commentary in the years immediately following the Act suggests that the Act successfully established a 'social' identity for the profession. In a symposium held by the Medical Protection Society, Royal College of General Practitioners, and RCOG, participants stressed that doctors, as gatekeepers to abortion, bore a responsibility to find out everything about a patient's circumstances in situations where 'there are not obvious clear-cut medical reasons for abortion', and to relay this information to other consultants involved (Dudley-Brown, 1969: 5). This apparent acceptance of the social role of doctors also recalls the paternalistic, doctor-knows-best image underlying parliamentary debates on the Act. Indeed, the gendered aspect of appeals to medical authority was made more explicit by one participant who objected to his patients' desire for privacy, describing such patients as 'hysterical and demanding' (Tooley, 1969: 11).

Many MPs feared that, under the Act, the argument that early abortions are safer than carrying a pregnancy to term (known as the 'statistical argument') could be used as legal justification for abortion on demand, giving greater control to pregnant women. However, this argument was used in the symposium to reinforce medical authority over abortion, on the grounds that if all first-trimester abortions are legal, it was for the doctor to decide whether they are appropriate (Tooley, 1969: 9). Such assertions persist with the image of the socially responsible doctor: far from being divorced from 'social' concerns, such a doctor makes it 'his' duty to adjudicate on them. This, of course, is predicated on the knowledge that the eventual decision to abort will remain in the hands of the doctor.

Perhaps the most compelling evidence of a shift in attitudes can be found in a *BMJ* leading article in 1971. In opposition to a pre-Act piece that worried about doctors making decisions 'on other than their expert knowledge' (*BMJ*, 1966: 1608), the article asserted that the decision to abort (or not) on 'social' grounds fell under a 'fundamental right to exercise professional judgment' (1971: 261). While adopting a disapproving tone towards women who are pregnant as a result of unprotected sex, the article conceded that 'It is no answer to say that women must pay for their mistakes and have the babies' and instead suggested that 'doctors should encourage the attitude that unless a child is really wanted sexual intercourse without contraception is an act of selfish irresponsibility by both parties' (1971: 261).

This is not to say that 'abortion on demand' or 'on request'[5] was widely regarded as legitimate at this time, even if 'social grounds' were increasingly accepted. Many doctors continued to express concern over the way the Act was being interpreted, especially in the private sector, allowing abortions 'for reasons of convenience' (Lewis cited in Keown, 1988: 112). However, this should not be mistaken for widespread rejection of a social role for doctors: rather, as is evident from the arguments relayed earlier, it was felt that doctors should be performing this role with more care and attention, and without simply granting the patient her wishes. The notion that the medical role was somehow being polluted by the intrusion of social concerns began to recede from public debate, with 75 per cent of doctors approving of 'social' abortions in 1974 (Keown: 1988: 121). By the mid-1970s, both the BMA and RCOG had accepted the legitimacy of abortion on social grounds (Marsh and Chambers, 1981: 73–7).

Social questions, medical answers

Early parliamentary debates on legal abortion demonstrate lawmakers' assumption that women are vulnerable, potentially irresponsible, and in need of paternal protection, while doctors were meanwhile represented as women's paternal guardians. The Act was also very clearly aimed at a certain type of woman – working-class, poor, perhaps in a bad or abusive marriage, and at risk of having 'delinquent' children. However, what is also clear is that the Act required a great deal of negotiation between disparate elements; it did not draw upon a ready-made affinity between lawmakers and the medical profession. Crucially, this negotiation involved a transformation of the identity of the medical profession, requiring an account of abortion linking women, doctors and the law together in a particular way. Reformists insisted that 'it was within the doctor's sphere of duty and competence to promote this type of health, i.e. not only *should* the doctor take into account social factors, but he *could* measure and evaluate them' (MacIntyre, 1973: 125).

Clearly, the prospect of taking on a 'social' role was a bitter pill for many doctors to swallow, despite accounts demonstrating that the medical profession has in fact *always* had a social role (Zola, 1972; Lupton, 1997). Before the Act, medical discourse on legalized abortion was preoccupied by the need to preserve a certain role for doctors. Even doctors in favour of abortion on social grounds attempted to situate such abortions within 'our duty to relieve suffering'. While these concerns began to recede after the Abortion Act 1967 came into effect, this chapter does not suggest that the Act simply forced the profession to accept a 'social' identity in spite of its scepticism. If this had been possible, the original incarnation of the so-called social clause might have remained intact. Rather, the contention is that the repeated redrafting of the Silkin and Steel Bills, especially of this clause, constituted a sustained attempt to achieve the legalization of 'social' abortions in a way that gelled with doctors' pre-existing understanding of their role and identity as 'relieving suffering' but above all as 'protecting health'. The increasingly broad definition of 'health' expounded by Steel as the debates went on, combined with the gradual erosion of explicit provisions for 'social' conditions, allowed doctors to approach an understanding of abortions as necessary for 'health' in a wide range of circumstances, and of themselves as responsible for 'health' in its broadest sense. In the context of the Abortion Act 1967 as a whole, 'health' may also be interpreted in a eugenicist sense – as preventing the birth of 'abnormal' babies and discouraging 'undesirable' groups from reproducing (Greenwood and Young, 1976).

Medicalization transformed medical professionals into quasi-governmental agents, responsible not only for adjudicating pregnant women's decision to abort, but also for assisting in the compilation of statistics that render abortion observable and knowable. However, it also made women into subjects with a duty to manage their own bodies in a certain way. This was achieved by the transfiguration of women seeking abortions into *patients*. Again, it must be stressed that the Abortion Act 1967 does not represent a hard-won *right* to have an abortion. At the time of writing, it is still illegal to 'self-abort';[6] abortions are only legal when certified by two registered medical practitioners and notified to the Department of Health. As Sheldon observes, this serves to make abortion identifiable and treatable. Moreover, the construction of women as (properly) patients is not incidental but an express aim of the Act: Steel and others remarked frequently during debates that one of its most desirable effects would be to encourage women to consult their doctors.

In the debates, lawmakers assumed themselves to be responsible, in a paternalistic sense, for the well-being of women and doctors. Participants in favour of reform listed wrongs and social problems that 'we' must put right (for example, Vickers, Short in Hansard, 1966: 1109; 1158–61). The Act thus constructed a 'paternalistic-patriarchal' (Yeatman, 1997) role for government and Parliament, concerned with defending an idealized vision of motherhood with heavy class connotations and protecting women from social evils, but not with granting women bodily autonomy. At the same time, however, a limited role was proposed for government in the actual business of deciding the circumstances in which abortion could be carried out, and this was the subject of prolonged debate (for example,

Hansard 1967c: 896–906; 940–59). Dissidence was quelled by invoking medical authority: doctors, as experts on health, would of course know better than Parliament whether an abortion should take place. Nonetheless, the same participants argued in favour of mechanisms such as notifications to act as a check on the irresponsible or immoral doctors who might abort purely for financial gain. Hence a tension emerged between the image of the moral, paternal and responsible doctor who could be given free rein to carry out abortions, and that of the immoral, profit-hungry racketeer who should remain the subject of state vigilance. This tension became a focal point for those in favour of further restrictions to legal abortion.

The overriding effect of medicalization was to reinscribe abortion with meaning, making it less threatening. This was achieved, firstly, by constructing abortion as a 'health' issue, but also through a particular gendering of health. To justify abortion, the Act's supporters repeatedly invoked distinctly feminized and classed modes of suffering (of the frightened young woman, the overburdened working-class mother, or the tragic victim of the back-street abortionist), which might damage (mental) health and impair women *in their function as women* (that is, as wives and mothers). Hence, the possibility that abortion might signify autonomy, self-determination and bodily integrity was constrained, and abortion instead came to signify a return to sanctioned feminine roles. Medicalization has thus operated to contain abortion's unsettling or radical implications.

4

Feminism Enters the Debate

Despite legalization, abortion remained relatively difficult to access in the 1970s, and women frequently had to travel to other regions of the UK to access abortion (Halfmann, 2011: 112). Access problems notwithstanding, political attacks on the Abortion Act 1967 were frequent, underpinned by the perception that widespread 'abuses' of the Act were occurring in the private sector. The alleged abuses ranged from abortions being carried out 'on demand' despite Parliament's intentions, to obscenely high charges, to low standards of care for women undergoing abortion. Public outrage over these claims heightened in 1974 after a series of articles was published in the *News of the World*, and later as the book *Babies for Burning* (Litchfield and Kentish, 1974), by freelance journalists Susan Kentish and Michael Litchfield. The journalists made several shocking allegations: that samples of both journalists' urine received positive results at pregnancy testing centres who refer for abortion (Kentish was not pregnant, and Litchfield was of course unable to become pregnant); that many abortion doctors were Nazi sympathisers; that viable foetuses were being destroyed; and that at least one doctor had agreed to sell foetuses to be made into soap. These claims were to be called into question in a *Sunday Times* report, which discovered, for example, that one of the alleged 'Nazi sympathisers' was Jewish and had lost his wife and son at Auschwitz (Francome, 1984: 166–8).

Nonetheless, these and other allegations influenced several MPs to introduce anti-abortion Bills during this period. Such claims served to undermine the notion of the 'socially responsible' doctor that was central to the Act's logic of medicalization. However, there was another powerful image underlying the Act: that of the weary, vulnerable women in need of paternal guidance. Up to this point, the Act's supporters had been able to present themselves as the protectors of these women, meaning that those attempting to amend the Act had a 'woman problem' (Amery, 2015a) to grapple with. This chapter charts the various attempts to 'solve' this problem by depicting women as threatened not by adverse social conditions and their inability to access abortion legally, but by exploitation by 'legitimate' abortion providers.

While feminist arguments were not really a feature of debates over the Steel Bill, distinctly feminist voices were heard in the 1970s debates. The Abortion Act 1967 was, of course, a huge improvement on the pre-Act situation in which richer women were able to access abortion covertly in private clinics, but poorer women had to resort to much more dangerous methods. However, as the Act placed abortion under medical control rather than allowing abortion on demand, it sat uneasily with calls for a right to choose. This placed feminist MPs in a difficult position: the gendered implications of the Act were troubling, but at the same time it was essential to defend it from attack by opponents of legal abortion. This difficult position meant that pro-choice and feminist arguments were often replete with inconsistencies.

Contesting the Abortion Act 1967

While sponsors of the amending Bills introduced in this period often claimed that their aim was simply to 'improve' the Abortion Act 1967, each of these Bills in some way undermined the logic of medicalization that the Act had formalized in law. The first such Bill was sponsored by Conservative MP Norman St John-Stevas in 1969 (Hansard, 1969). As a Ten Minute Rule Bill, it had little chance of progressing past its first reading, and St John-Stevas's aim was simply to air his views to the House. The Bill's one provision would have required one of the two doctors who certify an abortion to be either a consultant gynaecologist in the NHS, or a doctor of equivalent status approved by the Minister of Health. In doing so, it would have arrogated to the government the ability to decide which doctors were to be considered sufficiently qualified to make decisions on abortion. This amendment had already been discussed at length and defeated during the Committee stage of the Steel Bill, and St John-Stevas was denied a first reading by 210 votes to 199 (Marsh and Chambers, 1981: 21–2).

In his speech at First Reading, St John-Stevas explained that his Bill's purpose was to confront the 'rackets' developing in abortion provision. In doing so, he appealed to a widespread perception that multiple abuses were occurring in the private sector, with a number of doctors focusing on profit above all else and 'not observing the normal standards of medical care' (in Hansard, 1969: 412). St John-Stevas framed the issue as one of public morality, appealing to a 'moral consensus' that abortion should not be banned, but that abortion on demand should not be allowed either (Hansard, 1969: 411–2). This consensus, he argued, was being violated, and legislation was needed to address 'the demands of the social, moral and medical strength and reputation of the country' (Hansard, 1969: 414). A central aspect of the speech was its division of doctors into two distinct classes. On the one hand was the figure of the responsible and ethical gynaecologist – 'a responsible medical person, highly qualified and highly placed' (Hansard, 1969: 413). On the other hand there were 'racketeers' – irresponsible doctors who cared more about profit than duty and whose actions 'amount[ed] almost to medical negligence' (Hansard, 1969: 412–3). The speech attempted to undermine the medicalization of abortion by appealing not to a unified, self-regulating medical profession but to a range of disparate doctors, from the unethical, medically negligent and poorly qualified to the responsible, qualified and knowledgeable.

St John-Stevas's speech and Bill thereby attacked the key assumptions of the Act. They challenged its treatment of the medical profession as a self-regulating whole, capable of dealing with these matters on its own. Instead, the Bill attempted to establish a place for further, formal state intervention. In addition, and perhaps more damagingly, the speech challenged the image of the socially responsible doctor established during the Steel Bill's passage through Parliament. Rather than the benign paternal guardians the Act's supporters had envisioned, private doctors in St John-Stevas's speech were construed as irresponsible, profit-hungry and immoral. The Bill therefore represented an attempt to divest certain segments of the medical profession of their role in abortion provision and reconsolidate power in the more 'traditional' arms of government.

However, the speech was less thorough in its challenge to the gendering of the Act. In fact, St John-Stevas barely mentioned women until the end of the speech other than to joke that 'an agnostic mother of nine' might have been a more fitting person to introduce the Bill (Hansard, 1969: 411). The final words of the speech, however, indicated an uneasy acceptance of the image of the tired, vulnerable woman underpinning the Act, acknowledging the importance of tending to 'the needs of the individual mother, for whom we should certainly have concern and compassion' (Hansard, 1969: 414). Of course, St John-Stevas quickly returned to his conservative moral stance, adding that these needs must be balanced with the moral demands of society. Nonetheless, these closing words seem to indicate a belief (or at least a desire to be seen to acknowledge) that the psychiatric discourses and social concerns behind the Act were, to an extent, legitimate.

Subsequent attempts to amend the Act also targeted the alleged abuses taking place in the public sector and similarly distinguished between classes of doctors deemed appropriate or inappropriate for the certification of abortion. Proposals for doing so included the requirement that one of the two doctors who approve abortion should be a consultant gynaecologist (as in the St John-Stevas and Irvine Bills) or have been registered as a medical practitioner for at least five years (as in the Benyon Bill), and stringent conditions for the approval of clinics (the White and Corrie Bills). Some of these Bills would have also restricted the grounds for legal abortion or lowered the upper time limit to 20 weeks' gestation (see Table 4.1).

These Bills all challenged the medicalization underpinning the Act, although they did this in different ways. However, when it came to the place of women in their arguments, they were on less certain ground. The image of the tired and vulnerable woman who needs an abortion to avoid becoming a 'mental wreck', along with that of the women butchered by the back-street abortionist, had been firmly established in the parliamentary imagination during the passage of the Abortion Act 1967, and indeed remained an important feature of pro-choice discourse. Moreover, the burgeoning feminist movement of the 1970s had provided powerful arguments in favour of liberal abortion laws and 'a woman's right to choose', arguments that began to enter parliamentary debate in the mid-1970s. The sponsors and supporters of amending Bills had to grapple with this 'woman problem' if they were to successfully alter the Act.

Defending the status quo

Those opposed to any alteration of the Abortion Act 1967 already had a whole repertoire of arguments at their command. In parliamentary debates, the continued use of psychiatric discourses and horror stories of 'back-street butchers' allowed opponents of these Bills to present themselves as the protectors of vulnerable women. In addition, these MPs challenged the image of a divided medical profession employed by the would-be reformists, stressing rather the unity of the profession and the potential damage caused by heightened government intervention. Backing up these accounts was the Lane Committee, appointed in 1971 to examine the workings of the Act. The Committee's eventual report was committed to upholding the medicalized regulatory system and stressed the need for cooperation between doctors and the government rather than the coercion of the former by the latter.

Table 4.1: Abortion Bills, 1969–80

Bill	Stage reached	Key provisions
St John-Stevas, 1969	First Reading	Require one of the two doctors who certify an abortion to be a consultant gynaecologist in the NHS.
Irvine, 1969–70	Second Reading	Require one of the two certifying doctors to be a consultant gynaecologist in the NHS, or a medical practitioner of equivalent status approved by the Secretary of State for Social Services.
Hunt, 1971	First Reading	Prohibit the charging of fees for referring or recommending persons to medical services or treatment (specifically aimed at abortion advisory services).
Grylls, 1974	Standing Committee	Similarly prohibit the charging of fees for referring or recommending persons to medical services or treatment.
White, 1974–5	Select Committee	Increase surveillance of private clinics, laid down statutory conditions for their approval, and prevented them being financially associated with referral bureaux. Prohibit abortions from being carried out on non-resident women, lower the upper time limit from 28 weeks to 20 weeks and require that the pregnancy must present a 'grave' risk to the life or health of the pregnant woman for an abortion to be carried out.
Benyon, 1977	Standing Committee	Require one of the two certifying doctors to have at least five years' clinical standing; prevent financial links between referring organizations and abortion clinics; introduce statutory conditions for the licensing of clinics; and reduce the upper time limit to 20 weeks. Introduce new protections for conscientious objectors.
Braine, 1978	First Reading	Lower the time limit for legal abortion to 20 weeks; clarify the law regarding conscientious objection; prevent financial association between abortion clinics and pregnancy advisory bureaux.
Corrie, 1979	Report stage (adjourned)	Tighten the licensing of abortion clinics and ensure that they could not be financially associated with referral agencies; lower the time limit for legal abortion to 20 weeks; insert the words 'grave' and 'serious' into the Abortion Act 1967; amend the conscience clause of the Act to allow greater protections for conscientious objectors.

Source: Hansard; Marsh and Chambers (1981)

Parliamentary debates

Opponents of the Bills often accepted that 'one or two' doctors in the private sector (Steel in Hansard, 1969: 416) might be behaving unethically, but minimized the significance of this. Such abuses, they argued, would be more appropriately solved by tighter administrative controls rather than by new statutory measures. Overall, they rejected the idea that there were different 'classes' of doctors:

> A doctor is a doctor. What can be more absurd than to have special categories of doctors in circumstances like this? As soon as a man is registered he becomes responsible for affairs of life and death every week, every day, yet for the purposes of termination of pregnancy he has to have a five years' registration. (Cronin in Hansard, 1975: 1826)

The heightened level of state control of doctors the Bills would have established was especially disturbing to some:

> Is it suggested that a termination is lawful if it is done by a consultant gynaecologist in the Health Service and near murder if it is done by a gynaecologist outside it? ... Have we reached the stage, in this field and in none other, to force people into the National Health Service? Is this a new monopoly in State medicine being suggested from the benches opposite? This is the astonishing thing. Is this a new tyranny coming from the opposition? (Houghton in Hansard, 1970: 1701)

Opponents of the Bills continued to back an approach to abortion provision in which government intervention was minimal and the medical profession was considered capable of self-regulation. The benefits of this were argued to be many. Some pointed out, for example, that the 1967 Act had resulted in more, not less, regulation of abortion provision (for example Short in Hansard, 1970: 1669). For the most part, however, opponents revisited the liberal-paternal arguments that had proved successful in justifying legal abortion in the first place. Such 'social' arguments ranged from the concern that the Bills might result in higher maternal mortality rates due to significant delays in NHS provision (Steel in Hansard, 1969: 417), to noting the downturn in 'illegitimacy' rates (Hansard, 1970: 1692–6), to warning of a whole range of social ills:

> I believe very much in the sanctity of life. I think that is one of the central issues for all of us, whichever side we take on this Bill. I do not want to see a situation in which we have more physically and mentally handicapped children; more sick and handicapped mothers; more deaths in childbirth; more unwanted children, with all the social problems that will involve; more child abuse from those who are unable to care for their children and did not want to have them; more broken lives, and more broken families ... That is my view of the sanctity of human life. (Ennals in Hansard, 1979: 908–9)

Such concern for fixing social problems – especially those ostensibly caused by poor people having children – was articulated alongside narratives of the trauma to the mental health of women who had 'more children than they could emotionally, rationally or financially cope with' (Fairbairn in Hansard, 1977: 1853). The figure of the back-street abortionist continued to loom large in these speeches, with the 'untold physical and emotional harm' (Ennals in Hansard, 1979: 906) caused by illegal abortionists serving as a caution against the Bills. While these speakers sometimes distanced themselves from 'right to choose' arguments (Steel in Hansard, 1975: 1770), these narratives of trauma allowed opponents of the amending Bills to present themselves as the protectors of vulnerable women, and the Bills' supporters, by implication, as 'against' women. As David Steel, quoting the *Lancet*, put it in his speech against the St John-Stevas Bill: 'Things were certainly much easier for the gynaecologists before the public and Parliament had made their wishes known in the Act – but they were much harder for women' (Hansard, 1969: 420).

The Lane Committee, 1971–74

After considerable pressure from the anti-abortion lobby for the 1967 Act to be re-examined, the Lane Committee was appointed in 1971 with the Hon Mrs Justice Lane, the first female High Court judge in England, as chair. However, the same lobbyists were critical of the Committee and the eventual report it produced. Firstly, its composition was felt to be skewed in favour of legal abortion. Secondly, its terms of reference only included administrative questions about the working of the Act. Consideration of the morality of abortion was outside its remit (Marsh and Chambers, 1981: 23). The Committee produced its report in 1974. The report was mainly favourable towards the Act, although it did recommend non-statutory measures be taken to counter private sector abuses. The only legislative change it recommended was that the time limit for legal abortion be lowered from 28 to 24 weeks (Lane Committee, 1974).

Like participants in parliamentary debates, the report elaborated a logic of medicalization underpinned by psychiatric discourses and assumptions of female vulnerability. Its opening pages situated the Abortion Act 1967 with reference to the social changes of the preceding decades and the social ills ameliorated by legal abortion: 'the burden of often repeated, unwelcome and debilitating child-bearing' and 'the serious mental stress which may result from an unwanted pregnancy' (Lane Committee, 1974: 4). The report went on to detail the consequences of failure to achieve a wanted abortion. The risk of a 'reactive depression' (1974: 53) was foregrounded, as was the adverse effect on the chances of marriage for the 'mother of an illegitimate child' (1974: 60), although the possible effects on schooling and training were also mentioned.

The report's recommendations regarding practitioners relied heavily on the principle of medical freedom. Proposals that only certain categories of doctors might be allowed to certify abortion were regarded as an 'injustice' to 'responsible doctors' (1974: 66). The report rejected this kind of government intervention in favour of an emphasis on the ability of the profession to self-regulate:

> We consider that it should properly be for the medical profession to set and enforce its own standards of ethics and practice, and that this should be done without excluding from any particular branch of medical work practitioners who have not offended against these standards. (1974: 66)

Thus, the report promoted cooperation between doctors and the government, rather than the coercion of the former by the latter. However, the same vision of a responsible and self-regulating medical profession was used to recommend against allowing abortion on demand or request. This stance was justified, firstly, with regard to 'good medical practice' (1974: 65) and the ideals of sociomedicine: 'that a patient should be treated as a whole person viewed in the light of personal physical and mental health and social conditions and not merely as one suffering from a particular disease or condition requiring amelioration or cure' (1974: 64).

Secondly, the Report justified its recommendation against abortion on request by appealing to the potential effects on, and character of, women seeking abortion:

Further, some women would find the burden of making their own decision, unsupported, a heavy one and in such cases the operation might well be followed by emotional turmoil and feelings of guilt. Additionally, they would be more vulnerable to pressure from parents, husbands or boy-friends. Another advantage of permitting abortion on demand might in some cases be to encourage neglect of contraceptive precautions. (1974: 65)

In this passage, women appear as *either* vulnerable – susceptible to psychological trauma and manipulation – *or* irresponsible – unlikely to manage their bodies responsibly without paternalistic guidance. The report's recommendations concerning medical practice therefore illustrate that the medicalization of abortion cuts both ways. It guards against heightened state control over and restriction of access to abortion, but its paternalistic logic undermines the notion of a 'right to choose' and represents women as incapable of responsibly exercising this right.

Feminism in the debate

Parliamentary feminism during this time comprised a radical contestation of gender regimes in Parliament and beyond, but was also committed to defence of the Abortion Act 1967 and its underpinning principles. Steering a course between being overly celebratory and overly pessimistic, this section shows that pro-choice women MPs clearly articulated a feminist agenda – often hostile to what one termed the 'maleocracy' of Parliament (Colquhoun in Hansard, 1977: 1847) – in each debate and contested the gender regimes operating in Parliament and society. However, the same MPs tended not to examine the workings of the 1967 Act with the same critical lens and produced narratives of female vulnerability and 'acceptable' abortion that ultimately undermined their commitment to the principle of 'choice'. Nonetheless, these arguments must be viewed in context: in defending the Act, feminist MPs were forced to defend the assumptions about women seeking abortion that underpinned it.

Narrating 'acceptable' abortion

Lesley Hoggart (undated), examining pro-choice activism during the 1970s, notes that forging alliances with Parliament and trade unions had significant consequences for feminist activists. This contact with 'political reality', she argues, resulted in the National Abortion Campaign (NAC) neglecting its feminist principles and radical politics. This was a precursor to what she sees as a wider deradicalization of feminism – 'the price feminists paid for becoming involved in state agencies and mainstream political institutions in the 1980s'. In the mid-1970s, NAC was firmly in favour of a woman's right to choose and opposed to the liberal paternalism of the Act, its stated aim 'not only to reject familial policies but actively to challenge the authority of the state to govern women's choices' (Hoggart, undated). According to Hoggart, however, NAC's radicalism proved difficult to sustain. Firstly, NAC was dragged into engagement with parliamentary politics, in spite of its wish to remain outside of formal politics. This caused some tensions in the movement:

> The revolutionary feminist policies of NAC moved it to reject the tactics of a parliamentary pressure group, but there was always a contradiction between NAC's inclination towards such a rejection and the knowledge that policy struggle over existing legislation is necessarily centred on Parliament ... Whilst NAC pointed to the inadequacies of the 1967 Abortion Act, the concern expressed in the House of Commons was to make the 1967 Act work effectively as a public health measure within definite limits.
> (Hoggart, undated)

As a result, radical demands were sidelined in favour of a strategy of defending the Act. NAC's leadership judged that a working alliance with the labour movement, notably the Trades Union Congress (TUC), would be vital to achieve this goal and, by 1979, it was aware that its radical aims were unlikely to mobilize this group. The Campaign Against Corrie was launched to fight against a Bill introduced by the Conservative MP John Corrie. The Corrie Bill would have allowed abortion only in cases where the woman's life was in 'grave' danger or where there was a 'substantial' risk of 'serious' injury to the woman's physical or mental health. As such, it presented a significant threat to abortion access. The Bill would also have lowered the time limit for legal abortion to 20 weeks' gestation, tightened the licensing of abortion clinics and ensured that they could not be financially associated with referral agencies, and amended the conscience clause of the Act to allow more scope for conscientious objection to assisting in abortions.

The Campaign Against Corrie was broad-based, involving both NAC and trade union activists (Hoggart, undated; Nielsen quoted in Orr, 2017: 163–4). Unlike NAC, however, the Campaign did not situate abortion rights in the broader context of women's rights and women's liberation. Rather, it played on the same 'social' concerns as the debate over Steel's Bill, emphasizing the possibility that the Bill would disproportionately affect working-class women, potentially meaning a return to back-street abortions. This strategy was successful, and Corrie withdrew his Bill on 26 March 1980 once it became clear that it would not succeed. Hoggart identifies two sets of politics operating within NAC during this period: firstly, the call for free abortion on demand situated within the broader context of women's liberation and, secondly, the inclusive, defensive politics of the Campaign Against Corrie. A Campaign poster demonstrates this well (Campaign Against Corrie, undated). The poster mimics a *Peanuts* comic strip, but the characters discuss the Corrie Bill, focusing on the proposed restriction of the upper time limit for legal abortion to 20 weeks' gestation. Abortion, the characters stress, 'is a great emotional trauma – it needs a lot of thinking about'. The poster emphasizes the vulnerability of women with unplanned pregnancies, and the possibility that unwanted children might be abused: 'if women are forced to have children, they may batter them through nervous strain or resentment'. The poster is obviously designed for broad public resonance, and there is no mention of a 'right to choose' or other feminist language. Rather, it translates feminist demands into a format that resonates with medicalization.

This is a good example of what Jeannie Ludlow has termed 'the trauma-tization of abortion' (Ludlow, 2008). Ludlow identifies a 'hierarchy of abortion narratives' at work in pro-choice rhetoric. Firstly, there are the narratives deemed 'politically necessary' to tell: those involving trauma and women's vulnerability – to rape, incest and domestic violence as well as to back-street abortion. Secondly, there are the narratives considered 'politically acceptable'. These concern contraceptive failure rates, women's financial difficulties, and foetal anomaly. Finally, there is a third category of narratives – 'the things we cannot say' (2008: 30). These include narratives of failure to use contraception (correctly or at all), of multiple abortions, of grief after abortion and of the economics of abortion provision. The latter category is, according to Ludlow, the most familiar to clinic workers, but the most downplayed in public pro-choice discourse.

Feminism in Parliament

While Ludlow's work focuses on pro-choice activism in the US, a similar emphasis on 'acceptable' abortion can be observed in UK abortion politics. A feminist contingent was beginning to develop in Parliament during this time and, by the time of the White Bill's Second Reading, there were several women willing to speak up in Parliament and explicitly frame abortion as a feminist issue. According to Elizabeth Vallance, the Bills were seen as a serious threat by Labour women MPs. Angry that their male colleagues seemed so indifferent to such an important issue, these women were galvanized by the abortion debates. Vallance argues that the threats to the Abortion Act 1967 were largely responsible for the group identity women MPs managed to forge in this period (Vallance, 1979: 75; 88–90).

Probably the most active pro-choice woman speaking in these debates was Renée Short. Short was no stranger to abortion debates, having sponsored a Ten Minute Rule Bill dealing with abortion before the Steel Bill was introduced. Other notable participants included Short's fellow Labour MPs Lena Jeger, Jo Richardson and Maureen Colquhoun. In these women's arguments, abortion was explicitly framed as a *women's* issue, and connected to questions of women's parliamentary representation. The idea that these women, minority as they were in the House of Commons, were acting for women outside Parliament featured prominently as a theme:

> It is, above all, a subject that concerns women. Practically all the women on this side of the House support the original 1967 Act and oppose this proposed amendment. I am sorry that there are not women on the other side of the House who are apparently anxious to take part in this debate, for this is a matter that concerns women very much indeed. (Short in Hansard, 1975: 1813)

> I speak for women in the House and outside. When I speak about women outside the House I refer to women in our own organised movement and in the Labour and trade union movement who also support the Act. (Short in Hansard, 1975: 1814)

> We have heard a lot of statistics today. I sometimes wonder whether we are talking about women at all. Perhaps if there had been more women Members of Parliament present today on the Opposition benches, we might have heard a wider variety of contribution. I must remind the House that this is International Women's Year. (Jeger in Hansard, 1975: 1830)

In addition, these MPs frequently articulated this feminist agenda together with a labour movement agenda, pointing out that women from the upper classes had never had trouble obtaining abortions, and that it was working-class women who would suffer most from any restrictions (e.g. Short in Hansard, 1975: 1814; Jeger in Hansard, 1977: 1829). However, by far the most explicit articulation of pro-choice demands into a chain of feminist demands was made by Colquhoun, who explicitly connected the issue of abortion to issues of women's representation, discrimination and equal pay.

> We seem to be considering constantly anti-women measures, which preoccupy this male-dominated Chamber. Perhaps I should suggest to the Prime Minister that he appoint a woman Minister with Cabinet rank to guard the rights of women. Then perhaps we should not have the kind of legislation that is constantly cropping up in this House to prevent women from having the right of abortion. (Colquhoun in Hansard, 1977: 1847)

> As a woman and as one of the small minority of women Members, I protest about the legislation that is set out by men. We have had the fundamentally weak Sex Discrimination Act and the Equal Pay Act, which have been of almost no significance to women when they get down to the nitty-gritty of having to use these laws, which have engendered a hardening attitude towards women. There are constant attempts to change the 1967 legislation in order to make it clear to women that their bodies are definitely not their own. They are the subject of laws to be made in this House, by and large, by the maleocracy. Whichever way one looks at it, the House of Commons is not a democracy but a maleocracy. (Colquhoun in Hansard, 1977: 1847)

Women MPs explicitly linked access to abortion with other women's movement causes: in particular, the matter of women's representation in Parliament, but also, in Colquhoun's speech, those of equal pay and ending discrimination. These demands formed the basis of their group identity in opposition to the male-dominated House or 'maleocracy', which was figured as hostile or at least indifferent to women's interests. Implicit in this was an imaginative politics that envisioned a world in which there are more women in politics guarding women's interests – including women in the Conservative party, and in the Cabinet.

Women MPs' speeches in these debates certainly contested the 'maleocracy' of the House of Commons and the gender regimes operating in society as a whole. However, with the exception of Colquhoun's contributions, they were far less radical when it came to critiquing the norms underpinning the Abortion Act 1967. If anything, it was doctors' narratives rather than women's narratives that were centred. For example, Jeger asked the House to consider 'the awful decision which faced doctors in the days before the law was changed', and centred the doctor's perspective in the tale of a woman who died after having an illegal abortion:

> I speak as a doctor's wife, and my husband used to work in a very poor part of the East End of London ... I remember my husband being called out to see a girl who had undergone an abortion and who had interfered with herself in a horrible way. My husband got the girl into hospital and she died there. The next thing that happened was that a policeman arrived and said to my husband 'You sent her into hospital and were the last doctor to see her'. My husband replied 'I can only say that if I had carried out the operation it would not have gone septic'. (Jeger in Hansard, 1975: 1828–9)

Women MPs also actively articulated the interests of women and doctors together, assuming that these interests must necessarily be aligned:

> The other particularly dangerous provision is in Clause 9. It is incredible that this House, the so-called bastion of democracy, should be even thinking of giving power to the police to investigate records, take away doctors' files and break that confidential link which has always existed between doctor and patient and which we should jealously preserve. It is monstrous, not only because women and doctors are involved but from the point of view of civil liberties. (Richardson in Hansard, 1977: 1870)

> It is a denial of the rights of women to decide how many children to have and when she will bear them, and the thing I find equally objectionable is that is displays complete mistrust of the medical profession in a way that is truly astonishing. (Short in Hansard, 1977: 1799)

In addition, abortion was constructed as being like any other medical practice, with participants stressing the unity of medical practice in opposition to the logic of difference employed by the Bill's supporters (for example Short in Hansard, 1977: 1803). Sometimes, the medicalization of abortion was explicitly linked to narratives of trauma:

> I submit that it is an extremely traumatic experience for a woman to have to go through an abortion at all, and she must be particularly desperate to have to come to this country to have it carried out. She is in need of help and compassion. It is astonishing that we in the House of Commons should seek to celebrate International Women's Year by making this differentiation. If a foreign gentleman comes to London to have his prostate fixed, he does not get sent home. How can we divide the specialities of medicine? How can we try to single out one element in the practice of medicine and ascribe to it a different branch of legislation? (Jeger in Hansard, 1975: 1830–1)

Such attempts to establish a continuity between abortion and other medical procedures reinforced the notion that doctors, not pregnant women, know best when it comes to abortion. Overall there appears to be a tacit acceptance of the medicalization of abortion. While MPs linked abortion into a chain of demands concerning 'women's issues', this was not done in a way that contested the fundamental norms underpinning the Abortion Act 1967 and the provision of abortion. Considering the extent of the feminist critique of medicalization, this is a worrying omission; the problematic notions of gender underpinning the Act went unchallenged.

Pro-choice women were in a difficult position in these debates. Doctors' and women's interests were not only regarded as aligned by participants, but *constituted* that way by the Act, which solved the problem of women's access to abortion by transfiguring women seeking abortion into patients. Defending women's access to abortion therefore necessitated, to some extent, defending a medicalized status quo. Moreover, pro-choice participants in the debates did not necessarily accept medicalization wholesale. While Maureen Colquhoun was the only of these women to also overtly criticize the 1967 Act and call for legislation giving women a full right to choose (Hansard, 1977: 1847), tensions emerged in other feminist accounts as participants noted the existence of 'reactionary chauvinist doctors' (Short in Hansard, 1977: 1801) and patchy NHS provision.

Nonetheless, overall the contributions of these women served to reinforce, rather than to undermine, the logic of medicalization. A narrative of trauma-tization developed in their speeches, which constructed women as heavily threatened by male sexuality but even more so by 'back-street butchery' (McDonald in Hansard, 1979: 1882) and restrictive abortion law. These accounts deployed gruesome imagery:

> The knitting needle is no joke. Before the 1967 Act was passed I worked in an office where there was a young junior of 15. She came in late one morning. I asked her why she was late. She said 'It was my mum. She fell again. We had her jumping up and down off the kitchen table all night. She has one or two instruments and I hope they will do the job'. (Richardson in Hansard, 1979: 928)

It is no surprise that these narratives of back-street butchery should have been deemed politically necessary to tell by pro-choice MPs: many women died in appalling circumstances before the Abortion Act 1967 came into effect, and their deaths provide a powerful case for legal abortion. However, by contrasting the figure of the back-street abortionist to that of the responsible and ethical doctor (as for Jeger's husband: 'if I had carried out the operation it would not have gone septic'), these narratives presented medicalization as the only option. Narratives of trauma-tization mobilized against attempts to restrict the terms of the Act, but they also reinforced the logic of medicalization, as implicit in these narratives were images of the paternal and protective doctor who can protect women from such tragedies.

Pro-woman language in anti-abortion discourse

This section turns to 'reformist' discourse from the Irvine Bill to the Corrie Bill. The sponsors and supporters of these Bills were often avowedly anti-abortion but viewed a more gradualist approach as more likely to be successful, although some supporters claimed to be merely concerned with tackling 'abuses' of the Abortion Act 1967. Analysis of their contributions in parliamentary debate, however, reveals a shift away from the conservative concern with 'public morality' emphasized by St John-Stevas, towards a seemingly more progressive concern with the protection of vulnerable women. This latter concern seems designed to cut into the Act's supporters' monopoly on sympathetic accounts of women seeking abortion, which had been critical in bringing the Act through Parliament in the first place.

At the forefront of such contributions were narratives of 'villains and victims' (Lee, 2003; 2013). These accounts distinguished 'responsible' from 'irresponsible' doctors, 'specialized' from 'non-specialized', 'experienced' from 'inexperienced' and so on. One the one hand, this strategy served to undermine the pro-Act assertion that doctors could reliably self-regulate on the matter of abortion, instead emphasizing the need for state intervention to separate the wheat from the chaff. On the other hand, these narratives presented women as 'victims' of legal abortion, vulnerable to exploitation by villainous doctors – a significant shift away from St John-Stevas's assertion that individual women's interests might somehow be at odds with the moral demands of society. These arguments clearly represent attempts to weaken the claim of supporters of the Act to be 'on women's side'. Indeed, elements of the reformists' speeches very much resemble feminist rhetoric concerning women's rights and entitlements. However, some significant tensions remained.

The Irvine Bill, 1969–70

The Irvine Bill's Second Reading debate occurred in February 1970. Similarly to the St John-Stevas Bill, the Irvine Bill would have required one of the two certifying doctors to be a consultant gynaecologist in the NHS or, failing that, a practitioner of equivalent status approved by the Secretary of State for Social Services. The Bill was 'talked out' at Second Reading, meaning its allocated time was used up in debate with no vote ever being taken. Nonetheless, it had the support of the BMA and RCOG, which claimed to be concerned only 'to safeguard the interests of the health of the women concerned' (Hansard, 1970: 1655). This was the framing given to the Bill by its sponsors during the Second Reading debate.

Bryan Godwin Irvine's speech centred on the standards and safety (or lack thereof) of abortions carried out in the private sector. Like St John-Stevas, he designated different categories of doctors, from the 'racketeers' to the responsible specialists. The fear figure of the 'professional abortionist' (Hansard, 1970: 1657) who only cared to profit from abortion featured heavily in the speech. Opposed to this was the consultant gynaecologist with a 'responsible medical opinion' (Hansard, 1970: 1664), who was assumed to be able to 'give specialised attention to girls who require it' (Hansard, 1970: 1663). This divide-and-rule tactic served to legitimate calls for increased government intervention to separate the responsible specialists from the profit-hungry racketeers.

These arguments were familiar from the St John-Stevas Bill. However, Irvine's speech was much stronger in how it handled the 'woman problem', containing language very similar, in fact, to that used to legitimate the Abortion Act 1967. Irvine stressed the vulnerability of 'girls' who seek abortion and the need for paternalistic intervention:

> One girl came to see me last week. After three hours in a clinic she was sent home, and two days later she had to go to a National Health Service hospital, where she was desperately ill for six weeks. Another girl, about whom I heard yesterday, was in a clinic for one hour, and subsequently had to spend 13 days in a National Health Service hospital because of the problems which had arisen. Another girl said that the conditions in the place to which she went were rather like Piccadilly Circus. (Irvine in Hansard, 1970: 1664–5)

In this subversion of pro-choice discourse, the private sector abortionist replaced the back-street abortionist in the narrative of abortion exploitation and trauma. This narrative detached fears about female vulnerability from the argument for medicalized abortion and incorporated them instead into a narrative where women were threatened by *abortion doctors themselves* and paternalistic government intervention was necessary. Irvine was subsequently able to present himself, rather than his opponents, as the socially progressive protector of vulnerable women: 'I want to see that humanity is offered to girls in this condition, and that they get proper medical care' (Hansard, 1970: 1665).

Nonetheless, there remained tensions in this vision. These became more evident as St John-Stevas – who also sponsored the Bill – made his speech. St John-Stevas's speech began in the same vein as Irvine's, complaining of abortion 'mills' with poor standards of care (Hansard, 1970: 1675). However, following an intervention by Renée Short, St John-Stevas dismissed her 'theological view of the right of women to have abortions on demand' (Hansard, 1970: 1675). By the end of his speech, St John-Stevas had returned to the conservative framing of the Bill as an issue of 'the requirements of public morality', opposed to and privileged over 'the needs of women' (Hansard, 1970: 1683).

The White Bill, 1974–75

As the Lane Committee had come under considerable fire due to its remit and composition, its report did not serve to quell anti-abortion activity. By the time the White Bill reached its Second Reading in February 1975, the Department of Health had already taken administrative action to prevent the worst 'abuses' in the private sector. Nonetheless, these actions were not widely publicized, and many MPs were unaware of its efforts (Marsh and Chambers, 1981: 28–9). With the publication of Litchfield and Kentish's *Babies for Burning* the previous year, parliamentary support for changed abortion law remained considerable. However, by this time there was also a notable cohort of women MPs who explicitly framed abortion as an issue of women's rights.

The White Bill would have increased surveillance of private clinics, laid down statutory conditions for their approval, and prevented them from being financially associated with referral bureaux (this latter provision would have severely impeded the work of charitable providers). Unlike previous Bills, however, it would also have prohibited abortions from being carried out on non-resident women, lowered the upper time limit from 28 weeks to 20 weeks and removed a provision from the Act that provided an apparent basis for the 'statistical argument' (that early abortions are statistically safer than carrying a pregnancy to term, and therefore always legal), replacing it with one specifying that, for an abortion to be carried out, the pregnancy must present a 'grave' risk to the life or health of the pregnant woman. This would have rendered a large proportion of abortions illegal. It would also have challenged the inclusive definition of medicine underpinning the Act, in which a broad range of 'sociomedical' concerns may be seen to require intervention, and undermined the idea that doctors are capable of making this decision without state involvement. The Bill was forwarded to a Select Committee and lapsed at the end of the parliamentary session.

As with the St John-Stevas and Irvine Bills, the pro-Bill narratives separated responsible and irresponsible, qualified and under-qualified doctors. In these accounts, doctors' roles were polluted by the involvement of 'non-medical people' (White in Hansard, 1975: 1760) in advising and referring on abortion, justifying further state intervention. The issue of doctors' conscientious objection to abortion, which had been discussed briefly in previous debates, took up a significant amount of time at the Second Reading of the White Bill. Supporters of the Bill expressed their fear that doctors and nurses were being 'victimised in their own professions' (Delargy in Hansard, 1975: 1842) for not carrying out abortions.

While a separate matter from the private sector abuses, the conscience issue had the benefit of underscoring sponsors' emphasis on differences between ethical and unethical doctors, and further suggesting that doctors' proper medical roles were being polluted by abortion: 'There are gynaecologists who believe that their role is to bring life into this world and who find it too repugnant that their task should involve the ending of life' (Abse in Hansard, 1975: 1785). These doctors were thrown into sharp relief by the 'totally unscrupulous' (Grylls in Hansard, 1975: 1789) doctors who were 'openly boasting' (Braine in Hansard, 1975: 1856) about the availability of abortion on demand, with the implication that those in the latter category were not mindful of what medicine is really about.

With the White Bill also came another shift in the portrayal of women seeking abortions. White's opening speech indicated an acceptance of the narratives of trauma-tization promoted by the Act's supporters: 'Until such time as the "New Jerusalem" comes along with no bad housing, no poverty and no alcoholic husbands, I insist that abortion must be made available for women with problems' (Hansard, 1975: 1757). Significantly, however, the speech downplayed paternalistic narratives of vulnerability in favour of appropriation of the feminist language of rights and entitlements:

> Women who go into these clinics are entitled to feel sure that they are properly conducted medically and surgically and that they are within the law. Women are entitled to proper privacy, and to feel sure that they have had a genuine pregnancy test; society is entitled to be satisfied that the clinics are charging proper rates, keeping proper accounts and paying tax. (Hansard, 1975: 1759)

Interestingly, in this argument women's interests/'entitlements' and society's interests were once again aligned rather than opposed. Other supporters of the Bill continued to push the notion that women might be hurt by abortion, claiming an increase in psychiatric cases since the Act was passed (Jones in Hansard, 1975: 1765; Taylor in Hansard, 1975: 1835) and noting women's vulnerability to exploitation by private clinics: 'We have no illusions about the inexhaustible ingenuity of the evil men who for private gain will prey upon women in trouble' (Abse in Hansard, 1975: 1780). Supporters who used this line turned narratives of trauma-tization to their advantage, breaking off a privileged moment in liberal-paternal discourse on abortion (the vulnerable woman) and rearticulating it into anti-abortion arguments.

The Benyon Bill, 1976–77

The recommendations of the Select Committee which examined the White Bill were relatively restrictive. The Committee members most in favour of the status quo walked out, feeling that its recommendations were bound to undermine the Act (Marsh and Chambers, 1981: 32); meanwhile, ALRA and NAC refused to submit evidence (Select Committee on Abortion, 1976: 2). The Benyon Bill was based on the Committee's recommendations. Unlike the White Bill, it did not attempt to insert the words 'grave' and 'serious' into the Abortion 1967. However, it would have required one of the two certifying doctors to have at least five years' clinical standing; it would have prevented financial links between referring organizations and abortion clinics (again making the work of charitable bodies difficult); it would have introduced statutory conditions for the licensing of clinics; and would have reduced the upper time limit to 20 weeks. It also attempted to introduce new protections for conscientious objectors. The Bill completed its Committee stage but lapsed at the end of the parliamentary session.

The Bill, and subsequent debate, once again sorted doctors into categories. However, rather than emphasizing the difference between specialized and non-specialized doctors, the requirement for one of the certifying doctors to have at least five years' standing introduced the idea of a gradient of medical experience. The Bill's supporters argued that doctors 'fresh from training' (Kellet-Bowman in Hansard, 1977: 1843) could not be relied upon to make such important decisions, and that inexperienced doctors might take the decision 'in a cavalier way' (Abse in Hansard, 1977: 1883). In addition, participants depicted the medical profession as somehow tainted by the profits (potentially) involved in abortion provision (Kellet-Bowman in Hansard, 1977: 1843), a taint that extended to their ability to offer impartial counselling and advice (Benyon in Hansard, 1977: 1786; Braine in Hansard, 1977: 1829). When pointedly asked why he was against profit-making from abortion 'when he supports profits in virtually every other matter', the Conservative MP Bernard Braine retorted that abortion was 'not like any other medical procedure', as it involved the destruction of life (Hansard, 1977: 1830). Conscientious objection remained a point of contention, with supporters of the Bill again describing 'responsible' doctors as victimized by the Act and by legal abortion.

In this debate there was less effort made to appropriate feminist discourses of rights and entitlements, although supporters continued to present themselves as the protectors of vulnerable women: 'the important thing is that the woman should be helped to come to the right decision and that she should not be pressurised in any way whatever' (Benyon in Hansard, 1977: 1786). Benyon stressed the Bill's benefits to women and argued that his proposals would give the

Department of Health and Social Security an opportunity to improve the standards of after-care for women undergoing abortions (Hansard, 1977: 1787). Others emphasized the 'shattering' nature of abortion for women (Braine in Hansard, 1977: 1834). This emphasis on potential harm caused by abortion allowed supporters of the Bill to dismiss calls for abortion on demand as 'extreme' (Braine in Hansard, 1977: 1827), and to portray easy access to abortion as the result of 'abuses' rather than the realization of a right:

> The inevitable result has been the development of a large and flourishing sector in which, because the motivation was not care of the woman but the making of profit, the 'social' clause has been interpreted so freely as to constitute abortion on demand. (Braine in Hansard, 1977: 1827)

In such arguments, the concept of abortion on demand was disconnected from feminist arguments concerning reproductive rights and instead conceptually linked to anti-women practices and exploitation.

The Corrie Bill, 1979–80

The Corrie Bill, like the White Bill, was also aimed at abolishing the 'statistical grounds' for abortion, and, as such, was more far-reaching than the Benyon Bill. It went all the way to Report stage, but eventually ran out of time and failed. During his speech at Second Reading, Corrie clearly saw himself as continuing the work of sponsors of previous Bills, noting that the subject of abortion had 'been well debated, but no conclusion has ever been reached' (Corrie in Hansard, 1979: 892). Like others before him, Corrie framed his Bill with reference to public 'outcry' about the 'effects' of the Abortion Act 1967 (Hansard, 1979: 892). He touched upon the familiar theme of exploitation in the private sector but foregrounded the apparent prevalence of abortion on demand. Doctors who favoured this practice, he noted, could use the 'statistical argument' to justify carrying out abortion on demand in the first 12 weeks of pregnancy without fearing prosecution (Hansard, 1979: 892–3). That the said behaviour was 'unethical' was of course implicit in this argument. However, Corrie's speech focused not on the character of such doctors but the difficulty of controlling them: 'whatever a politician's views are, the medical person is the one who sees the patient and who will make the decision in the end' (Hansard, 1979: 894). The risk that doctors might go against the wishes of Parliament was thus used to justify further state intervention, undermining the concept of the socially responsible doctor who operates best with minimal interference.

Regarding women seeking abortions, Corrie emphasized the risks to their health and well-being from abortion (Hansard, 1979: 896). This was echoed by his supporters. Braine, for example, stressed the need to guide 'frightened young girl[s]' down the right path (Hansard, 1979: 963–4), while Ancram talked of the importance of prioritizing women's 'health, well-being and protection from exploitation' (Hansard, 1979: 912). He continued: 'Abortion is not a simple act for a woman to undergo. It is not simply a social convenience; it is a medical act. In many cases it is a medical operation, with medical, biological and psychological implications' (Hansard, 1979: 916).

These potential dangers to women helped stress the need for a purer and more 'scrupulous' (Ancram in Hansard, 1979: 917) medical care, the provision of which would be facilitated by legislative intervention. Notably, Corrie appropriated to himself the ability to speak and act 'for women':

> I have received many letters from unhappy women. Many of them bitterly regret having had their abortion and express in their letters the importance of counselling. If only they had known what it all entailed, they would not have gone through with the abortion. (Corrie in Hansard, 1979: 896)

This claim had the double effect of undermining pro-choice feminists' claims to be speaking for women beyond the House of Commons and decoupling abortion rights from women's rights. However, there remain some tensions in such accounts, as evidenced by Corrie's brief discussion of 'fathers' rights' in abortion:

> We have the strange position at the moment that the rights of the woman are total. It is she, and she alone, at the end of the day, who can decide whether to keep the baby. The father has no say whatever. (Hansard, 1979: 896)

In this statement, there is obvious anxiety that women's reproductive rights might jeopardize the status of fathers-to-be. Yet this seems at odds with the general emphasis on women's vulnerability: are women threatened by abortion, or threatening? This undecidability can be observed throughout debates on abortion, as the following section demonstrates.

Female vice and virtue in the debates

Some ambiguities in anti-abortion discourse during this period have already been observed. Firstly, there was a disconnect between earlier conservative accounts of abortion, which opposed 'the needs of individual women' to 'the needs of the nation', and emerging accounts of the vulnerability of women apparently hurt by legal abortion. These tensions were further exposed by uneasiness over fathers' rights and fathers' status with regard to abortions. This section details additional tensions in the construction of women seeking abortion. Firstly, it outlines images of the 'brazen' abortion patient, who seems to be the polar opposite of the 'broken' woman envisaged by Steel's supporters: boastful and un-traumatized by her circumstances, she is prepared to lie and deceive to get what she wants. Secondly, the section discusses anxieties over 'foreign' women travelling to Britain for abortion: these women were alternately portrayed as vulnerable and exploited victims or as criminals taking advantage of British medical services.

These tensions in the construction of women seeking abortion were connected to anxieties concerning female virtue and vice. In abortion debates, women were alternately presented as virtuous mothers who had done everything 'right' or as moral corrupters leading the country into vice – the 'tarts and tired housewives' noted by Sheldon (1997: 32). Such fears are often connected to ideas about national identity and doubts about the future of the nation. Women's child-bearing and child-rearing capacity has meant they have often been situated as the nation's moral guardians (Yuval-Davis, 1997), especially while raising the next generation – but this in turn stimulates anxiety about women's capacity for vice. Female virtue and vice may therefore be policed particularly closely due to the effects they are seen to have on the nation (Boryczka, 2012). The connection of female vice to concerns about national identity are particularly apparent in the panic over the influx of 'foreign women' to Britain for abortion.

'Brazen' and 'broken' women

In the debates over the Steel Bill, women seeking abortions were often depicted as somehow 'broken': worn down physically and emotionally and at risk of becoming a 'mental wreck' if forced to continue with the pregnancy. The women in these narratives had generally done everything 'right' – they had had several children, worked hard to look after them, and simply could not bear the strain of any more.

In other words, due to their virtuous nature, these women 'deserved' abortions. As we have seen, in the 1970s MPs continued to use this construction to defend the Abortion Act 1967, while their opponents appropriated the figure of the virtuous, vulnerable woman to their own ends.

However, the Lane Committee's report reveals anxieties bubbling under the surface. The report states that the Committee received complaints about 'hectoring' and demanding patients who believed they were entitled to an abortion under the Act or were willing to lie or make threats of suicide if they were refused abortion (Lane Committee, 1974: 9). Some abortion patients, the complaints continued, had a 'brazen' or 'boastful' attitude, which upset other patients in hospital wards (1974: 110). Women seeking successive abortions were singled out in this regard (1974: 83). These women, it appears, were not thought to be traumatized 'enough' by their circumstances or by the prospect of abortion, and their immoral behaviour was thought to be enabled by the Act.

The Lane Committee report thus exposed some deep-seated anxieties about female vice connected to the issue of abortion. The report's response to these criticisms was perhaps more progressive:

> It seems to us that such women are often among those most in need of sympathetic attention and of abortion. The very fact that a woman is prepared to undergo repeatedly what, to most women, is a distressing experience and one to be avoided in future, may point to some psychological or other problem affecting her health. (1974: 83–4)

Nonetheless, in resorting to psychiatric discourses to 'defend' women who had multiple abortions, the report also de-normalized them and indeed all women who did not appear as traumatized by abortion as popular wisdom dictated they should. Dominant abortion discourses only allowed constructions of women as either virtuous and vulnerable, or vicious.

Abortion 'scandals' and national identity

A significant element of the abortion 'scandals' in the 1970s was the perception that a high number of abortions were being performed on non-resident women, due to the criminalization of abortion in other countries and the UK's relatively high upper time limit. In particular, MPs were concerned about taxis 'touting' at airports for women seeking abortion and driving them to expensive private clinics. This concern was fed by media stories about 'package deals' on abortion in the UK being offered in other countries (Steel in Hansard, 1970: 1697; Houghton in Hansard, 1970: 1702). These suggestions were only a murmur at the time of the St John-Stevas Bill – the sponsor noted these 'disturbing' stories but stressed that his concern was chiefly with the Act's impact on the British (Hansard, 1969: 412) – but during the Irvine Bill debates, MPs expressed their fears that London was now seen as an 'abortion capital' by the rest of the world (Hansard, 1970: 1656).

By the time of the White Bill, the outcry had swelled to a crescendo.[1] The Bill contained a provision prohibiting abortions being carried out on non-resident women. Crucially, the outcry spoke to anxieties over national identity and the future of the UK, with MPs pondering the question of what kind of society 'we' were becoming and how the rest of the world saw 'us'. These anxieties were not only held by the Bill's supporters: even David Steel was concerned that some doctors had 'brought considerable reproach on this country, both at home and abroad' (Hansard, 1975: 1769). Concerns regarding abortion and national identity had also been expressed to the Lane Committee, which received complaints that the private sector had brought the country 'into disrepute' (Lane Committee, 1974: 132), particularly by touting at airports and advertising abroad (1974: 133).

Nonetheless, the Committee's report was ambivalent in its treatment of women. In much of its summary of the evidence, women seem to be indulging in vice: they are breaking the law in their own countries, and it is impossible to know whether they are lying to doctors about their circumstances (1974: 141). The Report, moreover, noted 'powerful arguments' that it is morally wrong for doctors to 'lend themselves to the commission of such offences' (1974: 141), although it eventually concluded that it would be extremely difficult to legislate against this (1974: 141–3). In this construction, women's vice threatened the medical profession by leading it into disrepute. However, this account clashes with accounts of female vulnerability in the report, such as the observation that many non-resident women seeking abortion were being 'hijacked' by touts, meaning they were driven to a clinic other than the one to which they had intended to go and charged extortionate fees (1974: 131; 136–7).

Similar tensions can be observed in the debate over the White Bill. The idea that 'foreign' women were being exploited of course fit the overall portrayal of women as endangered by abortion, and White stressed the need to protect women 'lured' to the UK for this purpose:

> I must stress this foreign traffic, not because I am anti-German, anti-French or anti-Italian, but because of one of the comments in the Lane Report. I disagree with a good deal of the report, but I agree with it when it says: 'It would undoubtedly be more difficult, if not impossible, to ensure their implementation in respect of non-resident women.' The reference there is to counselling, after-care and making sure that these women get the attention they should have. (Hansard, 1975: 1758)

However, White's supporters decried the 'repugnance' of this behaviour (Abse in Hansard, 1975: 1783), stressed its criminal aspects (Braine in Hansard, 1975: 1856), and argued that such women 'take advantage of our medical services' (Winterton in Hansard, 1975: 1816). As Renée Short wryly noted, these women were seen as 'polluting' (Hansard, 1975: 1830) by many MPs. As a result, tensions remained in anti-abortion discourse even as it attempted to appropriate narratives of trauma-tization: women were at once portrayed as exploited and in need of help, and as polluting elements leading the country into vice.

Dealing with the 'woman problem'

The Abortion Act 1967 relied on the dual construction of doctors as socially responsible and women seeking abortion as vulnerable. The discussion in this chapter demonstrates the lasting effects of this gendering: anti-abortion speakers have had to find ways to deal with their 'woman problem', but something of a woman problem has also been present for feminists seeking to defend the Act. For the most part, pro-choice women declined to contest the logic of medicalization underpinning the Abortion Act 1967, even though it conflicted with the logic of a right to choose they espoused. It is too simplistic to either celebrate feminist activity on abortion as entirely 'successful' or present a sweeping narrative of the decline of feminist radicalism (see Dean, 2010 on these tendencies in academic feminist critique). An extensive feminist agenda *was* articulated in the debates, and this was maintained into the 1980s and 1990s. However, this was married with a 'politics of protection' (Brown, 1992; Yeatman, 1997) emphasizing women's vulnerability and trauma and the need for government regulation, and thereby reinforcing the paternalistic-patriarchal state intervention legitimated by the Act.

As soon as feminist discourses entered the debates, they were adapted by anti-abortion speakers, demonstrating feminism's vulnerability to appropriation. This period saw the emergence of attempts at a 'woman-friendly' but still broadly anti-abortion discourse that ranged from extolling women's 'entitlements' to portraying women as hurt and damaged by abortion and by abortion clinics. Sponsors of the Bills often claimed to be acting on behalf of women who had written to them. As their opponents made similar assertions, the claim to be acting 'for women' became somewhat emptied of meaning. While none of the Bills passed, this does not mean that anti-abortion efforts during this period were not significant; some of the Bills commanded a great deal of parliamentary support but fell foul of the usual difficulties afflicting Private Members Bills. The Corrie Bill in particular failed mainly due to time constraints, although the strength of Corrie's opposition and the government's refusal to give the Bill extra time also played a part (Marsh and Chambers, 1981). Nonetheless, anti-abortion discourse remained ultimately ambiguous and confused in its relationship to women and feminism. Supporters of the Bills alternated between portraying women seeking abortion as exploited victims and portraying them as immoral criminals. Anxieties concerning female virtue and vice were further elaborated in evidence to the Lane Committee. Portrayals of female virtue and vice are important, not only because of their role in mobilizing for and against the Abortion Act 1967, but because they became an important feature of feminist discourses on abortion in the 1980s and 1990s.

Conspicuously absent from the debates was any awareness of the racialized nature of abortion. During this period, there were allegations that some doctors were treating women differently according to their race, with eugenic intentions – such as the case of a black woman who was approved for an abortion, but later discovered white women who visited the same doctor were denied both abortions and contraception (McGrane and Nicholls, 1977). Black feminists continued to draw attention to the fact that abortion provision might have different significance to different women during the 1980s (Bhavnani and Coulson, 1986). However, such an awareness was not to enter the debate until the 21st century, and even then with significant problems.

5

Backlash and Appropriation

The abortion debates of the 1980s and 1990s came to focus on the problem of 'late' abortions above all else. Recent advances in medical technology meant that premature babies were surviving at earlier stages of gestation, and many people had come to see the 28-week upper limit for legal abortion as outdated. Advances in foetal imaging technology had also resulted in a proliferation of images of the foetus, used by opponents of abortion as 'evidence' of foetal personhood. This 'technicization' of abortion was one of the most important developments in abortion rhetoric during this period (McNeil, 1991: 157). The debates took place on the watch of the government of Margaret Thatcher that was increasingly coming to be seen as 'uncaring' due to its cuts to the NHS and failure to provide high-tech facilities (1991: 150). These cuts meant that those seeking abortions on the NHS were faced with many difficulties and delays; in this sense, 'late' abortions were to an extent a creation of the system. However, many of the Bills introduced in this period would have 'solved' the problem by policing abortion patients, not the NHS, more closely (1991: 150) (see Table 5.1).

Academic accounts note that the debates took place in a new moral climate involving heightened fears about sexuality, where abortion was viewed as a symptom of moral decline. These fears became evident in the idea that women might suffer from 'post-abortion syndrome' – the implication being that a price must be paid for separating women's sexuality from reproduction (McNeil, 1991: 157–8; Lee, 2003: 85). Such accounts are indicative of the broader backlash against feminism taking place in the 1980s and early 1990s. According to Susan Faludi's influential book on the subject, the backlash had two elements: first, attempts to halt or turn back the tide on advances in women's equality; and, second, attempts to blame feminism itself for women's unhappiness (Faludi, 1991: 9–10).

Table 5.1: Abortion Bills, 1981–99

Bill	Stage reached	Key provisions
Richardson, 1981	First Reading	Require health authorities to provide abortion facilities free of charge.
Lord Robertson, 1982	First Reading	Require pregnancy to present a 'serious' risk to a woman's health, 'substantially' greater than the risk presented by abortion, for an abortion to be carried out.
Bishop of Birmingham, 1986–7	Lords Select Committee	Reduce the upper time limit to 24 weeks.
Bruinvels, 1987	First Reading	Reduce the upper time limit; required the father of the foetus to be consulted before abortion could be carried out.
Leigh, 1987	First Reading	Require a medical practitioner treating a non-resident woman to give notice of abortion to a medical practitioner in her home country.
Winterton, 1987	First Reading	Require medical practitioners referring women for abortion to make a declaration that they had no financial interest in the place where the abortions were performed.
Alton, 1988	Report stage (adjourned)	Reduce the upper time limit to 18 weeks.
Widdecombe, 1989	First Reading	Require a medical practitioner treating a non-resident woman to give notice of abortion to a medical practitioner in her home country.
Widdecombe, 1989	Second Reading (adjourned)	Reduce the upper time limit to 18 weeks.
Hargreaves, 1989	First Reading	Require ancillary workers to give a positive indication of assent before being required to perform or assist at an abortion (in order to protect the rights of conscientious objectors).
Amess, 1989	First Reading	Require doctors and nurses to give a positive indication of assent before being required to perform or assist at an abortion (in order to protect the rights of conscientious objectors).
Bennett, 1989	First Reading	Require medical practitioners referring women for abortion to make a declaration that they had no financial interest in the place where the abortions were performed.
Braine, 1989	First Reading	Amend the grounds on which an abortion could be carried out.

Table 5.1 (cont.)

Bill	Stage reached	Key provisions
Lord Houghton, 1989	Lords Third Reading	Took up Bishop of Birmingham (1987) Bill, with Committee amendments.
HFE Bill, 1990	Became HFE Act	The Bill's main purpose was to deal with advances in reproductive technology. However, several amendments dealing with abortion were tabled. The eventual Act lowered the upper time limit to 24 weeks.
Lord Braine, 1995	First Reading	Prohibit the use of dilation and extraction ('partial-birth' abortion).
Viscount Brentford, 1996	First Reading	Prohibit the abortion of foetuses with Down's syndrome.
Peacock, 1996	First Reading	Prohibit the use of dilation and extraction ('partial-birth' abortion).
Amess, 1996	First Reading	Amend the grounds for legal abortion so that the pregnancy would have to present a 'substantial' risk to a woman's health in order for an abortion to be carried out.

Source: Hansard; Sheldon (1997)

For Faludi, the anti-abortion movement in the US was an exemplar of backlash politics. Abortion and birth control were seen as threatening, as they gave women the freedom to have sex on their own terms (1991: 412), and were therefore subject to antifeminist attack. Faludi notes that the imagery used by the anti-abortion movement in the 1980s 'bore all the hallmarks of the New Right ideology that had preceded it' (1991: 414), involving moralistic language and portrayal of feminism as the enemy. While their campaigns were often hostile towards women seeking abortion – dubbed 'babykillers' – they also frequently depicted women, along with foetuses, as the 'victims' of abortion (1991: 414–15). This chapter explores the impact of the backlash in the context of UK abortion politics. Although anti-abortion actors in the parliamentary debates of this period did not often explicitly blame feminism for the problems facing women and society, their activity was still saturated by the politics of backlash. Simultaneously, opponents of legal abortion began to appropriate feminist arguments by criticizing men's sexual behaviour.

A significant change happened in this period in the form of the Human Fertilisation and Embryology (HFE) Act 1990. The HFE Act was an item of government legislation dealing with new developments in human reproductive technology. However, several MPs tabled amendments to the HFE Bill to reduce the time limit for legal abortion from anything from 26 weeks to 18 weeks, or to change the grounds on which abortion could be allowed. Some of the defeated amendments were substantially liberalizing. For example, an amendment tabled by the Labour MP Harriet Harman would have allowed abortion up to 12 weeks' gestation for any reason, with the consent of only one doctor. Another would have extended the Abortion Act 1967 to Northern Ireland, but this was defeated by 267 votes to 131. Despite the re-establishment of direct rule, the UK government had little desire to align Northern Ireland's abortion laws with the rest of the UK (Thomson, 2016). Indeed, the Troubles – the violent sectarian conflict from about 1968 to 1998 in Northern Ireland – were sometimes cited by parliamentarians, reasoning that the people of Northern Ireland were for once united in their opposition to abortion, as a reason why the Act could *not* be extended (Alton in Hansard, 1990a: 1143).

While Parliament eventually voted to lower the upper time limit to 24 weeks,[1] this was a result of the decision that in certain cases the Infant Life (Preservation) Act did not apply to abortion law, meaning that exceptions could be procured to permit women to obtain necessary abortions (McBride Stetson, 2001b: 151). Since a potential limit of 18 weeks had been successfully avoided, this was regarded as a success by the pro-choice movement (Hohmeyer, 1995: 42; McBride Stetson, 2001b: 151). However, the debate also signified a wholesale acceptance of medicalization by pro-choice actors, who emphasized medical knowledges in constructing their arguments and accepted that foetal viability should be the principal concern when deciding whether an abortion should be allowed. The mutually accepted framework of the abortion debate increasingly posited the issue as a narrow medical question, revolving exclusively around the status of the foetus and at what (medically determined) point its claim to protection becomes paramount. To accept an essentially medical framework for debate seems doubly dangerous given that many of the problems faced by women seeking termination are related to medical control (Sheldon, 1997: 106; see also Steinberg, 1991). Moreover, the overly technical nature of debates has discouraged grass-roots involvement (Cooper, 2016: 23–57).

The early 1980s: continuity and change

In the early 1980s, Labour MP Jo Richardson introduced a Ten Minute Rule Bill that aimed to improve women's access to abortion through the NHS (Hansard, 1981). However, this was quickly followed by a

Lords Bill sponsored by Lord Robertson of Oakridge, which, similarly to the Corrie Bill, would have only allowed abortion if a pregnancy presented a 'serious' risk to a woman's health, 'substantially' greater than if an abortion were carried out (Hansard, 1982). In some senses, these debates are an extension of the debates of the late 1970s. The issues raised reflect those of earlier debates: medical irresponsibility and 'abortion on demand' remain prominent fears. However, they also represent significant developments in two ways. Firstly, the Richardson Bill was the first attempt to improve women's access to abortion since 1967 using a legislative measure, although other attempts to liberalize abortion law by amending the HFE Bill would be made later on. Secondly, there was a slight shift in the argumentative strategy of opponents of legal abortion. In these arguments, it was not only abortion clinics who exploited women but men in general, mirroring similar claims made by feminists.

The Richardson Bill, 1981

Richardson's National Health Service Act (Amendment) Bill was an early attempt to bring a liberalizing agenda to Parliament. The Bill, which had its First Reading debate in July 1981, aimed to improve the availability of abortion on the NHS by making it a duty for health authorities to provide abortion facilities free of charge. As a Ten Minute Rule Bill, it had barely any chance of becoming law. However, it was denied a First Reading by 215 votes to 139. In her speech, Richardson argued that patchy provision of abortion meant that the NHS had failed in its duty to women. She observed that better provision on the NHS would lead to fewer delays, allowing abortions to be performed as early as possible. This emphasis on the need for abortions to be carried out early foreshadows the distinction between 'early' and 'late' abortion that would become pivotal in later debates.

Richardson's speech conspicuously drew upon medicalized logic. Throughout, she portrayed women as patients, and women's rights and needs as the demands that patients could legitimately make of the NHS: 'it is indefensible that the NHS should not provide treatment for women who are legally entitled to treatment under the law' (Hansard, 1981: 877). Accordingly, abortion was constructed as a medical necessity that the NHS was failing to provide. Richardson backed this argument up with statistics relating to the patchiness of abortion provision in different areas, and implied unfairness (Hansard, 1981: 877). Like reformists before her, Richardson framed the Bill as a matter of protecting women, emphasizing the need for a 'humane' attitude towards women who need 'sympathetic treatment' (Hansard, 1981: 879). If Parliament and the NHS failed to do this, she warned, women might once again turn to the back streets.

Conservative MP Jill Knight spoke against the Bill, using arguments familiar from the 1970s. She challenged the medicalized framework used by Richardson, arguing firstly that abortion was unlike other medical services provided by the NHS: 'abortion is not supposed to be available to all comers' (Hansard, 1981: 879). Abortion was here contrasted to 'real' medical necessities – 'kidney failure, mental health care, cancer and scores of others' (Hansard, 1981: 880) – which, according to Knight, had a far greater need of funding. Knight did accept that *some* abortions might be medically necessary, but utilized a much narrower definition of 'medical necessity', observing that abortion was already available on the NHS for women with a *real* need. Wider availability of abortion in the private sector, she argued, was due only to the actions of irresponsible doctors complying with the letter of the law but not its spirit (Hansard, 1981: 879).

The Robertson Bill, 1982

Lord Robertson of Oakridge's Bill was similar to the Corrie Bill in that it would have eliminated the 'statistical argument' for abortion and rendered most abortions carried out on 'social' grounds illegal. However, an amendment moved by Lord Houghton to delay the Bill's Second Reading by six months was passed, and the Bill never progressed further. At the Second Reading debate in December 1982, Lord Robertson framed the Bill as a solution to the 'problems' of abortion on demand and abortion for 'trivial' reasons (Hansard, 1982: 57). Doctors, he argued, were acting irresponsibly, facilitated by a government that was failing to take action against them:

> It cannot be disputed that considerable numbers of doctors used the Act as a basis for granting abortion on demand, and no action is being taken to stop them. Doctors promoting such a policy justify their actions by the so-called statistical argument which claims that the statistics show that the risk to the life of the pregnant woman is smaller if the pregnancy is terminated in the early months than if it is allowed to continue. (Hansard, 1982: 56)

Such arguments were familiar from 1970s attempts to undermine the logic of medicalization by stressing the differences between doctors.

However, Lord Robertson's speech also indicated some emerging themes in anti-abortion rhetoric. Most evident of these was its vivid description of foetal development:

> For that baby, life started in some form at the moment of conception. The early weeks of her existence in the womb saw the physical development of her body happen almost incredibly quickly. By 30 days her main organs were already in recognisable form and she had a heart pumping blood she had made herself. In other babies, electric brainwaves have been recorded as early as 40 days, and this must indicate that the mind has started to develop. In this connection, Professor Sir William Liley, generally regarded as the father of foetological medicine, has stated: 'We know the baby is responsive in utero to touch, to light, to sound and to stimuli which at least you and I would consider painful'. (Hansard, 1982: 58–9)

This argument utilized the new knowledge and imagery made available by developments in medical technology. While the protection of 'the unborn' had always been a feature of anti-abortion rhetoric, the use of such imagery heralded the emergence of a 'foetal subject' (Squier, 1996) who would become central in later debates and, in doing so, challenged the logic of medicalization by stressing that it was vulnerable foetuses, not women, who needed protecting. The speech also indicated a new tactic for undermining feminist arguments, by simultaneously disavowing feminist claims and appropriating them to an anti-abortion agenda. Lord Robertson opened by arguing that women's right to control their own fertility did not exist in law and was not at stake in the debates (Hansard, 1982: 55–6); however, he later went on to use ideas about women's sexual and reproductive freedom to justify his Bill:

> It must surely be obvious that women today are treated by men in a more cavalier way than ever before. It is more difficult for a woman to say 'No' to the sexual act than it used to be, not least because abortion is held up as an extension of contraceptive measures. When the so-called worst happens, and a pregnancy occurs, it is only too easy for the man concerned to wash his hands of the whole business and put the woman under pressure to have an abortion, regardless of the dangers to her health or of her own convictions. (Hansard, 1982: 58)

This rhetoric clearly echoed earlier feminist arguments concerning women's treatment at the hands of men. However, in comparing gender relations now to gender relations as they 'used to be', it implicitly blamed societal changes and the sexual revolution – and, by extension, feminist values – for this treatment. Such rhetoric demonstrates both the resourcefulness of anti-abortion actors in appropriating elements of feminist arguments and the continuing tensions as these actors simultaneously attempted to reject and blame feminism.

Defending the Abortion Act 1967

In debates from 1987 onwards, opponents of restrictive Bills used many familiar arguments. Women seeking abortion were generally represented as vulnerable and needy, 'frightened, unwise, indecisive, uncertain, anguished, full of second thoughts, and impoverished' (Hansard, 1988: 1258–9), seeking abortions 'for reasons beyond their control' (Hansard, 1987: 1428). These arguments relied heavily on narratives of acceptable abortion, and used accounts of personal trauma, rather than bodily autonomy or reproductive freedom, to justify the need for 'choice' (e.g. Hansard, 1988: 1247). Such narratives led participants to emphasize the horror of back-street abortions as the only alternative to the status quo. The figure of the back-street abortionist was explicitly connected to women's vulnerability:

> A return to back-street abortions will mean a return to deaths and trauma, and the people who will suffer are those whom the House should most want to protect. The vulnerable, the not very intelligent and the inadequate will be driven to the backstreet abortionists, who will be laughing all the way to the bank. (Hansard, 1988: 1238)

> The things that were going on in back streets, the hardship and cruelty that women – sometimes young and ignorant, sometimes suffering from a situation which they did not understand – were deplorable. (Hansard, 1989b: 1492)

Imagery of vulnerable women was nothing new. However, these participants also introduced a new category of people affected by late-term abortions: women carrying severely disabled foetuses (and, crucially, their families). Those in favour of relatively liberal access to abortion emphasized the importance of giving women the 'choice' of whether to have a disabled child, and the ability to monitor the likelihood of disability using new technology. Such arguments did not necessarily stem from a belief in a fundamental right to bodily autonomy, but from the belief that disability should exempt the pregnant woman from the usual moral concerns. In doing so, they legitimized abortion in 'eugenic, rather than woman-centred terms' (Steinberg, 1991: 187).

Moreover, participants justified post-viability abortions on the grounds that they might restore women to motherhood. According to these arguments, if a woman is compelled to carry a severely disabled foetus to term, 'there is no way in which she will bring another child into the world' (Hansard, 1987: 1430–1).

> We have had many letters from medical bodies urging us not to support the Bill. More impressive than those is a short letter that I received from a constituent who said: 'Having had a late termination (about 19–20 weeks) because it was discovered my baby had severe abnormalities I know what I am talking about. It was a disturbing event for me but not as bad as giving birth after 9 months to a baby the doctors said would not have lived anyway. Parents must have the choice to make their own decision in cases like this. I know I personally could not have coped with a full term baby being born like this. I have had a healthy daughter since this tragic event but I am sure I would never have had the courage to become pregnant again if I knew that I would have to go 9 months and not be offered a late termination had the baby had the same abnormalities'.
> (Hansard, 1988: 1241)

Abortion was hence legitimated on gendered grounds, as a measure to encourage women to have more children. Thus, the more radical implications of legal abortion – such as women's ability to reject motherhood – were curtailed. The argument that abortion might actually *help* women fulfil their role as mothers is familiar from debates over the Steel Bill. However, concerns about foetal abnormality in the late 1980s gave it new focus.

Feminism, medicine and female virtue

Feminists reacted forcefully to the restrictive Bills and amendments. According to the then Labour MP Alice Mahon, fighting such Bills involved coordination between women of all parties, whereas Labour men were often 'less than helpful' and obstructed their efforts.[2] The

1990 HFE Bill involved two attempts by women to liberalize access to abortion by doing away with the two-doctor rule, although neither of these were successful. This section covers the explicitly feminist demands these women made in the debates, as well as the ways in which their speeches constructed women seeking abortion.

Feminist demands

Pro-choice women MPs frequently situated their arguments in relation to their status as a minority in Parliament. Moreover, they often referred to the need for the women in Parliament to work together and to forge a group identity in order to protect women's rights. As Mahon told me, in reference to divisions within the Labour movement over women's reproductive freedoms: 'there were enough of us to persuade them to get their hands off our sexual and reproductive rights. They were ours, not theirs.'[3] This combative language and sense of a strong divide between men and women was reflected in the Parliamentary debate:

> Women must say – honourable Members who are women must say – that we have consciences and that we exercise them daily as women and that women exercise their consciences when making choices about abortion. We do not need the men in the Chamber to borrow our consciences for us and to take that decision. (Primarolo in Hansard, 1990b: 247)

> The remarkable consensus on this issue stretches from every woman Labour Member right across to the Conservative Women's National Committee. That consensus arises not because we have suddenly all become the same sort of people, but because as women we share some life experiences. (Wise in Hansard, 1988: 1291)

> [The House of Commons] is overwhelmingly male, and it is important to remember that fact when discussing abortion. ... Conservative Members who have spoken against all forms of abortion are the enemies of women. (Mahon in Hansard, 1990b: 233)

Parliament's preoccupation with female reproductive capacity was neatly subverted by Dawn Primarolo, who suggested that to restrict access to abortion would be akin to forcing men to be sterilized (Hansard, 1990b: 246–7). Such observations were articulated alongside an explicitly feminist agenda linking together a series of demands, exemplified in this contribution by Mildred Gordon:

> The whole question of abortion is closely linked to other campaigns that women have been fighting for many years ... [W]e need improved sex education. We need contraceptives of all kinds, freely available and free. We need better housing and employment and training opportunities. We need safer childbirth – our record is not among the best in the advanced world. We must do away with some of the more recent 'conveyor belt practices' connected with childbirth in hospitals, which have a traumatic effect on the baby during birth. We want nursery provision for young children. We want money for medical research into foetal abnormalities to discover them at an earlier stage. We need money for disabled people and money to provide facilities for them. We need money from the Government, as of right, for women who are carers of children, the disabled, the sick and the old. (Gordon in Hansard, 1988: 1284)

Others called for improved family planning services (Mahon in Hansard, 1990b: 233; Harman in Hansard, 1990b: 260), increased maternity support (Richardson in Hansard, 1988: 1273) and changes in men's attitudes towards women (Gorman in Hansard, 1990b: 230). Attempts to restrict access to abortion, moreover, were linked to heightened anti-woman activity on the part of the New Right:

> The underlying reason is that the new Right in America goes around bombing abortion clinics, photographing women who go there for abortions and sending the photographs to their neighbours. That is the kind of crude behaviour that comes from the new Right. The growing new Right in Britain is saying that women should stay at home and bear children and care for elderly and disabled people. They are not in favour of public expenditure; they want to push women back into a traditional role and deprive them of the freedom to control their lives. (Short in Hansard, 1988: 1262)

Clare Short's observation that anti-abortion activity was connected to an anti-feminist backlash was insightful. But it is also a fitting example of the ways in which women participants in the debates situated their demands in relation to broader chains of demands and a far-reaching rejection of the status quo. As Mahon put it:

> Let me tell you something, with women's issues. They're backing off on other prejudices now, and this gay marriage bill [of 2013] I think's brilliant, personally I think it's brilliant. But it always comes back with women ... it's the most enduring inequality, is the one between the sexes.[4]

Medicalization and technicization

As in the 1970s, pro-choice MPs did criticize the workings of the Abortion Act 1967, although this was generally done indirectly, by referring to the difficulties and unnecessary delays that might face women seeking abortion (Richardson in Hansard, 1988: 1272). The most explicit critique of the Act was advanced by Emma Nicholson (Conservative), who had attempted to amend the HFE Bill to allow self-referral up to 12 weeks. Nicholson did not use the explicitly feminist language of some of her peers. However, unlike other women MPs, she did explicitly contest the norms underpinning the Act, arguing that 'the Act places a succession of minor hurdles in the way of the pregnant mother trying to obtain an abortion' (Hansard, 1990b: 250) that could lead to a delay of months before an abortion could be carried out. Nicholson stressed the vulnerability of women, whose credibility might be 'wrecked' by the delay, and accepted the need for some medical control 'so that society can satisfy itself that [women are] not using the medical profession as a source of late contraception'. Nonetheless, her contribution was significant, as she placed the blame for delays squarely on the Act (rather than the NHS or restrictions on the private sector, as others did), and pointed out that abortions are not always carried out for health reasons (Hansard, 1990b: 249–51). This is not to say that other pro-choice MPs were not critical of the Act. Mahon expressed regret that further liberalization of abortion law had not been achieved:

> I don't like this idea that you've to go to two doctors. I mean, what is wrong with just going along to your local clinic and seeing a nurse practitioner even? Or a doctor, we're allowed this. So what is this psychological pressure on women? 'Naughty girls, you must go in front of the doctor!'[5]

For the most part, however, the speeches indicate the continued adherence of the logic of medicalization. Once again, the interests of women and doctors were articulated together, and both construed as equally threatened by restrictive amendments (Richardson in Hansard, 1988: 1277). Furthermore, the figure of the medical professional was frequently appealed to in justifying women's 'choice':

> I would leave it to the woman, her medical adviser and her family to make the decision. (Gorman in Hansard, 1990b: 232)

> The medical decision and the woman's decision are what is relevant. (Primarolo in Hansard, 1990b: 247)

> It is my view ... that up to 12 weeks the mother's wish, in conjunction with her general practitioner's decision, should be sufficient to allow her an abortion. (Nicholson in Hansard, 1990b: 250)

'Choice', in these arguments, does not appear to be a right; rather, it seems to be dependent on the approval of the doctor. The construction of abortion as 'a medical matter ... to be argued medically' (Wise in Hansard, 1988: 1289) resulted in women's rights being transmuted into *patients'* rights, and the demands women could legitimately make being restricted to the demands a patient might make of the health service. Delays and difficulties accessing abortion were as such blamed on NHS 'obstruction' (Richardson in Hansard, 1990b: 187; Short in Hansard, 1990b: 257).

These arguments were commonly framed by appeals to medical science rather than to rights or freedoms. This involved centring the issue of foetal viability as the cutting-off point for when abortion should be legal. Pro-choice MPs observed that advances in medical science meant that abortions after 24 weeks' gestation were already becoming rarer (Short in Hansard, 1988: 1261; Short in Hansard, 1990b: 256–7) and stressed that the weight of medical opinion was behind a 24-week limit (Harman in Hansard, 1990b: 262). While these arguments were deployed to defend against anti-abortion initiatives, they nonetheless accepted in theory the distinction between 'early' and 'late' abortions that was becoming central to pro-life arguments (Steinberg, 1991: 177–8).

Female virtue and acceptable abortion

What is most striking about pro-choice contributions in these debates is the heightened use of narratives of female vulnerability and acceptable abortion. These narratives tended to feature young and frightened 'girls', post-menopausal women who may not have realized they were pregnant until late in the pregnancy, women with serious health conditions and women carrying foetuses with severe abnormalities (Short in Hansard, 1988: 1246; 1261; Richardson in Hansard, 1988: 1273; Richardson in Hansard, 1990b: 186–7; Harman in Hansard, 1990b: 261–2). Accounts of female vulnerability were bolstered by readings from personal correspondence and tragic cases involving the MPs' own constituents, for example:

> One of my constituents is a simple parent with a violent husband. She has three children, the oldest of whom is aged 14½. They live in a freezing, hard-to-let house. The house is so cold that they live effectively in one room. Last December, the 14-year-old daughter gave birth to a premature baby. The baby is ailing. The local hospital cannot keep it in, although its health demands that it returns to hospital frequently. That baby has been born and is physically perfect, although it is weak. Some people have tremendous stresses and strains on their lives. They might have forgiven that 14-year-old girl, and her mother, for having an abortion in those circumstances. I certainly would, and I hope that hon. Members who do not always agree with me would. (Richardson in Hansard, 1988: 1273)

Female vulnerability has always been a feature of pro-Act discourse. However, pervading feminist narratives in this period were ideas concerning female virtue and innocence. In such narratives, the women seem to do everything 'right': they are either middle-aged mothers (carrying out their duty by having already had children) or vulnerable (and therefore not 'frivolous') girls. Their contraception failed, or they had been diagnosed as menopausal. They may well have been under great stress or even scared, or they may have discovered that the foetus was severely disabled. This concern with the morality of 'late' abortion is most explicit in this contribution from Baroness Lockwood:

> A wife may find herself pregnant and realise that she is carrying a child which could be born with the AIDS disease *through no fault of her own*. It may be the fault of her husband, but *it is not her fault*. ... Some 50 per cent. of late abortions are to young people under 20, according to the study of the Royal College. *The pregnancies of some*

> *of these girls are not necessarily due to promiscuity or curiosity.* Sometimes it is a consequence of abuse or rape and that leads to difficult circumstances. This is a group that needs our understanding and sympathy. (Baroness Lockwood in Hansard, 1987: 1437–8; emphasis mine)

Speeches emphasizing the 'faultlessness' of women seeking abortion were a feature of the debates in both the Lords and the Commons. Narratives asserting the rights of women who did not use contraception, had multiple abortions, or were not traumatized by the prospect of abortion – 'the things we cannot say' (Ludlow, 2008: 30) – were missing. That feminist participants might soften their stance by emphasizing women's vulnerability rather than women's rights or freedoms is understandable. Parliament during this period was often extremely hostile towards women speakers. When asked about her experiences of being a woman in the House of Commons, Alice Mahon stated that 'the place reeks of male dominance … it comes out of the panelling'.[6] In her time in Parliament, she had been mocked for her Yorkshire accent, the lobby of Parliament lacked a women's toilet, and comments were frequently passed on women's clothing. This hostility can be difficult to observe when reading Hansard, the parliamentary archive, as interruptions and jeering are typically not recorded, but sometimes it becomes evident, such as in Clare Short's response to one interruption to her speech: 'Honourable Members may laugh. They always laugh and sneer when we talk about the status of women and their freedom. The behaviour of honourable Members is absolutely consistent' (Short in Hansard, 1988: 1262). What can also be difficult to discern from Hansard is participants' sense of anger and outrage at what had happened to women before the Abortion Act 1967 came into effect and at what might happen if restrictive amendments were passed. This outrage came across forcefully during an interview with Mahon, as she recounted her experiences as a nurse before 1967:

> If a woman's made her mind up, that she don't want to carry that baby, for a variety of reasons, they're not going to make her change it … I remember specialing[7] a woman one night, and she died actually, a teacher. And walking out, after they laid her out, I could see her little brother and her mother, sitting waiting to go in and look at her. That stays with you, that kind of thing. You don't lose that. She'd just decided, this young woman, she wasn't going to have that

child. She'd made a couple of attempts, and eventually she succeeded, but she killed herself in the process.[8]

Anti-abortion discourse

Many of the themes of anti-abortion discourse in the 1980s are familiar. Anti-abortion actors continued to reject the notion of doctors as social agents, creating narratives about untrustworthy doctors performing abortion 'on demand' and depicting abortion clinics as exploiting the women who visited them. These participants also expressed concern about the capacity of doctors and nurses to refuse to perform an abortion, and 'persecution' of conscientious objectors. All in all, these arguments reveal an enduring logic in which doctors' roles and identities are threatened by the 'corrupting and degrading business' (Alton in Hansard, 1988: 1233) of abortion. As Deborah Steinberg notes, there were several significant developments in anti-abortion discourse during the debate on then Liberal MP David Alton's Bill, which would have reduced the upper time limit to 18 weeks (Hansard, 1988):

> an unprecedented scientific dimension to the construction of fetal personhood ... the growth of the currency of the language of rights; and the incorporation and subversion of the language and concepts of the women's liberation movement (including the language of women's 'reproductive rights'). (Steinberg, 1991: 175–6)

The claim that women who had abortions would suffer from 'post-abortion syndrome', a kind of post-traumatic stress,[9] was also popularized in this era, and fed into attempts to undermine the image of abortion as a women's rights and health issue (Lee, 2003). Steinberg also observes that anti-abortion rhetoric began to distinguish between 'early' and 'late' abortion. 'Late' abortion was a new concept, framed by Alton supporters as a new kind of criminality, and graphic images of such abortions were used as a way of undermining the legitimacy of abortions generally. Outlawing 'late' abortions would only have been the tip of the iceberg: 'the Bill was deliberately styled to initiate an incremental erosion of legal abortion, beginning with "late" abortions' (1991: 176).

Virtue, vice and 'frivolous' abortion

Anti-abortion participants continued to push the idea that abortion harms women. Most commonly, they argued that abortion itself caused women physical and emotional damage. Alton argued that his Bill would mean fewer women would be 'emotionally and psychologically scarred' (Hansard, 1988: 1230) by abortion, and others continued this line of argument (Braine in Hansard, 1988: 1245; Viscount Massereene and Ferrard in Hansard, 1989b: 1480; Viscount Buckmaster in Hansard, 1989b: 1481; Cormack in Hansard, 1990b: 208). These arguments once again took up the theme of exploitative clinics who 'run a profitable industry in human weakness' (Kellet-Bowman in Hansard, 1988: 1232). They also suggested that women 'in a traumatic state' may be vulnerable to being talked into an abortion they would not otherwise want (Smyth in Hansard, 1990b: 240–1).

Female virtue and vulnerability also played a part in the construction of 'certain categories of women' (Cormack in Hansard, 1990b: 207) who were to be allowed an abortion in all cases, women who were 'in dire need and distress' (Braine in Hansard, 1990b: 219). Similarly to feminist constructions of female virtue, these women had done nothing 'wrong' – they were victims of rape, incest or faulty genes, and 'a pregnancy that was never wanted or never sought' had been 'thrust upon' them (Cormack in Hansard, 1990b: 208). However, unlike in feminist discourse, the subject of female vice came up frequently in these contributions. The distressed, virtuous women in their arguments were placed in opposition to women who sought abortions for 'frivolous' reasons. These involved the familiar 'social' reasons; however, these arguments were also fuelled by fears of an epidemic of abortions for minor disabilities:

> Should any handicap – a club foot, deafness, blindness or any other handicap – mean that the child should be aborted? Is it a sufficient reason to get rid of a child? (Knight in Hansard, 1988: 1250)

> Not long ago there was a great to-do in the national press because Guy's hospital advertised for mothers to come forward with children suffering from hare-lips and facial deformities to have pre-natal surgery, of which we are all in favour. They asked those mothers to come forward because they were considering abortions for those reasons. (Widdecombe in Hansard, 1990b: 197)

Anti-abortion participants also challenged the claim that restrictions on 'late' abortions would primarily affect frightened young girls and weary mothers, pointing to statistics apparently showing that the majority of abortions after 18 weeks were carried out on single, childless (and, by implication, less deserving) women (Paisley in Hansard, 1990b: 237; Duffy in Hansard, 1990b: 253). In this way, those in favour of abortion restrictions appealed to female purity, dividing women into the categories of 'deserving' and 'undeserving' and thus challenging the depiction of the Abortion Act 1967 as a measure to help the vulnerable. Deserving women were those who had behaved in a morally correct manner and were simply the victims of circumstance, while undeserving women sought abortions for trivialities – whether personal inconvenience or eugenic purposes – without having performed any maternal duties. This logic demonstrates the danger inherent in appealing to female virtue in order to justify legal abortion: ideas about female virtue can easily be subverted by arguing that virtuous women will 'choose life' when given the right support, or undermined by demonstrating that women seeking abortion are not particularly 'virtuous' after all.

Foetal subjects

As previously noted, the debates took place in the context of advances in foetal imaging technology and advances in medical science that allowed foetal life to be sustained outside the uterus at an earlier stage of gestation. As Rosalind Petchesky observed in her pivotal work on the topic, anti-abortion activists were quick to use this imagery to transform the foetus into a 'person' in the popular imagination. The 1984 US film *The Silent Scream* depicts an abortion, purporting to show the foetus attempting to escape the cannula and screaming silently. The film was framed as new knowledge allowed by a new 'science of fetology', allowing abortion to be witnessed 'from the victim's vantage point' (Petchesky, 1987: 266). While *The Silent Scream*'s claims were rebutted by various members of the medical community, it has had a large influence on the abortion debate in the US. Petchesky attributes this to the seemingly 'objective' nature of photography – its assumed ability to capture 'literal reality' – in spite of foetal imagery's tendency to depict the foetus as suspended in mid-air, abstracted from the pregnant body (1987: 268–9). Because it depicted the foetus in this way, this imagery was pivotal in allowing the foetus to be constructed as a separate, autonomous being and subject in its own right:

> the autonomous, free-floating fetus merely extends to gestation the Hobbesian view of born human beings as disconnected, solitary individuals. It is this abstract individualism, effacing the pregnant woman and the fetus's

dependence on her, that gives the fetal image its symbolic transparency, so that we can read in it our selves, our lost babies, our mythic secure past. (1987: 270)

Such images were also disseminated in the UK. As Sarah Franklin notes, supporters of further restrictions on legal abortion in the 1980s skilfully used such imagery to produce 'a social category of fetal personhood which has an enhanced ontological validity and specificity' (1991: 196). To a much greater extent than in the 1970s, parliamentary debate in this period involved graphic descriptions of both foetal development and 'late' abortion. Anti-abortionists depicted the 18-week foetus as 'fully formed' (Smith in Hansard, 1988: 1257) and therefore little different from a full-term baby. Such descriptions were often accompanied by vivid and horrifying accounts of late-term abortions in which the aborted foetus allegedly had 'its limbs torn from its body and its head crushed' (Braine in Hansard, 1988: 1245) while 'writhing in agony' (Alton in Hansard, 1990b: 226–7).

Some of these contributions explicitly referenced *The Silent Scream*, presenting it as a factual account of abortion (for example Viscount Buckmaster in Hansard, 1989b: 1481). By transforming the foetus into a 'baby' who is 'fully formed' and can feel pain, anti-abortion participants were able to construct it as a patient in its own right who can make the same demands of doctors that a woman can and is under threat from female vice. In keeping with their emphasis on female vulnerability, these participants often referred to the foetus itself as female:

> 600 abortions are undertaken every working day, some even on the grounds of the gender of the child, simply because it is a little girl. (Alton in Hansard, 1988: 1230)

> One is talking not just of the woman's choice – and one must remember that the foetus might be female. At times, the debate has resembled a contest between male and female. The tragedy is that the selective abortion techniques that are now available could be used not only to breed heirs for the Upper House but to reduce the number of women in a society that did not value them as much as our society does today. (Smyth in Hansard, 1990b: 242)

This strategy recalls the advice of a US anti-abortion handbook of the same period, which explicitly advised activists to borrow feminist language and apply it to the aborted female foetus (Faludi, 1991: 414).

While this manifestation of the claim that abortion harms women was not explored very far in the 1980s debates in Parliament, it would become a much larger point of contestation in the 21st century, as the following chapters show.

Appropriation and backlash

Some of the anti-abortion speeches made use of some very obvious borrowing from feminist discourses. The speakers used several strategies that subverted feminist strategies on abortion, which involved arrogating the ability to speak 'for women' to themselves (Robertson in Hansard, 1987: 1421) and privileging (or claiming to privilege) women's experiences in their arguments. One key difference from the anti-abortion/'pro-woman' rhetoric of the 1970s was a new emphasis on men's sexual behaviour as problematic:

> Men must, of course, approach the debate with humility and sensitivity. We rarely have to suffer the practical day-to-day experience of an unwanted child. We rarely hear about unmarried fathers, only about unmarried mothers. We do not hear about men having illegitimate children, only women, and how often men smugly talk about fallen women. We never hear about fallen men. Women are frequently pressurised into abortions by men. Men too often leave a woman in the lurch, having used their sexuality without responsibility. Those who maintain that abortion is purely a woman's issue do women no service; it allows men to evade their responsibilities, and without changes in men's attitudes women will not be truly liberated.
> (Alton in Hansard, 1988: 1235)

> Free and easy abortion is in the interests of men because it removes the problem of pregnancy, and women are well aware of that. (Duffy in Hansard, 1990b: 253)

In such arguments, female vulnerability was no longer just a matter of exploitation by doctors, but also of men's mistreatment of women. Awareness of feminist ideas was demonstrated throughout, and Alton's opening speech in the Second Reading debate of his Bill quoted a feminist author who called abortion 'killing' (Hansard, 1988: 1231). However, what is striking about these speeches is not only the tendency to borrow from feminism, but that it went hand in hand with attempts to indirectly *blame* feminism for the troubles now facing women and society. Men's unacceptable behaviour was not, as in feminist arguments, linked to centuries of male dominance. Rather, it was implied that women's mistreatment at the hands of selfish men was a consequence of the erosion of traditional values linked to feminism and the sexual revolution:

> Many of the things that most hon. Members would hold dear are held a little more tenuously than they were 23 years ago. ... One has to face the fact that marriage is no longer the central institution that it was. One has only to do some canvassing, as I did in Mid-Staffordshire recently – not that it did much good – to realise that for two people of different sex to live in the same house in different names is much more common that it was 20 years ago. One has only to consider the statistics for children born out of wedlock, or the increasingly powerful demands, which I shall not expand on at the moment because it would be out of order, from some sections of the community for women to be allowed to have children without any thought of marriage, to realise that there have been many changes. (Cormack in Hansard, 1990b: 210–11)

> At the heart of the debate about contraception and family planning ... is the need to recognise that when love and a sense of responsibility is removed from sexual relations, there will always be tragedy. (Alton in Hansard, 1990b: 221)

Such remarks demonstrate the deeply conservative nature of anti-abortion activity and reveal that many participants saw abortion as at once a cause and signifier of social change, as discussed in Chapter 2. As the Conservative MP Nicholas Bennett put it: 'freely available abortion has changed the nature of society' (Hansard, 1988: 1261). This is classic backlash politics: from the claim that 'society' would be better off if the changes associated with feminism were reversed, to the claim that feminism and feminist demands have actively harmed women.

The 1990s: anti-abortion politics in decline?

After the HFE Act 1990 passed there was little parliamentary activity on abortion for several years, aside from a 1991 adjournment debate (where no measure is put to the vote) on early medical abortion and a handful of Private Members' Bills, none of which reached Second Reading. Sheldon argues that early medical abortions present a difficulty for anti-abortionists as the foetus is much less recognizable as a 'baby' at this stage of gestation, thereby detracting from the focus on the foetal subject (1997: 130). This assessment seems accurate: in the mid-1990s, two Bills were introduced that dealt with a particularly gruesome method of late-term abortion, thereby shifting focus back onto the foetus, although only Elizabeth Peacock's was debated. This section deals with the RU486 debate, the debate on the Peacock Bill, and another anti-abortion Bill introduced by David Amess.

Early medical abortion

Mifepristone, earlier known as RU486, is a drug used to induce abortion in the early stages of pregnancy. It was licensed for use in abortion in the UK in 1991 and is used in the first nine weeks of pregnancy (Sheldon, 1997: 126–9). As taking mifepristone is a relatively simple, non-surgical procedure, the drug had the potential to shift the balance of power during the abortion procedure in women's favour. Its licensing provoked the fear among anti-abortionists that abortion was becoming too easy or trivial, and arguments against mifepristone often implied 'that women need to suffer in order to be deterred from reoffending' (Sheldon, 1997: 131). However, in the parliamentary debate over mifepristone, anti-abortion MPs chose to represent women seeking abortion in a different way. Participants who opposed the licensing of mifepristone either implicitly challenged the notion of increased agency by depicting women not as choosing subjects but as unwitting 'guinea pigs' (Winterton in Hansard, 1991: 895) of the pharmaceutical industry, or depicted increased agency in abortion as itself traumatizing (Hind in Hansard, 1991: 886).

Such arguments challenged medicalization by undoing its construction of abortion as a measure to protect the vulnerable. However, pro-choice commentators had their own concerns about the introduction of mifepristone, noting that, in practice, it resulted in more medical control of abortion, not less: the administration of mifepristone involves heightened medical supervision entailing multiple visits to a clinic (Sheldon, 1997: 133–9). Furthermore, in the parliamentary debate supporters of the decision to license mifepristone were careful to stress that its use would not diminish medical control of abortion, and that its administration would be in accordance with the terms set out in the Abortion Act 1967 (Sheldon, 1997: 134). It is worth noting that parliamentary pro-choice discourse continued to construct women as patients, and articulate the interests of women and doctors together:

> The drug will save theatre time and theatre staff. It will save the surgeon's time. It will save anaesthetists, theatre nurses and anaesthetic nurses. It will save porters, equipment and anaesthetic agents. I hope that that considerable saving of resources and the freeing of resources will be redirected into providing a comprehensive national health service for abortion, with less delay for women ... I support self-referral for abortion in the first three months of pregnancy. I realise that that view is not shared by everyone. That practice would ease NHS delays and, for the first time, would give women rights to decide whether to continue with a pregnancy. (Richardson in Hansard, 1991: 893)

This is an interesting statement that requires some unpicking. On the one hand, it is an explicit call for demedicalized abortion provision and a right to choose. On the other, it is also fairly obviously an attempt to translate women's interests or goals into a format compatible with the objectives of medical providers and health administrators. This was a creative use of discursive resources on Richardson's part, and allowed her to demand not only self-referral for abortion but also vastly improved NHS provision. However, it risked suggesting that women's rights are worth pursuing only in so far as they fit with governmental objectives.

While mifepristone provision was at the time highly medicalized, there were reasons to be optimistic about its use. Sheldon argues that mifepristone may radicalize understandings of abortion because it allows women to be more in control during the actual process of abortion itself: it does not require women to be hospitalized or undressed in the presence of a stranger (1997: 139–40) and allows women to take a more active role and doctors a more passive one. Moreover, in practice its administration has sometimes involved only minimal supervision as doctors do not always strictly abide by rules regarded as medically unnecessary (1997: 143). Providers and medical organizations ultimately came to favour demedicalization of such abortions and allowing them to happen at home. Nonetheless, the extent to which this was resisted by the Department of Health demonstrates that medicalization was still important to politicians, if not to the medical profession.

A final important feature of the mifepristone debate is the unique difficulty it presented for anti-abortion participants. Drugs inducing an early medical abortion 'make it more difficult for the anti-choice movement to rest their arguments on considerations of a foetus which is less easily represented as a recognisable "baby" at this stage of gestational development' (Sheldon, 1997: 130). Instead of focusing on the foetus, opponents of mifepristone focused on alleged dangers to women's health and the potential 'trauma' resulting from abortion. Sheldon implies that this shift in focus away from the foetus might be part of a broader shift towards the use of 'medical' discourses above all else. Nonetheless, in later debates in the 1990s and in the 21st century, anti-abortionists found new ways of focusing on the foetus.

Keeping the debate alive

When asked about the potential for further restrictive legislation to be brought in, former Labour MP Brian Iddon predicted that 'people will keep chipping away, keeping the thing alive through the Ten Minute Rule Bills'.[10] This is in essence what happened in the 1990s after the low-key RU486 debate. Several restrictive Bills were introduced between 1991 and 1996 (see Table 5.1). Firstly, Conservative MP David Amess introduced a Bill to prohibit the use of techniques for selecting foetal sex. Amess pledged that the Bill would not seek to amend the Abortion Act 1967 (Hansard, 1993: 769); however, its focus on apparent risks posed to 'little girls' by reproductive technology would be echoed in later Bills. In 1995, Lord Braine introduced a Bill to prohibit 'partial-birth' abortions and, in 1996, Viscount Brentford attempted to prohibit the abortion of foetuses with Down's syndrome. However, neither of these Bills received a Second Reading debate. More successful – in airing the issue in Parliament if not in becoming law – were two Ten Minute Rule Bills introduced by Conservative MP Elizabeth Peacock and David Amess in 1996.

Peacock's Bill moved to prohibit so-called partial-birth abortions. More commonly called dilation and extraction (D&X), these abortions involve the dilation of the cervix so that the foetus can be removed intact. D&X has attracted controversy, particularly in the US, due to the nature of the procedure, which requires the brain of the foetus to be suctioned out. Nonetheless, this procedure is only rarely used in the US, and never used in the UK – neither at the time Peacock's Bill was introduced nor in the 2000s (Hansard, 2003). This, however, did not deter Peacock from introducing her Bill. In her speech at First Reading, she noted that 'there is nothing to stop the general practitioner from using' D&X, and that 'there is no legal requirement for practitioners to notify the use of the technique' (Hansard, 1996a: 1041). While the object of contention was somewhat new, this line of argument recalls earlier challenges to medicalization, which depicted doctors as irresponsible and impossible to control, rather than benign and socially responsible. Also familiar from 1980s debates is the graphic depiction of the abortion procedure:

> The practitioner, guided by ultrasound, pulls the living unborn child through the mother's vagina, except for the child's head, which is deliberately kept just within the uterus. The practitioner then puts surgical scissors or another medical instrument into the back of the skull, inserts a catheter and sucks out the brains. (Peacock in Hansard, 1996a: 1041)

Peacock's speech, unlike earlier speeches of mifepristone opponents, had an obvious affinity with 1980s depictions of violence against 'the unborn'. Since the Bill had no actual practical purpose, as D&X was not used in the UK, I suggest that Peacock's Bill represented an attempt not to change the law but to refocus abortion discourse on the foetus, the 'horror' of abortion, and the danger of medical power – as Labour MP Ann Clwyd put it in her opposing speech, 'to shock and repulse people' (Hansard, 1996a: 1043). Focusing on the foetus of course challenges the logic of medicalization, which relies on a dual depiction of doctors as responsible and women as vulnerable. Instead, these graphic accounts of abortion depict the foetus as the true victim, and doctors as either butchers or themselves victims of legal abortion. Female vice also rears its head in these accounts: Peacock claimed that most 'partial-birth' abortions 'are purely elective ... another name for abortion on demand' (Hansard, 1996a: 1042).

This renewed focus on the foetus does not mean that anti-abortion legislators had abandoned medical arguments. Two weeks later, Amess introduced a Bill that, like previous Bills, would have amended the grounds for legal abortion so that the pregnancy would have to present a 'substantial' risk to a woman's health in order for an abortion to be carried out (Hansard, 1996b). There was little new in Amess' speech: he worried about abortions being performed for 'purely social reasons' and went on to stress the potential risks to a woman's physical health (an alleged increased risk of breast cancer) and mental health (from 'post-abortion trauma') (Hansard, 1996b: 776–7). Neither Amess' nor Peacock's Bill was pressed to a vote.

Tackling the backlash

Pro-choice and feminist MPs had clearly been pushed into a defensive position by the volume of attacks on abortion rights. Their arguments relied heavily upon narratives of female virtue and vulnerability in order to justify women's access to abortion. This strategy seems reasonable at first: images of women aborting for 'trivial' reasons such as club foot or personal inconvenience were rife in the arguments of anti-abortionists, and there may well have been an urgently felt need to counter them. Yet 'attributing value to one category of people still occurs at the expense of denying it to another' (Boryczka, 2012: 61). Due to the dualistic nature of virtue and vice, the argument that some women need abortions 'through no fault of their own' implies another category of women who *are* at fault, and therefore *do not* deserve access to abortion.

As earlier chapters have demonstrated, the medicalization of abortion regulation – and therefore the Abortion Act 1967 – is sustained by narratives of female vulnerability. This means that feminists forced to defend the Act have found it difficult to escape such narratives. It would be unfair, however, to argue that medicalization went completely unchallenged by feminists during this period. Liberalizing amendments to the HFE Bill proposed by Harriet Harman and Emma Nicholson demonstrate that medicalization was in fact somewhat contested. Nonetheless, important parts of its logic remained unchallenged and this generated tensions for feminism. Constructing women seeking abortion as primarily *patients* allowed feminists to argue that obstructions to abortion access meant that the state and medical profession were failing in their duty to women. However, over-reliance on medical necessity to justify abortion results in questions of women's rights, reproductive freedom and bodily autonomy being eclipsed (Purdy, 2001; Skinner, 2012). As Janet Hadley has observed, 'the woman as an active social agent, a decider, a person with the capacity to determine her own future, fades from view' (Hadley, 1997: 242). Appeals to medical necessity also render advocates of legal abortion vulnerable to claims that abortion is not a 'real' need or is indeed harmful to women.

Meanwhile, anti-abortion discourse generally attempted to undermine the idea that abortion is medically necessary, counterbalancing with stories of women aborting for 'trivial' reasons. These stories indicate the danger of narratives of 'acceptable' abortion, which are easily subverted and undermined. The arguments of the anti-abortionists also frequently appropriated elements of feminist rhetoric, claiming to speak on behalf of women and to be interested in ending women's exploitation. Nonetheless, these arguments at the same time utilized a conservative morality, implying that feminism and the social changes of the 1960s and 1970s had in fact been bad for both women and society in general. Anti-abortion discourse in the 1980s was in this way just as conflicted as feminist discourse, attempting to simultaneously appropriate and scapegoat feminism. While none of the amendments sought by anti-abortionists came to pass, they should not be discounted. The Alton Bill in particular came close to becoming law before being eclipsed by the HFE Act. Furthermore, the arguments established in these debates were revisited by anti-abortion forces well into the 21st century.

6

Into the 21st Century

After a huge swing to Labour in the 1997 general election – including an unprecedented intake of female MPs – the issue of abortion went quiet for almost nine years. This election saw 120 women MPs elected, many of whom sought specifically to further women's interests (Childs, 2000; 2002). As a former Labour MP from this cohort told me, the high intake of women 'started to change the culture' of Parliament, making it easier for women to express certain views.[1] Many of these women would later be highly active in defending the Abortion Act 1967 – or even pushing for further liberalization. Despite the lack of political activity, however, abortion provision began to change in practice. In the past decade or so, a gap had opened up between the law and practice as doctors became increasingly liberal in their attitude towards abortion and less inclined to stand in the way of the abortion decision. Meanwhile, more and more abortions were carried out in the charitable sector (with NHS funding), making abortion more widely available than ever before. However, many women still face logistical barriers to access to abortion (Aiken et al, 2018).

Medicalization continued to present problems in other ways. In 2011, the British Pregnancy Advisory Service (BPAS) made a bid to allow women to undergo early medical abortion in their own home. Early medical abortion requires a woman to take two medications, mifepristone and misoprostol, 24–48 hours apart. Until 2017 in Scotland and 2018 in England and Wales, women had to take both pills in a clinic under medical supervision, meaning that those who had to travel long distances to reach a clinic could begin to miscarry on their journey home. BPAS argued that the law could be interpreted such that both pills would be prescribed in a clinic, but patients would be allowed to take the second pill at home, as in many other countries. However, the Department of Health opposed this move, and a High Court judge ruled that both pills must be taken under medical supervision (Greasley,

Table 6.1: Abortion Bills, 2005–12

Bill	Stage reached	Key provisions
Robertson, 2005	First Reading	Prohibit abortion except in the case of rape or incest or if the woman's life was endangered by the pregnancy.
Dorries, 2006	First Reading	Require women seeking abortions to receive mandatory counselling followed by a 'cooling-off' period before medical practitioners would be allowed to certify an abortion.
Winterton, 2007	First Reading	Require women seeking abortions to receive mandatory counselling followed by a 'cooling-off' period before medical practitioners would be allowed to certify an abortion.
Dorries, 2007	First Reading	Require women seeking abortions to receive mandatory counselling followed by a 'cooling-off' period of seven days before medical practitioners would be allowed to certify an abortion.
HFE Bill, 2008	Became HFE Act	Several restrictive and liberalizing amendments concerning abortion were proposed. However, none made it into the eventual Act.
Health and Social Care Bill, 2011	Became Health and Social Care Act	Nadine Dorries and Frank Field tabled an amendment that aimed to strip providers of the ability to offer counselling, requiring instead that it be provided by an independent organization. However, the amendment failed.

Source: Hansard

2011). This ruling appeared to reflect the ongoing conviction that abortions must be closely observed and controlled, even if this caused suffering. (As the following chapter discusses, the Department of Health relented in 2018, after the devolved administrations in Scotland and Wales both moved to allow women to take the second pill at home.)

Alongside these clashes came a flurry of anti-abortion activity in Parliament, starting from the mid-2000s (see Table 6.1). This perhaps reached its apex in 2012 when the Care Quality Commission (CQC) conducted surprise inspections on a number of clinics amid allegations that regulations were not being followed (Department of Health, 2012). Nonetheless, the terms of parliamentary debate remained similar. As Ellie Lee (2013) has noted, anti-abortion discourse was dominated by a dichotomy between 'villains' (abortion providers) and 'victims' (women who have abortions).[2] However, this and the following chapter describe new anti-abortion strategies that emerged in the 2000s and went beyond the familiar topics of viability, abortion clinic profiteering and conscientious objection. These include attempts to introduce various provisions relating to pre-abortion counselling, justified using the language of 'a woman's right to know'.

Prohibition, counselling and cooling off

Between 2005 and 2007, Conservative MPs Ann Winterton and Nadine Dorries introduced Bills that would have required women seeking abortions to receive mandatory counselling followed by a 'cooling-off' period of seven days before medical practitioners would be allowed to certify an abortion (Hansard, 2006; 2007). Both were Ten Minute Rule Bills that did not progress past First Reading, although Dorries later introduced a second Bill that was not debated but was subject to a Department of Health impact assessment (Department of Health, 2007). Similarly assessed was a Bill, introduced by Laurence Robertson (Conservative) but not debated, which would have prohibited abortion except in the case of rape or incest or if the woman's life was endangered by the pregnancy. Nadine Dorries in particular requires introduction here, as she has maintained a high profile in abortion debates. While Dorries describes herself as pro-choice and a feminist, her campaigns have been attacked by abortion rights advocates (Abortion Rights, 2012). The counselling Bills came under fire for the delays and impediments they would have placed in the way of those seeking abortion. These Bills represent a continuation of anti-abortion strategy in their depiction of abortion as something that harms women, but are also innovative in their use of the concept of a 'right to know'.

Medical purity, progress and a 'right to know'

In their speeches at the First Reading debate of each Bill, both Dorries and Winterton situated their Bills within a narrative of progress. This is somewhat at odds with the conservative values expressed by some anti-abortion participants in earlier debates. However, it is perhaps unsurprising as, since at least the 1980s, anti-abortion activism has made use of, and been boosted by, new technologies surrounding prenatal care and the foetus. Dorries suggested that that medical knowledge had 'moved on' since the HFE Act 1990, and that 'ground-breaking foetal monitoring techniques' could be used in abortion care (Hansard, 2006: 155). Moreover, this narrative was explicitly tied up with ideas about 'what doctors want': Dorries stated that 'doctors do not like foeticide and they do not like late abortions' (Hansard, 2006: 156), while Winterton asserted that younger doctors were 'refusing to have anything to do with the operation' (Hansard, 2007: 138–9). This may seem surprising, given past anti-abortion emphasis on medical irresponsibility. However, the idea that abortion victimizes doctors and goes against medical ethics has always been a facet of anti-abortion arguments. Dorries and Winterton simply emphasized this aspect over the image of the irresponsible, uncontrollable doctor that featured heavily in past debates. Indeed, Winterton went on to suggest that these doctors would soon become a thing of the past, 'seen out' by a 'more enlightened' generation (Hansard, 2007: 139–40). Such claims stressed the differences between doctors, challenging both the notion of a medical consensus on abortion and the underlying assumption of the Abortion Act 1967 that abortion provision was consonant with medical roles and identities.

Dorries and Winterton's depiction of women in their speeches was innovative. Like previous anti-abortion actors, they appropriated and subverted both liberal-paternal conceptions of female vulnerability and elements of a feminist discourse of rights and empowerment. As in previous debates, women's vulnerability and the risks of abortion were highlighted, and Dorries and Winterton both referenced a study purporting to show that women who have abortions have vastly increased risks of subsequent mental health problems (Hansard, 2006: 156; Hansard, 2007: 140). The findings of this study are contested; other research has not found evidence that 'post-abortion syndrome' exists (for example Robinson et al, 2009; Munk-Olsen et al, 2011). Nevertheless, the notion that abortion harms women has long been a feature of anti-abortion arguments, as it challenges the conception of the Act as a protective measure. What was innovative about these speeches – and the push for 'informed consent' in abortion provision more broadly – however was the way they tied the portrayal of women as vulnerable and at risk from abortion to a feminist rhetoric of empowerment. This coupling of feminist and anti-abortion ideas hinged on the concept of *knowledge* and the right to be properly informed:

> The latest piece of major research on the possible effects of abortion on women's mental health was carried out in New Zealand and was led by a scientist who supports abortion on demand. Evidently, however, he also supports *a woman's right to know what she is choosing*. (Winterton in Hansard, 2007: 139; emphasis mine)

> I call that [mandatory counselling and 'cooling off'] a woman's right to know and to choose, because *without information, what choices does a woman have?* A period of informed consent is about empowerment—it is about whether or not the decision to abort is fully thought through. It is about making an informed decision. (Dorries in Hansard, 2006: 156; emphasis mine)

This strategy represented an attempt to decouple abortion rights from feminism, thereby undermining the credibility of feminists speaking in favour of the status quo and situating Dorries and Winterton as those truly concerned with protecting women's rights. Indeed, Winterton's speech took aim at pro-choice feminists, whom she termed 'the abortion sisterhood' (Hansard, 2007: 138). As well as emphasizing the 'right to know', Winterton attacked the 'sisterhood' for their criticism of 'crisis pregnancy centres',[3] depicted as neutral organizations simply seeking to provide help and support to women (Hansard, 2007: 138). Likewise, she described birth control activist Margaret Sanger – seen by some as a feminist pioneer (Chesler, 2007; Coates, 2008) – as a eugenicist who 'was not interested in women's rights' (Hansard, 2007: 139). In this way, her speech sought to blame feminism, or at least pro-choice feminists, for women's suffering, while at the same time attempting to arrogate elements of feminist arguments to herself.

Feminists respond

Speaking to oppose the Dorries and Winterton Bills were two Labour women MPs, Christine McCafferty and Laura Moffatt. Both challenged what they saw as the assumption that women seeking abortion do not know their own minds, emphasizing that most women seeking abortion have made up their minds long before speaking to a medical professional (Moffatt in Hansard, 2007: 141) and should be allowed to make this choice on their own terms (McCafferty in Hansard, 2006: 159). In doing so, they depicted women as reasonable and competent – a far cry from the image, often found in the contributions of early supporters of legal abortion, of women as frightened and irrational. On the other hand, these accounts are coloured with assumptions about female virtue and faultlessness. Take McCafferty's insistence that women seeking late abortions 'have *compelling reasons* and often face *extremely difficult or unusual circumstances*, perhaps the catastrophic long-term illness of another, older child' (Hansard, 2006: 158; emphasis mine). This is yet another narrative in which the woman seeking abortion is a victim of circumstance who did everything 'right' — and is possibly already a loving mother.

Nonetheless, these speeches did situate their claims about abortion with respect to a broader sequence of feminist demands. Both McCafferty and Moffatt called for improved sex education and access to contraception as better ways to tackle the problems identified by Dorries and Winterton:

> As I have said many times in the House, the best way of reducing the number of unintended pregnancies is to improve women's access to contraception, as well as educating women and men about sexual health. This cruel Bill — for it is a cruel Bill — is an attack on women's reproductive rights. (McCafferty in Hansard, 2006: 159)

> A delay in treatment results in abortion taking place later and at greater emotional and financial cost. It would undoubtedly force some women to continue a pregnancy against their wish, but the best way to reduce the numbers of unintended pregnancies is to improve women's access to contraception, as well as educating women — and men — about sexual health. (Moffatt in Hansard, 2007: 141–2)

These demands were more limited than in earlier debates, during which feminists linked together demands for liberal abortion laws with demands for better housing, employment and maternity support, to name a few.

The Department of Health responds

Under the Labour government, the Department of Health produced impact assessments of Robertson's Bill and Dorries' second counselling Bill (Department of Health, 2005; 2007). While these were very different Bills — Robertson aimed to prohibit abortion entirely, with very few exceptions, while Dorries claimed to be in favour of legal abortion — the assessments are similar enough that they are worth mentioning here, as they demonstrate how ideas about female vulnerability have become inscribed in the process of 'evidence-based policy-making' (EBP). The assessments sought to calculate the 'impact' (Department of Health, 2005: 2) or 'effect' (2007: 3) of the proposed Bills. They are suffused with the language of EBP: women and providers feature as 'stakeholders' and the effects of the Bills are figured in terms of risks and costs. The assessment of the Robertson

Bill found that the risks it posed to women involved, among others, suicide, feigned suicidality (in order to convince doctors that the woman concerned needed an abortion), death from illegal abortion and damage to mental health from being forced to continue the pregnancy (2005: 7–8). The predicted costs were estimated to be £750 million a year in medical costs, welfare, social care, education and others. The assessment of the Dorries Bill found that it would have involved risks to mental health, a small number of self-induced pregnancies, and financial difficulties for those living in poverty, among other risks (2007: 9–10). In addition, the Bill was estimated to involve a cost of £74 million a year in costs to the NHS, counselling costs and benefits.

Of course, these assessments were useful to the pro-choice cause, as their findings supported the case against the Bills. Nonetheless, they considerably flatten the terrain of abortion politics by seeking only 'what works' (Parsons, 2002; Sanderson, 2003). This is most evident from the 2005 assessment's reduction of the complexity of ideas involved in anti-abortion sentiment to 'a socio-moral benefit to members of the public that are pro-life' (Department of Health, 2005: 14). The 'evidence-based' approach may also be detrimental to pro-choice politics. By formulating the 'problem' of abortion in terms of a calculation of the 'risks' and 'costs' incurred by 'stakeholders', they effectively exclude questions of rights, autonomy and liberation. Instead, the 'impact' of a proposed item of legislation can only be figured as that which is directly observable and can be measured. This in turn necessitates the portrayal of women as essentially vulnerable, as the only women visible to evidence-based impact assessments are those who are deemed to be 'at risk'.

The Human Fertilisation and Embryology Bill 2008

In the mid-2000s, the Labour government became aware of a need to update the HFE Act 1990. The Human Fertilisation and Embryology Authority (HFEA), the statutory body regulating human embryo research and reproductive technology, had been 'making the law on the hoof'[4] while trying to keep up with technological advances, and it was recognized that new primary legislation was needed. As in 1990, anti-abortion parliamentarians attempted to attach amendments to bring the upper limit for legal abortion down to anywhere between 22 and 12 weeks (including a campaign by Dorries for a reduction to 20 weeks) and to require the provision of counselling. However, the outcome was heavily influenced by a report of the Science and Technology Committee on legal abortion (2007b), which found there to be little evidence suggesting foetal viability rates had improved below 24 weeks' gestation. In a series of divisions, Parliament voted to keep the 24-week limit.

Several MPs also attempted to attach liberalizing amendments to the Bill. These amendments would have removed the rule requiring two doctors to certify before an abortion could be carried out, extended the Act to Northern Ireland where it still did not apply, permitted nurses to carry out abortions where suitably trained, and extended the range of locations where abortions could take place – including allowing women to complete early medical abortion at home. However, the government tabled a programme motion[5] that changed the order in which amendments were called for discussion, and guillotined the time allowed for debate. This ensured that there was no time to debate the liberalizing amendments (Sheldon, 2009: 4).

Report of the Science and Technology Committee

In the mid-2000s, the Labour government had realized that the HFE Act 1990 was in need of updating, and wanted the help of the House of Commons Science and Technology Committee in doing so. This led the Committee to produce a report on human reproductive technology in 2005 (Science and Technology Committee, 2005), which was followed up by reports into chimaera and hybrid embryos (2007a) and abortion (2007b). These reports led in turn to the formation of an ad hoc Joint Committee with the House of Lords, resulting in the publication of the Human Fertilisation and Embryology Bill. The Committee had not initially planned to discuss abortion at all. However, it came to conduct an inquiry into abortion after the government suggested that since anti-abortion actors were likely to attempt to insert abortion amendments into the Bill, it would be worthwhile to consider whether there had been any scientific developments relating to abortion since 1990. The Committee explicitly ruled out consideration of ethical and moral issues surrounding abortion (Science and Technology Committee, 2007b: 5), and attempted to emphasize evidence from those seen to be the most neutral. Nonetheless, it received a large volume of evidence from both pro-life and pro-choice campaigners.[6]

The inquiry looked for evidence pertaining to four key areas: the upper gestational limit for legal abortion, abortion for foetal abnormality, the potential impact on the aborting person's health and issues surrounding access and procedure. Regarding the upper gestational limit, the report found that survival rates below 24 weeks had not improved since 1990, although they had improved from

24 weeks onwards (2007b: 22). The inquiry also considered the issue of consciousness and foetal pain, again concluding that there was little evidence that pain is consciously felt by the foetus, especially below 24 weeks. It also looked at reasons why women might present for 'late' terminations, stressing that many women did not realize they were pregnant until a late stage in the pregnancy. However, it also found that 41 per cent of women present for late abortions because they 'struggle to take the decision to have an abortion' (2007b: 28).

The section of the report relating to foetal abnormality focused on whether further clarification of the definitions of 'abnormality' and 'handicap' in the Act were necessary. The report indicated that some submissions to the inquiry had expressed concern over abortions for clubbed feet and cleft palates, although it concluded that it would not be feasible to create an exhaustive list of conditions legitimating abortion (2007b: 29–31). Regarding the risks to mental health posed by abortion, the report found the evidence inconclusive (2007b: 47), and one former Committee member suggested to me that more research needed to be done in this area.[7] However, it found that the physical health risks of abortion were minimal, that the RCOG's guidelines in this area were correct, and that abortion patients were generally well informed of any risks (2007b: 48–51).

The Committee's recommendations concerning access and procedure contrast sharply with those of the Lane Committee of the 1970s, which justified its support for medical control of abortion by depicting women as irrational, vulnerable and incapable of responsibly exercising a right to choose. The 2007 report framed issues of access to abortion in terms of the need for abortions to be carried out as early as possible, and recommended a loosening of medicalization in several ways, including allowing a more active role for nurses in the provision of abortion (2007b: 38–9), and letting women undergo medical abortion at home[8] (2007b: 42). However, its observations concerning the two-doctor rule are the most significant. The Committee suggested that the need for two doctors be removed on the basis that it might cause delays (2007b: 35). Evidence submitted to the inquiry generally cited medical reasons for removing the rule, noting that 'no other medical or surgical procedure' requires two signatures (2007b: 33). Moreover, evidence from Sally Sheldon suggested that the requirement for two signatures runs counter to the principle of patient autonomy (2007b: 33).

These arguments might be seen as medicalizing due to the translation of women's rights into patients' rights. On the other hand, they simultaneously indicate the destabilization of the medicalized framework for abortion regulation. Medicalization was achieved in

1996–7 by describing abortion as 'like other medical procedures', but recent criticism of the two-doctor rule uses the same argument in order to undermine the basis for strict medical control. Medical organizations themselves criticized the need for two doctors in their evidence to the Committee (2007b: 33), and a BMA document published in the same year recommended the removal of the two-doctor rule and the need for women seeking abortion to meet specified medical criteria, 'so that first trimester abortion is available on the same basis as any other medical treatment – on the basis of informed consent' (BMA, 2007: 5). Meanwhile, the pro-life group SPUC advocated retaining the rule on the basis that prescribing a medical procedure 'for a social reason or a psychiatric reason ... is highly unusual in medicine' (Science and Technology Committee, 2007b: 35).

Strikingly, this argument appeals to medical purity – the notion that there is a clear distinction between the 'social' and 'medical' realms – in order to justify medical control of abortion. This is markedly different from the concerns of anti-abortion politicians in the 1966–7 debates, who argued that decisions on 'social' matters should not be committed to the hands of doctors. This reversal suggests a move away from medicalized rationales for abortion regulation. Medicalization may have been based on the idea that 'doctor knows best', but if doctors themselves are recommending a shift away from medical control, it is unclear what this now means.

Anti-abortion arguments

Two members of the Committee, Nadine Dorries and Bob Spink, published a dissenting minority report indicating concern over how the inquiry had selected evidence. While Brian Iddon and Des Turner (both former Committee members), along with the report itself, emphasized the attempt to find a neutral ground in the inquiry, the minority report suggested that the process of evidence selection had been shaped by 'ideological and financial interests' (Science and Technology Committee, 2007b: 71). However, it was not made clear what these interests were. Dorries and Spink criticized several aspects of the report. Firstly, they took issue with the validity the key study informing the Committee's conclusions on foetal viability (2007b: 73–4). Secondly, they emphasized what they saw as significant health risks of abortion and stressed the need for a 'right to know' (2007b: 78–9). Finally, they expressed anxiety that allowing women to undergo abortion at home would result in 'a more relaxed attitude' among young women concerning abortion and contraception. This brings to mind Sheldon's observation that the anti-abortion project requires women to suffer 'in order to be deterred from reoffending' (1997: 131).

Similar concerns were expressed in the 2008 debate. Anti-abortion participants continued to situate restrictive amendments in the context of 'new evidence' regarding the foetus and 'advances in modern medical science' (Leigh in Hansard, 2008: 227), arguing that liberal abortion laws are 'perhaps outdated now, given the advances in science in recent years' (Pritchard in Hansard, 2008: 233). There was also a sustained use of graphic descriptions of foetal development, presenting the foetus as a person and subject in its own right:

> Scientific evidence increasingly suggests that unborn children feel pain at 16 weeks. That is not simply a stress response; it is a physiological response, perhaps not the same as in a fully grown adult, but a physical and even emotional response beyond the norms of passive reflex. Pain is felt, which is why specialist, gifted surgeons who perform surgery on babies in the womb use anaesthetic. Now, 4D imaging reveals that 16-week-old unborn babies are very much alive and kicking, although their limbs are too small to be felt by the mothers. (Pritchard in Hansard, 2008: 234)

These descriptions were again found alongside shocking descriptions of abortion depicting violence against the foetal subject:

> the baby was given a lethal injection of potassium through the mother's abdominal wall, into the baby's heart. The process was supervised by an ultrasound scanner, so that the doctor could see exactly where the needle was going – into the foetal heart. The baby died and 24 hours later went through the process of surgical dismemberment and removal. (Dorries in Hansard, 2008: 259)

As Childs et al (2013) note, anti-abortionists also drew upon the image of the 'social' abortionist who lacks a sense of responsibility, noting that 'social' abortions account for the vast majority of abortions (Leigh in Hansard, 2008: 226) and take place 'for the convenience of the parents' (Curtis-Thomas in Hansard, 2008: 231). Female vice was implicit in these arguments, which challenge the pro-choice depiction of women presenting for late abortions as virtuous and vulnerable. John Pugh (Liberal Democrat), for example, picked up on statistics concerning reasons for late abortions published in the Committee report, observing that over 40 per cent of late abortions 'result, in a sense, from late choices' (Hansard, 2008: 252). In a similar vein, Dorries complained that some women 'demand' a late termination 'with no good reason' (Hansard, 2008: 261), recalling old fears that women are not traumatized 'enough' by abortion.

Yet at the same time, anti-abortion participants continued to stress the harm done to women by abortion, whether in the form of an increased physical risk or in terms of damage to mental health (for example Curtis-Thomas in Hansard, 2008: 228–9; Pritchard in Hansard, 2008: 234). On one occasion, an MP brought attention to the harm done to 'girl' foetuses (Leigh in Hansard, 2008: 227) – foreshadowing future attempts to restrict access to sex-selective abortion. These participants also presented themselves as acting 'for women', continuing to call for a 'right to know' (Curtis-Thomas in Hansard, 2008: 228) about alleged health risks and even making explicit appeals to feminism: 'a cursory glance at 19th-century and even early 20th-century social history reveals that it was the feminist movement, alarmed by a male-dominated medical profession, that led the charge against liberalising abortion laws' (Pritchard in Hansard, 2008: 233). That such arguments existed alongside narratives of female vice and irresponsibility suggests an on-going tension in anti-abortion politics between the desire to appeal to a conservative vision of gender roles, and the need to grapple with the 'woman problem' presented by the Abortion Act 1967. What is most notable about anti-abortion contributions in this debate, however, is the near absence of the 'irresponsible doctor' theme. Although this theme was still present among the Lords (Childs et al, 2013), MPs displayed an apparent acceptance and encouragement of the pastoral role of medical providers in guiding men and women onto the 'right' path. Two separate MPs compared the role of doctors in abortion care to that of GPs in approving a vasectomy:

> When a man presents for a vasectomy at a doctor's surgery, the doctor does not say, 'Come in, sit down and take your trousers off.' He says, 'I think you ought to think about this for a little while.' If the man involved is under the age of 30, childless and not yet married, the doctor may well say to him, 'I think you ought to think about this seriously'. (Curtis-Thomas in Hansard, 2008: 229)

> I had a vasectomy on the national health. I went to see my GP, who said, 'I want to speak to your wife.' My wife and I both sat there and agreed that a vasectomy was the way

forward for us as our own personal form of contraception. The GP then sent us away for three or four days, after which my wife and I both saw the consultant, and again we both agreed that a vasectomy was the way forward. I entirely agree with the hon. Lady that if that time for thought is right for a man having a vasectomy … there must be a provision for more time to think and consult when it comes to such a serious decision as having an abortion. (Penning in Hansard, 2008: 242–3)

These very similar accounts suggest that during this period parliamentary abortion opponents did not abandon the figure of the 'socially responsible' doctor. This is the novelty of counselling amendments: they subvert feminist arguments by transforming 'a right to choose' into 'a right to know', but also subvert the notion that the 'socially responsible' doctor will *enable* abortions. These kinds of arguments can result in contradictions and tensions in anti-abortion arguments, as the following chapter indicates.

Feminist arguments

Like those speaking in support of restrictive amendments, pro-choice feminists prioritized medical evidence in their arguments. Dawn Primarolo, by this time Minister of State for Public Health, spoke in support of existing time limits, emphasizing her focus on the evidence concerning foetal viability even when directly challenged about the morality of abortions in specific circumstances (Hansard, 2008: 248). However, Primarolo also made it clear that she was consciously situating her arguments with respect to how Parliament had decided the matter in the past (Hansard, 2008: 245). Others similarly prioritized scientific evidence. However, interviews with former MPs suggest that this was at least in part done strategically:

> I think they were much more receptive to the medical evidence. I think that was the thing that won it, that kept things at bay. I don't think the feminism and the women's issues would resonate with some people in Parliament.[9]

The perception that it was evidence 'that won it' was shared by my other interviewees, who believed that anti-abortion actors were unlikely to win the argument in Parliament without evidence that viability rates were improving.[10] Turner observed that the evidence may not have been the deciding factor for many people whose moral and political views played a part, but that it gave people the 'confidence' to resist restrictive amendments, especially Primarolo in her role as a minister. Labour MP Kate Green, who was not an MP at the time but has been active in abortion politics since her election in 2010, expanded on this. For Green, arguments concerning evidence are not only *necessary* in order to counter anti-abortionists' claims regarding foetal viability, but also an *easy* way to address the issue, as anti-abortionists are 'disingenuous in their use of evidence'.[11]

However, Green also noted that the factors concerning a woman's decision to abort were just as important, if more difficult, to discuss. This view seems to have been shared by pro-choice MPs active in the 2008 debate, many of whom centred women and women's rights in their speeches (Childs et al, 2013) and explicitly represented the debate as about 'women's right to choose' (McCafferty in Hansard, 2008: 245; Morgan in Hansard, 2008: 269–70). While Julie Morgan stated her belief that abortion should be more accessible (Hansard, 2008: 268), there was very little else by way of critique of the Abortion Act 1967– far less so than in the 1990 debate. However, some context is required here: the 1990 debate took place against a backdrop of cuts to the NHS that caused delays in accessing care, whereas by 2008 charitable sector provision of abortion had expanded, rendering abortion far more accessible. Moreover, participants in the 1990 debate were able to discuss an amendment to end the two-doctor rule, but similar discussion was guillotined in 2008. Nonetheless, it is still the case that feminist arguments continued to appeal to the figure of the doctor as a justification for 'choice', with many stressing that the decision should be 'between the patient and her doctor, just like any other medical treatment' (McCafferty in Hansard, 2008: 238; see also Morgan in Hansard, 2008: 269).

Demands for maintaining abortion access were again situated within a broader chain of demands. However, these demands were, as in the 2006 and 2007 debates, rather truncated compared to previous decades:

> What has been proven to reduce abortions is comprehensive sex education and unrestricted access to effective contraception and early safe abortion services. (McCafferty in Hansard, 2008: 237)

> Many of us … would seek to improve sex education, relationships education and contraception. (Mallaber in Hansard, 2008: 254)

Feminist speakers continued to represent women seeking abortion as vulnerable. Again, it was late-aborting women who were primarily deemed to be vulnerable in these contributions (Morgan in Hansard, 2008: 234; Primarolo in Hansard, 2008: 246–7). In addition, the mandatory counselling amendments were seen as potentially victimizing women by forcing them to receive information they were not in a state to hear (Primarolo in Hansard, 2008: 249). These speakers also drew upon narratives of acceptable abortion to support their case, such as in this letter read out by Labour MP Judy Mallaber:

> I was 19, my father had died and I was looking after my 8 siblings with my mother who could barely afford to keep us. I couldn't face telling my mum about my pregnancy—things were so difficult. If I couldn't have an abortion I'd have killed myself. Now I've been able to go to college, learn to read and write, play a full role in society and bring up a family of my own. (Hansard, 2008: 256)

While such stories may be important to tell, as Childs et al (2013) note, missing from pro-choice discourse were arguments that presented abortion as a normal part of life that a diverse range of women experience. Narratives of acceptable abortion also frequently centred on the issue of foetal abnormality as justification for 'late' abortions. In these narratives, women were depicted as responsible and reasonable choosers, often deciding to abort because they know it is best for the families and often for the foetus: 'Any reduction below the current 24-week limit would leave little or no room for women and couples to make a responsible, considered choice when a potentially serious abnormality is detected' (McCafferty in Hansard, 2008: 239). Unlike other arguments that focus on the vulnerability of women who seek abortion, these narratives do construct women as agents: active choosers rather than victims of circumstance. Yet, to reiterate Steinberg's (1991: 187) point, this is justified not on the grounds of a 'right to choose' (which would not dictate 'acceptable' reasons for termination) but on the grounds that disability is a 'special case' that legitimates abortions that might otherwise be unethical.

Northern Ireland

As the Abortion Act 1967 was never extended to Northern Ireland, at this time it remained governed by the Offences Against the Person Act 1861, meaning that almost all abortions were illegal. The question of abortion was raised in the debate around the Northern Ireland Act 1998, which provided for devolved government in Northern

Ireland following decades of direct rule. At the time, government ministers pledged that a change in abortion law would not be imposed on Northern Ireland (Colthart, 2009: 4–5). The HFE Bill 2008 nonetheless saw a serious attempt at Westminster to introduce legal abortion in Northern Ireland,[12] driven by Labour MPs including Diane Abbott, who tabled an amendment that would have extended the Abortion Act 1967 to Northern Ireland. Calling for reform, Abbott condemned the inequality inherent in existing legislation, which she described as treating Northern Irish women as 'second class citizens' (quoted in Thomson, 2018a: 96).

The amendment was given a heightened sense of urgency due to the understanding that further powers relating to policing and justice were due to be devolved to Northern Ireland, limiting Westminster's ability to intervene. Still, abortion rights activists in Northern Ireland were hopeful that it would pass and become law (Thomson, 2018b: 171). However, the proposal was pushed down the agenda by the government's programme motion, meaning there was no time for a debate or a vote and the amendment could not pass (Thomson, 2018a: 95–6; Thomson, 2018b: 172). Many assumed that this happened as part of a deal between the government and Northern Ireland's anti-abortion Democratic Unionist Party (DUP) in return for the latter's support for efforts to increase the legal detention period for terror suspects (Thomson, 2018a: 97).

After the HFE Act 2008

Unlike in previous decades, the debate on abortion does not seem to have died down following the failure of high-profile attempts to amend the Abortion Act 1967. Nadine Dorries secured an adjournment debate on counselling in 2010 (Hansard, 2010), which was followed by an attempt to amend the coalition government's Health and Social Care Bill in 2011 (Hansard, 2011a). The amendment failed after Dorries' co-sponsor Frank Field (Labour) withdrew his support and Public Health Minister Anne Milton stated that legislation would not help address Dorries' concerns; but the government promised to launch a consultation. Nonetheless, abortion counselling was again discussed in an adjournment debate later in the year (Hansard, 2011b).

The political climate seemed to shift further in favour of anti-abortion sentiment in 2012. First, a *Daily Telegraph* 'sting' indicated that some doctors might agree to perform abortions because of the sex of the foetus (Watt et al, 2012). This was followed by allegations that doctors were 'pre-signing' abortion certificates before seeing patients, despite providers alleging that this was done for 'good clinical reasons' to improve services (Kavanagh quoted in Orr, 2017: 169). The Department of Health subsequently ordered the CQC to conduct a series of unannounced inspections on independent abortion providers (Department of Health, 2012). Later in the year, there was another adjournment debate during which several MPs expressed anti-abortion sentiments. However, during the debate the new Public Health Minister Anna Soubry announced that the government had dropped the planned consultation into abortion counselling (Hansard, 2012). The Department of Health's sexual health framework, published in 2013, suggested that there were few problems with charitable providers' own provision of counselling (2013: 35–6). Nonetheless, suspicion of providers was reawakened and providers began, for the first time in years, to seriously consider the possibility that abortion doctors and their patients might be prosecuted (Kavanagh quoted in Orr, 2017: 168–70).

The Dorries and Field amendment would not, unlike Dorries's previous Bill, have imposed mandatory counselling or a 'cooling-off' period. Rather, it aimed to strip providers of the ability to offer counselling, requiring instead that it be provided by an independent organization. While presented by Dorries as a pro-woman rather than anti-abortion amendment, abortion rights groups worried that it would introduce delays in the process of obtaining an abortion, and that anti-abortion organizations might be contracted in order to provide counselling (Abortion Rights, 2011). Dorries's speeches in this and other debates seemed designed to reignite suspicion of doctors, especially those involved in abortion provision. While opponents recognized that the amendment was unlikely to become law, it was perceived as part of a broader strategy of 'chipping away' of abortion rights by 'creating a climate of scepticism about the way in which abortions are carried out'.[13]

The debates again saw Dorries focusing on the vulnerability of women (for example Hansard, 2010: 896), who may even be 'coerced' into abortion (Hansard, 2012: 74). These arguments in places seem to invert the narratives of personal crisis and trauma told by many pro-choice feminists:

> I ask Members, just for a moment, to put themselves in the shoes of a 16-year-old girl who turns up at that clinic and does not know what to do. She is pregnant and panicking. Some of her friends tell her to have an abortion and some tell her not to. She does not want to tell her parents because

she is scared of doing so. Her boyfriend is saying to her, 'You've got to have an abortion and get rid of it'. (Hansard, 2011a: 370)

Dorries continued to present herself as a feminist, citing her respect for Harriet Harman and 'what she has achieved for women and humanity' (Hansard, 2011a: 363), claiming to be acting on behalf of women who had asked her to propose new legislation (Hansard, 2011a: 373–4; 377) and even evading an attempt by the more openly pro-life DUP MP William McCrea to refocus the debate on the foetus, as 'the amendment is not about the unborn child; it is about the woman accessing counselling' (Hansard, 2011a: 375). However, Dorries's contributions also pointedly attacked abortion providers, who, she argued, 'flout the law' (Hansard, 2012: 70) and are motivated by profit, not by caring for women:

> BPAS has advertised for business development managers, whose primary function is to increase its market share – those are its own words in the advert. If an organisation advertises that it wants to increase the number of abortions, can we trust it to provide vulnerable women who walk through that door with the counselling that they need? (Hansard, 2011a: 377)

In the later 2011 debate, Conservative MP Gavin Shuker expressed similar opinions, reciting stories of 'disinterested' counsellors, who 'presented [women's] abortion options like it was a sweet shop' (Hansard, 2011b: 629). The debates elicited a strong feminist response, and a strong articulation of feminist demands:

> Women – both individual women and women in general – have been called in aid in this debate, and indeed they face very real problems in this society, here in 2011. They face spiralling employment as a direct consequence of the coalition's policies and the sexualisation of our culture, which affects younger and younger female children. (Abbott in Hansard, 2011a: 381)

> I am sure we would all prefer a world in which there are fewer abortions; in which men and women have access to sex education, support and advice to make the right decisions for themselves; in which, should partners choose to engage in sexual relations, there is safe and confidential

access to contraceptives; in which there is no rape or incest; and in which, if a woman becomes pregnant, she is not so afraid of family and community that she is unable to seek early advice and support. (Malhotra in Hansard, 2012: 80)

These speeches go beyond the demands for sex education and contraception expressed in 2008. On the other hand, such contributions did still tend to privilege medical knowledges (Malhotra in Hansard, 2012: 80; Elliott in Hansard, 2012: 83–4), present abortion as primarily a medical decision that 'must, at the end of the day, be between a woman and a doctor' (Abbott in Hansard, 2011a: 382), and depict the interests of women and doctors as aligned:

> the proposers of the amendment are asking us to believe, on the basis of purely anecdotal evidence, that tens of thousands of doctors, nurses and charity workers involved in the 190,000 abortions a year are wilfully ignoring both the law and the guidance of the British Medical Association and the Royal Colleges ... The proposers of the amendment, I might add, also seem to be arguing that thousands of women do not actually know what they are doing. (Abbott in Hansard, 2011a: 180–1)

Alliance with the medical profession means something different in the 21st century. Firstly, as previously noted, the medical organizations now favour further liberalization over medical control. Secondly, the growth of BPAS and other organizations has hugely changed the landscape of abortion provision, and leaders of the biggest providers have been longstanding advocates for change (Furedi, 2008; Rickman, 2012). As the following chapter will make clear, allegiance with the medical profession now, ironically, means allegiance with organizations that advocate for an end to, or at least loosening of, medical control over abortion.

Pro-choicers on the back foot

Abortion debate in this era remained overly technical and focused on foetal viability. Where human stories were told, they overwhelmingly prioritized narratives of acceptable abortion and female vulnerability. While of course these stories must be told, as Childs et al (2013) note, the sense that abortion is a normal if not universal part of life, and something that a diverse array of women experience, was generally missing from pro-choice parliamentary discourse. Moreover, the prioritization of such narratives tends to reinforce the notion that there is no option other than medicalization: since 1967, the figure of the vulnerable women has been heavily intertwined with that of the paternalistic doctor. Ideas about female vulnerability also contributed to the reluctance of some to allow abortion pills to be taken at home, due to a suspicion that women would not be able to 'cope' with their heightened agency in this process – even though research demonstrates that many women find home abortion preferable to abortion in a clinical setting (Cameron et al, 2010; Lohr et al, 2010).

Pro-choice activity in Parliament was sustained after the Human Fertilisation and Embryology Act 2008 by a cross-party group of MPs committed to fighting any attempts to restrict abortion access. According to one member, the Labour MP Kate Green, this group saw it as important to coordinate even when the threat was not considered very great:

> We felt it was so important at the time of Nadine's Bill to organise the voice in Parliament who are pro-choice. Not because we thought her Bill as such was necessarily going anywhere, but it was so important to show that there were a lot of people who would come back in this debate.[14]

The powerful campaign in the Republic of Ireland following the death of Savita Halappanavar in 2012 aided the pro-choice cause in the UK. Halappanavar died of a septic miscarriage after University Hospital Galway staff repeatedly refused her requests for a termination, even after she had been told the foetus would not survive. The case highlighted 'how utterly non-discriminating the need for a termination can be'[15] as well as how much can be lost when anti-abortion attitudes take hold. However, when I first started interviewing MPs and former MPs in 2013, there had been no recent attempts to push for liberalization. Interviewees were consistently critical of the operation of the Abortion Act:

> I think it's overprotective … the need for two doctors to certify implies that women somehow can't be trusted to make this decision, or that it's a hugely medically finely balanced decision, and I would like to see that examined again.[16]

> Why do you have to have a reason to have an abortion if you really decide you don't want to go through with it? … I just

> wonder whether having to have a reason, or having to have the two doctors, may be a bit of a mechanical exercise.[17]

> We [the Science and Technology Select Committee] suggested that nurses should sign this HSA1 form [notifying abortion to the government], we saw no reason why it should be doctors to organise the consent.[18]

> It's all too easy for doctors who fundamentally disagree with abortion to withhold their signatures, therefore leaving a pregnant woman faced with increased delay in seeking to obtain an alternative.[19]

While interviewees readily gave such opinions, it was a struggle to find them reflected in records of parliamentary debate. The government guillotine on the 2008 debate was a major reason for this, having removed a big opportunity for the merits of liberalizing amendments to be discussed. As a result, the 2008 debate put pro-choice parliamentarians in a reactive role, unable to move the discussion on. Yet there were other, pragmatic reasons for the lack of effort to liberalize the law. Although critical of elements of the Abortion Act 1967, those interviewed in 2013 suggested that attempts to reform the law would not work as the 'climate' in Parliament was wrong,[20] that 'opening the debate up' might backfire,[21] and that, in spite of its flaws, the Act was still 'reasonably liberal and workable'.[22] This prevailing attitude was not to change until 2017.

7

Towards Decriminalization? New Battlegrounds in Abortion Politics

Much has changed since I first started interviewing MPs about abortion. Most strikingly, in July 2019 Parliament voted to require the government to act to decriminalise abortion in Northern Ireland. Parliament has also considered two separate Bills aimed at repealing sections 58 and 59 of the Offences Against the Person Act 1861 (OAPA) – and therefore the removal of criminal sanctions associated with abortion in the rest of the UK – and hosted an emergency debate on the same topic (Hansard, 2017; 2018a; 2018b) (see Table 7.1). As backbencher initiatives, these had little hope of changing the law, but the cross-party support they enjoyed is surprising, given that until recently MPs felt it would be unwise to rock the boat by agitating for radical reforms. The case for reform was, in part, galvanized by the increasing ability and willingness of women to access abortion pills online, bypassing bricks-and-mortar clinics. But it was accelerated by the success of the Repeal the Eighth campaign in the Republic of Ireland, which culminated in Irish citizens voting to remove a 1983 amendment to the Irish constitution recognising the equal right to life of the pregnant woman and the 'unborn'. This in turn put the spotlight on the near-total criminalization of abortion in Northern Ireland. For once, the future of abortion rights in Northern Ireland became closely linked to that of abortion rights in Britain in parliamentary debate, as pro-choice MPs and campaigners began to blame the situation not on the failure to extend the Abortion Act 1967 to Northern Ireland, but on the criminal sanctions required under OAPA. Repealing the relevant sections of OAPA would remove these criminal sanctions

Table 7.1: Abortion Bills, 2013–19

Bill	Stage reached	Key provisions
Bruce, 2013	First Reading	Require the Secretary of State to compile statistics on the gender ratios of foetuses aborted and impose harsher penalties on those found to have assisted such an abortion.
Bruce, 2014	First Reading	Clarify the law relating to abortion on grounds of foetal sex (presumably to explicitly criminalize it).
Serious Crime Bill, 2015	Became Serious Crime Act	Two amendments were tabled relating to sex-selective abortion: Fiona Bruce's amendment explicitly criminalising the practice (which failed), and a further amendment requiring to government to collect evidence on sex-selective abortion (which passed).
Lord Shinkwin, 2016	Report stage (Lords)	Remove the clause permitting abortions in the case of severe disability after 24 weeks' gestation.
Johnson, 2016	First Reading	Repeal sections 58 and 59 of the Offences Against the Person Act 1861, decriminalizing abortion
Baroness Winterboune, 2017	First Reading (at the time of writing, Second Reading of this Bill was yet to be tabled)	Lower the time limit for legal abortion to 12 weeks' gestation.
Lord Shinkwin, 2017	First Reading	Remove the section permitting abortions in the case of severe disability after 24 weeks' gestation.
Johnson, 2017	First Reading	Repeal sections 58 and 59 of the Offences Against the Person Act 1861, decriminalizing abortion up to 24 weeks' gestation; introduce new offences relating to non-consensual termination of pregnancy; introduce new conscientious objection rights.
Northern Ireland (Executive Formation and Exercise of Functions) Bill, 2018	Became Northern Ireland (Executive Formation and Exercise of Functions) Act	Stella Creasy and Conor McGinn successfully tabled an amendment holding UK ministers accountable for their role in ensuring human rights compliance in Northern Ireland on abortion as well and marriage equality.
Northern Ireland (Executive Formation) Bill, 2019	Became Northern Ireland (Executive Formation etc.) Act, 2019	Creasy successfully tabled an amendment requiring the UK government to act to decriminalise abortion in Northern Ireland and introduce new provisions for abortion regulation if Stormont failed to reconvene by 21 October 2019.

Source: Hansard

in England, Wales *and* Northern Ireland (OAPA does not apply in Scotland, where abortion is a common law offence).

As the goals and tactics of pro-choicers shifted, so did those of anti-abortion activists. The longstanding claim that abortion harms women found a new – and perhaps more resonant than ever before – iteration in the form of claims that female foetuses were being aborted on a large scale in South Asian communities. While heavily contested, these claims were leveraged in support of attempts to further restrict legal access to abortion, and continue to be used to undermine calls for decriminalization. To a lesser extent, similar tactics were used in a campaign to abolish the exemption to the 24-week limit on legal abortion in cases where, were the pregnancy to be carried to term, the baby would be severely disabled. Sex selection and disability are useful to abortion rights opponents, as they can be deployed in such a way as to destabilize the perception of abortion as an issue of human rights and equality. But these cases should not simply be dismissed as mere matters of anti-abortion strategy; both raise issues that abortion rights advocates must address.

The changing climate of abortion opinion

Political debates now operate within a vastly different context than they did in the 1960s. Early abortions using medication rather than surgical methods are now commonplace – something never envisioned by the authors of the Abortion Act 1967. Yet, at the same time, hundreds of women in Britain have been turning to Women on Web, an international service which helps women order abortion pills online if they cannot otherwise access abortion (Aiken et al, 2018). This situation was greatly exacerbated by the ban on home use of abortion pills, ultimately lifted in Scotland in 2017 and in England and Wales in 2018. A handful of women have been prosecuted for self-administering abortions. In Britain, these are cases where a woman deliberately caused her own miscarriage in a late stage of pregnancy, while in Northern Ireland women have been prosecuted for self-administering abortions in the first trimester (BMA, 2017a: 16–17). These cases helped to drive shifts of opinion among the medical profession.

Medical opinion

As the previous chapter indicated, medical opinion on abortion regulation was already shifting by the time of the HFE Act 2008, and doctors involved in abortion provision have long felt that the law does not align with best practice (Sheldon, 2016b; Lee et al, 2018). Medical organizations reported to Parliament that they supported scrapping the two-doctor rule, and in some cases advocated abolishing the requirement for medical grounds for abortion entirely. However, these changes would all have taken the form of amendments to the Abortion Act 1967; no major medical organization was calling for the repeal of OAPA. This began to change in 2016, when BPAS, the largest abortion provider in the country, launched its 'We Trust Women' campaign with the support of the Royal College of Midwives, and Diana Johnson MP launched her first decriminalization Bill. The Royal College of Midwives was thus the first professional association to come out in support of decriminalization.

In 2017 and 2018, other major medical bodies threw their weight behind the campaign. The BMA was the first to officially change its position. In February 2017 it published a neutral 'discussion paper' to inform its members of the various cases for and against decriminalization (BMA, 2017a). At its annual representative meeting in June the same year, representatives voted to back decriminalization. BMA Medical Ethics Committee chair John Chisholm observed that 'decriminalization does not mean deregulation', that it also 'does not address the broader issue of when and how abortion should be available' and affirmed that existing BMA policy on abortion provision would remain in place (BMA, 2017b).

The RCOG underwent a similar process. Its Council voted in September 2017 to back decriminalization, with its president, Lesley Regan, similarly stating that 'decriminalisation does not mean deregulation' (RCOG, 2017). Its partner organization, the Faculty of Sexual and Reproductive Healthcare, followed suit after an October 2017 consultation indicated that 'the vast majority' of its members supported decriminalization (FSRH, 2017). A Royal College of Nursing consultation published in June 2018 found that 73.7 per cent of respondents were in favour of decriminalization – although only 1 per cent of members responded to the consultation (RCN, 2018a). The College released a position statement in December 2018 in support of decriminalization (RCN, 2018b). Finally, the Royal College of General Practitioners voted to support decriminalization in early 2019 (RCGP, 2019).

A search of the *British Medical Journal* (*BMJ*) reveals a similar groundswell of support for decriminalization around this time. Prior to 2016, abortion in the UK was rarely mentioned in the *BMJ*; rather, articles usually discussed abortion in the context of countries with far more restrictive arrangements, particularly in the wake of the

Zika epidemic of 2015–16. But from late 2016 onwards there was a flurry of articles covering decriminalization. Contributors variously described the law as 'hypocritical and anachronistic' (Wise, 2016), 'meaningless and moralising' (Parsons quoted in Howard, 2017) and 'either coercive (as in Northern Ireland) or impotent (as in the rest of the UK)' (Goldbeck-Wood et al, 2018). A key concern of critics of the Act was that while its stated aim was to protect doctors, it in fact placed doctors in danger of imprisonment (Rimmer and Coombes, 2017).

Analysis of debates among the medical profession reveals the curious reversal that has taken place since 1967 in understandings of medicalization and the role it plays (or does not play) in the 'protection' of vulnerable women. At the BMA's annual representative meeting, Eleanor Draeger, a genitourinary medicine consultant, appealed directly to women's vulnerability in order to make an argument *for* decriminalization:

> Because of the way the law says that two people have to consent to a woman having an abortion, our service folded after a year because we didn't have enough doctors who were willing to sign a form. That means that the women in my borough, which is one of the most deprived in the country, have less access to termination. There were women that I saw who had partners who would not let them use long acting contraception, who would not use a condom — women who did not have the choice to have sex or not and therefore did not have the choice whether to get pregnant or not. Because two doctors are required to sign the form ... some of those women will have a baby in a circumstance where having a baby is not the right choice for that woman. (quoted in Rimmer and Coombes, 2017)

In the 1960s debates over the Steel Bill, the depiction of women seeking abortions as poor and vulnerable worked in support of a restrictive and highly medicalized regime of abortion regulation that assumed that doctors were best placed to decide whether a woman 'really needed' an abortion. Here, it appears to do the exact opposite – criminalization (and with it, the two-doctor rule) is portrayed as placing vulnerable women in danger.

None of this is to say that midwives, nurses and doctors uniformly support decriminalization. In response to the Royal College of Midwives' support for the We Trust Women campaign, a group of midwives launched a counter-campaign, Not In Our Name, later echoed by members of the Royal College of Nursing who circulated a petition titled 'Not In My Name'. These campaigns described calls for decriminalization as 'extreme' and lambasted both the Royal College of Midwives for failing to consult its members on the change of position (Hart, 2016) and the Royal College of Nursing for not allowing members to vote on the exact wording of their position statement.[1] Many doctors agreed; by the time of the BMA meeting, 1,500 doctors and medical students had signed an open letter asking the BMA to reject the motion backing decriminalization (Rimmer and Coombes, 2017).

Devolution and abortion provision

Along with shifts in medical opinion came shifts in regulation and provision: chiefly, new rules allowing women to undergo early medical abortion in their own homes, and provision for those travelling from Northern Ireland to have abortions funded by the English, Welsh and Scottish NHS. These were driven not by the central UK government, but by the devolved administrations in Scotland and Wales (in the case of the former) and by UK Parliament backbenchers (in the case of the latter). The process began in 2015, when power over abortion legislation was devolved to the Scottish Parliament as part of a larger bundle of powers following the fractious independence referendum the previous year. While some expressed concerns that devolution could negatively impact abortion provision in Scotland, in late 2017 the Scottish government became the first to allow women to undergo early medical abortion at home (Moon et al, 2019).

This decision faced resistance. SPUC brought a legal challenge at the Court of Session, Scotland's supreme civil court, arguing, like the Department of Health had in 2011, that abortions must occur under medical supervision under the terms of the Abortion Act 1967. However, the judge, Lady Wise, ruled that home abortions were not illegal, as 'patients who self-administer medication at home may still be described as being treated by their medical practitioner, who remains in charge of that treatment' (BBC, 2018). The Scottish Parliament's decision triggered a similar change of policy in Wales, which began to allow home abortion from June 2018. The decisions of both administrations put pressure on the UK government, especially after the RCOG, the Faculty of Sexual and Reproductive Healthcare, and other medical organizations and women's groups joined the call (Lay, 2018). Meanwhile, activists and MPs campaigning for decriminalization repeatedly pointed out that more and more women were buying abortion pills online in order to avoid making repeated trips to a clinic. The Department of Health eventually relented and announced a plan to allow home abortions in England in August 2018.

The status of abortion in Northern Ireland attracted renewed attention in June 2017, when, following the shock loss of its parliamentary majority in that year's snap election, Theresa May's government entered an agreement with Northern Ireland's staunchly conservative and anti-abortion Democratic Unionist Party (DUP), which would provide the votes to pass its legislation in Parliament. Not long after the election, the Labour backbencher Stella Creasy sought to pass an amendment to the Queen's Speech[2] that would fund abortions for women travelling to England from Northern Ireland. Creasy's actions were in large part a response to lobbying by the London-Irish Abortion Rights Campaign, which had by that point been in communication with her for several months.[3] The amendment attracted considerable cross-party support, and the UK government, wanting to head off a damaging debate about its newfound allies, announced that it would fund abortions for Northern Irish women travelling to England (Thomson, 2018a: 102–3; Moon et al, 2019). Contrary to what has frequently been reported, this funding does not come through NHS England (as with most abortions) but rather from the Government Equalities Office (Elgot, 2017). As one activist pointed out, Northern Irish women are 'still not getting equal treatment, they still aren't accessing abortion on the NHS in the same way women in England and Wales are able to'.[4] Moreover, when the government's guidance on home abortion in England was published, it became clear that Northern Irish women were to be excluded from the new arrangements (Department of Health and Social Care, 2018a). Government funding also does not address the other costs associated with travelling for an abortion, and cannot possibly address the emotional costs. Funding for abortions for Northern Irish women was provided in Scotland from November 2017 and in Wales from November 2018 (this time funded by the NHS in both countries).

From this brief account it may seem as though devolution has been a positive driver of change in abortion policy, with reforms passing rapidly from one administration to another. However, research on devolution and abortion in the UK suggests that it has been a risky process, 'not only with regards to increased incoherence across the nations, but also risks of backsliding' (Moon et al, 2019: 2). While Scotland and Wales have in some cases outpaced the central UK government in driving reform forward, the same cannot be said for the Northern Ireland Assembly. Responsibility for abortion law has rested with the Assembly since 2010; however, the Assembly underwent a long period of suspension following the collapse of the power-sharing agreement between the DUP and the other largest party, Sinn Fein, in early 2017. Yet for a long time, the central UK government insisted that abortion was a matter for the Assembly – in spite of the successful Repeal the Eighth campaign south of the border, and a Supreme Court ruling that Northern Irish abortion law violated international human rights law (Moon et al, 2019).

Buffer zones

The other major development to occur between 2016 and 2018 concerned calls to introduce legal 'buffer zones' outside abortion clinics in order to keep anti-abortion protestors away from their doors. Major medical bodies alongside abortion rights advocates have promoted this idea for some time, alleging that protestors have aggressively harassed patients and staff at the clinics, filmed people leaving and entering, distributed misleading information about the clinical risks of abortion and generally created a distressing environment for those seeking abortion (BPAS, 2014a; RCOG and FSRH, 2018). Some research suggests that even when anti-abortion activists protesting outside clinics perceive their own behaviour as supportive, it is experienced by abortion patients as harassment (Lowe and Hayes, 2018). Anti-abortion campaigners have meanwhile decried the proposals as an attack on freedom of speech (Rudgard, 2018). In any case, progress on this issue has been extremely slow. Interviews with BPAS's campaigns team suggested that even having a sympathetic ear in the Home Office, provided by then Home Secretary Amber Rudd, had not been enough, as change was being blocked from on high:

> It's a nightmare because we've got a pro-choice Home Secretary, who's been to her BPAS clinic in Hastings, who still won't do anything about protests outside clinics, and it must be Theresa May. I mean, by process of elimination we think we've worked that out. She's putting a block on doing anything about it.[5]

It was suggested that the government's preoccupation with preparations for the UK to leave the European Union was blocking the creation of progressive legislation. Rudd did launch a consultation on protests outside abortion clinics in November 2017, inviting input from the public, police and abortion providers as well as protestors themselves. Yet before the consultation was complete, Rudd resigned as Home

Secretary due to the fallout from the Windrush scandal[6] and was replaced by Sajid Javid, an MP who lacks Rudd's pro-choice commitments. When the consultation concluded, Javid announced that there would be no national buffer zones: the consultation *had* uncovered evidence of harassment and intimidation, he admitted, but buffer zones would be disproportionate as 'predominantly, anti-abortion activities are more passive in nature' (Javid, 2018).

The decriminalization campaign

Decriminalization has long been an aim of abortion rights advocates. However, as previous chapters have demonstrated, parliamentarians have generally been extremely cautious about the prospects of liberalizing reform. Diana Johnson, the Labour MP who set the parliamentary campaign in motion, had originally planned on introducing a bill with a narrower scope for liberalization. Even so, she found herself 'warned off' by fellow MPs, even those who were pro-choice: 'a lot of the women politicians, in the House of Commons in particular, said to me, if you start opening up the Abortion Act you could end up in a worse position than we're in now'.[7] The idea to push for decriminalization was suggested to Johnson by Dr Kate Guthrie, a consultant gynaecologist who has worked in NHS abortion care and now works for Women on Web. Johnson introduced her first Bill in 2017 with the support of groups such as BPAS and Abortion Rights[8] as well as the abortion law scholar Sally Sheldon. The Bill aimed to repeal sections 58 and 59 of OAPA in England and Wales only; Northern Ireland was left out at this stage. It passed its First Reading by 172 votes to 142 but did not progress.

It was the resounding success of the Repeal the Eighth campaign in the Republic of Ireland, in combination with Creasy's earlier work on abortion funding, that brought Northern Ireland onto the agenda for British politicians. The Eighth Amendment of the Constitution of Ireland asserted the equal right to life of pregnant women and the unborn, but the campaign to repeal it was given new life in 2012 following the death of Savita Halappanavar. On 25 May 2018, a referendum on repealing the Eighth passed by 66.4 per cent. Shortly after the vote, the Irish Taoiseach, Leo Varadkar, suggested that women from Northern Ireland might be able to have abortions south of the border when new laws had been introduced (Rawlinson, 2018). Following the change of law, Northern Irish residents were required to pay hefty charges to access abortion in the Republic, and campaigners recommended that they travel to England instead (Simpson, 2019).

Nonetheless, the Irish referendum served to highlight Northern Ireland's own extremely restrictive abortion law.

Earlier in 2018, a UN Committee on the Elimination of all forms of Discrimination against Women (CEDAW) report had found that that UK was violating the rights of Northern Irish women by restricting their access to abortion. The report proposed the repeal of the relevant sections of OAPA in order to decriminalise abortion in Northern Ireland. It also recommended legislating to allow for abortion in cases of rape, incest, and severe foetal impairment and in any case where there is a threat to the physical or mental health of the person seeking abortion, as well as proposing a host of other changes to promote sexual and reproductive rights in Northern Ireland (CEDAW, 2018). Then, just weeks after the Irish referendum, the UK's Supreme Court considered an appeal brought by the Northern Ireland Human Rights Commission to examine the legality of Northern Irish abortion law. The Supreme Court rejected the case; however, this decision was based on a lack of jurisdiction to act, as the case had not identified an individual victim. The majority of judges stated that the lack of access to legal abortion in Northern Ireland was incompatible with European human rights law. A fresh case has been brought in the name of Sarah Ewart, a Northern Irish woman who had to travel to England for an abortion after discovering her baby had a fatal abnormality.

Following the Irish referendum, Stella Creasy – with the support of a cross-party coalition of MPs – successfully lobbied for an emergency parliamentary debate on abortion in Northern Ireland. This was the first point at which abortion law in Northern Ireland became linked, in the parliamentary imagination, to the decriminalization campaign. Instead of blaming the situation on the failure to extend the Abortion Act 1967 to Northern Ireland, Creasy instead blamed OAPA itself – a law made at Westminster in 1861 that still had bearing on Northern Ireland's criminal law. Diana Johnson's second decriminalization bill consequently included Northern Ireland within its scope; at this point Johnson no longer regarded Northern Ireland as in the 'too-difficult pile'.[9] The Bill passed by 208 votes to 123 but again could not progress.

Johnson's Bills were critical in rallying parliamentary support for reform, but without government support, they met the fate of most backbench legislation. It was, instead, amendments to government legislation that made the difference. The first of these, proposed by Creasy and the Labour MP Conor McGinn, was more modest in scope. This was a clause inserted into the Northern Ireland (Executive Formation and Exercise of Functions) Act 2018 – which was meant to assist in restoring devolved government to Northern Ireland – that holds UK ministers accountable for their role in ensuring human rights compliance in Northern Ireland, on abortion as well as marriage equality. But the second was radical: a successful amendment to another Northern Ireland Act, the Northern Ireland (Executive Formation etc.) Act 2019, requiring the CEDAW recommendations to be implemented in full, which was passed by 332 votes to 99. Building on their earlier collaboration, McGinn also successfully moved an amendment to extend equal marriage legislation to Northern Ireland.

Johnson's Bill, meanwhile, is fully drafted and 'ready to go' if Johnson or another backbencher is given the opportunity to introduce another decriminalization Bill for England and Wales. The Bill is long and thorough, with clauses that criminalize the non-consensual termination of pregnancy through violence or coercion. While campaigners wanted the removal of any time limit on legal abortion, the recent Bill leaves the 24-week limit intact, largely due to the desires of the professional bodies.[10]

Campaigning for decriminalization

The decriminalization campaign was drawn from a broad coalition of abortion rights activists, abortion providers, medical professionals and MPs, with some individuals blurring the lines between those categories. The We Trust Women campaign was announced in February 2016 by BPAS and the Royal College of Midwives, but enjoyed support from a wide range of women's groups, including the Fawcett Society, the End Violence Against Women (EVAW) coalition, Southall Black Sisters, Women's Aid and Rape Crisis. It called for complete decriminalization of abortion by repealing sections of OAPA, as well as, initially, completely removing the 24-week gestation time limit for abortion from statute, although the latter demand was later revised.

The campaign launched with a short video titled 'On the Shoulders of Giants'.[11] The video situated decriminalization firmly in the context of women's political history, moving through a timeline of milestones in women's political history – the creation of the suffragette movement, the entry of women into the workforce, the Dagenham Ford machinists' strike – as well as a number of political firsts, such as the election of the first woman MP Constance Markievicz, Margaret Thatcher's ascent to become prime minister, and the election of the first black woman MP Diane Abbott. Earlier generations of women, intones the narrator, 'fought to … create a world where we could thrive because of our ability, not be held back because of our biology'. Abortion is not explicitly mentioned until around two thirds of the way into the video, and the practical problems with existing law are not addressed. Instead, the video is framed as a call to action to 'continue the fight' against inequality: 'We have come so far. Changing this ancient law will be a symbol of just how far.'

The depiction of OAPA as an 'ancient' or 'archaic' law, an impediment to 'modern' values of gender equality and reproductive choice, is a constant in the campaign. We Trust Women describe the legislation as 'in line with the punitive values of mid-Victorian Britain', observing that 'no other medical procedure in the country is governed by legislation this old, or this out-of-step with clinical developments and the moral thinking of the modern world' and comparing it to the lack of criminalization in other countries, even ones with otherwise restrictive abortion laws (We Trust Women, 2018). A similar constant is the use of women-centric language. The narrative is one of feminist victory not yet won:

> Although often seen as a victory of the women's movement, the Act was passed very much in response to the growing public health problem of illegal abortions. It placed decision-making about abortion in the hands of doctors, not women. Abortion is still not a woman's choice and no woman has the right to end a pregnancy. (We Trust Women, 2018)

Campaign materials utilize the 'woman and doctors' framing familiar from earlier pro-choice defences of the Abortion Act 1967, appealing for example to 'women's welfare and best medical practice' (Abortion Rights, 2018). However, the emphasis is firmly on women's needs. The impact on the medical profession is primarily presented as a problem for women: if doctors are deterred from working in the field due to the risk of prosecution, abortion care standards will worsen (We Trust Women, 2018). Abortion is throughout portrayed as like any other medical procedure and deserving of the same treatment: 'No other routine medical procedure demands legal authorisation by doctors in addition to the normal requirements of obtaining informed consent' (We Trust Women, 2018). A vision of patient-centred, non-judgmental care is thereby set out. As Guthrie put it at an Abortion Rights-hosted public meeting on decriminalization: 'we do not walk in patients' shoes, and we have no right to do so'.[12]

An interesting development is that the uncontrollability of abortion is here, unlike in debates over the Steel Bill in the 1960s, taken as reason to legislate less, not more. According to We Trust Women:

> The use of the criminal law to punish women in the UK serves no purpose. It is not a deterrent, as any woman who feels desperate enough to try to end her own pregnancy will find a way to do so, and it cannot be seen as an appropriate punishment for a heinous crime, given that legal abortions are approved everyday. (2018)

The message here is that the attempt of a punitive abortion regime to force abortion into the 'open', where it can be 'contained, monitored and controlled' (Sheldon, 1997: 29) by gatekeeping doctors, has failed. Nonetheless, advocates of decriminalization stress, like the medical bodies, that 'decriminalisation does not mean deregulation' (Abortion Rights, 2018). BPAS produced a document on consent and safeguarding in abortion care, released in support of the decriminalization campaign and in response to allegations that decriminalization would dismantle safeguarding for vulnerable women seeking abortion. The document points out that abortion law itself does not provide for safeguarding or informed consent in abortion provision, and decriminalization would leave existing provisions and safeguards intact (BPAS, undated: 1). The document also covers 'domestic violence, including forced marriage and honour-based violence' (BPAS, undated: 6). This was, in part, a response to allegations regarding sex-selective abortion and its link to 'honour' violence, covered later in this chapter. The document heavily stresses the safeguarding processes already in place in abortion clinics. Overall, pro-decriminalization materials stressed that criminalization does not help vulnerable women, but rather can worsen standards of care (We Trust Women, 2018).

A heavier focus on vulnerability can be found in a document produced by EVAW along with several of its member organisations, Imkaan (campaigners against violence against BAME women and girls), Women's Aid, the Fawcett Society, Rape Crisis England and Wales and Southall Black Sisters. Their briefing document opens with a quote from a woman in an abusive relationship:

> I'm in a controlling relationship, he watches my every move, I'm so scared he will find out [that I'm pregnant], I believe he's trying to trap me and will hurt me. I can't breathe. If he finds out, he wouldn't let me go ahead [with the abortion], then I will be trapped forever. I cannot live my life like this. (EVAW, 2018: 1)

This sets the tone for the rest of the document, which stresses the difficulties faced by women in abusive relationships in accessing abortion. Like BPAS, the document stresses the need for safeguarding in abortion services and for training for clinicians to recognize signs of abuse. However, it goes further in observing that reproduction is particularly fraught for women in abusive relationships: they may be less able to control whether or not they get pregnant, may be exposed to more violence while pregnant, and find it more difficult to access abortion services, particularly when they want to keep this hidden from their partner (EVAW, 2018: 2). Crucially, EVAW (unlike some groups campaigning on domestic abuse) resists calls for criminalization and bans as a response to female vulnerability. Nonetheless, this is very different framing to the bulk of the material produced by abortion rights groups: instead of stressing the need for liberation, this document stresses the need for protection.

Campaigning against decriminalization

Anti-abortion groups variously described the decriminalization campaign and Johnson's Bills as 'radical' (Right to Life, 2018), 'extreme' (Life, 2018a) and 'morally repugnant' (Life, 2018b). They seized in particular upon the 'decriminalization up to birth' aspect of the campaign's original demands (Life, 2016), in spite of We Trust Women's assertion that removal of the legal time limit would not actually impact rates of abortion post-24 weeks (We Trust Women, 2018). The imagery used in their campaigns is familiar from anti-abortion attempts to undermine confidence in the Abortion Act 1967. First, there is the portrayal of women as victims. SPUC named its counter-campaign 'We Care About Women', citing 'adverse mental health outcomes for women following abortion' (SPUC, 2018: 2) and claiming that women 'suffer grievously because of liberal abortion laws' (2018: 7). Similarly, the charity Life claimed that decriminalization 'would place the health and welfare of women at risk' (Life, 2018a). This argument was perhaps put most forcefully by a protestor from the group Stand for Life, who disrupted an Abortion Rights public meeting in Parliament to shout loudly about the 'vulnerable women' who, he claimed, regret their abortions.[13]

Despite the pro-woman framing, the bulk of pro-criminalization material does not expound the hypothesized risks from abortion. Rather, echoing the *Babies for Burning* missives from the 1970s, it furthers the portrayal of abortion providers as untrustworthy, profiteering abortion mills. Life's Education Director, Anne Scanlan, asserted that Diana Johnson's Bills sought to 'remove the threat of potential legal action against the abortion industry as it seeks to grow and expand its market' (Life, 2017) and alleged that abortion providers would receive a 'financial windfall' as a result (Life, 2018a). Scanlan later claimed that the success of Johnson's later Bill at First Reading was 'a demonstration of the power this multi-million-pound industry, famous for its "cattle market" culture,[14] has at Westminster' (Life, 2018b). These arguments are certainly not new.

In opposition to the claim that 'decriminalization does not mean deregulation', SPUC argued that decriminalization would '[remove] an important restraint on the medical profession' and, further, that the medical profession itself could not be trusted to regulate abortion: 'The regulation of abortion should not be handed over to those who effectively constitute the abortion industry. This would be like putting the fox in charge of the chicken coop' (2018: 5). On the other hand, its briefing raised fears that, following decriminalization, exchange of abortion pills or other instruments 'could take place *anywhere*: in the pub or on the street' (2018: 4; emphasis in original) rather than in the safety of the clinic under medical supervision. As Pam Lowe has observed, there is a contradiction in how doctors are thus positioned in anti-abortion discourse: are they 'unscrupulous profiteers' or are they necessary gatekeepers to abortion (Lowe, 2018: 11)?

A final key claim of these campaign materials is that criminalization protects women from abuse. Scanlan observed that OAPA 'has enabled the prosecution and conviction of men like Gil Magira who laced his wife's sandwich and Edward Erin who spiked his lover's drink, with drugs to cause a miscarriage' (Life, 2018c). SPUC went even further, claiming that decriminalization would make it easier for abusive men to obtain abortion pills to force on their partner, and making a link to child sex abuse:

> Serious case studies of child sexual abuse rings in England found that vulnerable girls were certified for abortions and given the morning-after pill and contraceptives with no questions asked. This approach masked the reality that the girls were being abused. A culture of weaker governance of abortion, where many abortions would take place in an unsupervised, entirely private environment, would leave girls at greater risk from predatory men. (SPUC, 2018: 5)

Life's statement linking decriminalization to the Magira and Erin cases was published some weeks before Johnson published the drafted second Bill, which in fact contained clauses penalizing 'non-consensual termination of pregnancy' with a maximum sentence of life imprisonment. SPUC's briefing, meanwhile, was explicitly updated in response to the Bill's publication, but did not engage with these clauses.

In Parliament

Johnson's first Bill was first read in Parliament in March 2017. Johnson introduced her Bill by stressing the 'Victorian' nature of OAPA; as in the wider campaign for decriminalization, social change formed a central part of the Bill's justification. Like campaigners outside Parliament, she stressed that 'no other medical procedure is governed by legislation that old' (Hansard, 2017: 26), and highlighted in particular changes brought about by new technology, both the availability of pills that safely induce abortion, but also women's increasing ability to bypass clinics by accessing these online – 'something that no one would have imagined in 1967, let alone 1861' (Hansard, 2017: 26). Like the early reformists before her, Johnson therefore asserted the failure of criminalization to contain abortion: women can and will access abortions anyway. Johnson stressed (using the phrase 'decriminalisation will not mean deregulation' [Hansard, 2017: 27]) that existing laws governing the licensing and regulation of clinics would still be in place. Her speech relayed several accounts of women who had ordered abortion pills online. These accounts drew upon the familiar tropes of faultlessness and vulnerability, with the women concerned portrayed as scared and depressed, or finding it 'impossible' to access a clinic, or controlled by their partners or families. However, there were also nods to the wider social significance of decriminalization. Johnson ended by quoting the words of one commentator on the decision to remove criminal sanctions on abortion in Victoria, Australia:

> Decriminalisation has resulted in 'a profound shift in the relationship between the state and its female citizens. It changes both nothing and everything. Nothing, because the number, rate and incidence of abortion will not change. And everything, because for the first time women will be recognised as the authors of our own lives. With that comes our full citizenship'. (Hansard, 2017: 28; see also Wainer, 2008)

This first Bill was only intended to decriminalize abortion in England and Wales. But following the Irish abortion referendum and Stella

Creasy's emergency debate, Northern Ireland was hooked into the decriminalization cause. Repealing sections 58 and 59 of OAPA would serve the dual function of achieving the campaign's objectives in England and Wales while also greatly liberalizing abortion provision in Northern Ireland – according to those in favour, without treading on the toes of the devolved government. The emergency debate, and subsequent debates on proposed legislation, suggest something of a shift in pro-choice parliamentary rhetoric on abortion. In her opening speech, Creasy denounced the Abortion Act 1967 as based in a 'paternalism that says women are not to be trusted to make choices about their bodies' (Hansard, 2018a: 208); a critique that was repeated later in the debate (2018a: 225). This is a significant development. It indicates, for the first time in Parliament, a wholesale rejection of a key principle on which the Abortion Act 1967 was founded – that is, the principle that it is doctors, not women themselves, who are the appropriate gatekeepers of abortion.

This is not to say that parliamentary language on abortion had radically changed. Narratives of trauma-tization and 'acceptable' abortion still featured heavily in the debates; most personal accounts of abortion that were relayed involved cases of abuse, rape, or fatal foetal abnormality. Some of these drew attention to the egregious injustice of existing criminal law, such as the possibility that Northern Irish women 'seeking an abortion after being impregnated through a sexual crime, rape or incest, could face a heavier criminal punishment than the perpetrators' (Johnson in Hansard, 2018b: 142). Opponents of decriminalization also drew on similar narratives of trauma, this time at the hands of unscrupulous abortion providers and abusive men who, it was claimed, might take advantage of decriminalization to pressure their partners into having abortions (for example Caulfield in Hansard, 2017: 27–31). The lone pushback against trauma narratives was offered by the then-Conservative MP Anna Soubry, who stated:

> It is important not to forget that this is actually about the right of a woman to choose ... It is not confined merely to those who have foetal abnormalities or who have been raped or in some ghastly incestuous relationship; it is about women's rights and our right to control what we do with our bodies. (Hansard, 2018a: 224)

The other key line of discussion of course concerned whether repealing the relevant sections of OAPA would undermine devolution in Northern Ireland. The impending exit of the UK from the

European Union – and the thorny question of the 'Irish backstop' agreement that would keep the Irish border open if no other solution were found – loomed large in the debates. Some pro-repeal MPs suggested that the lack of legal abortion provision in Northern Ireland amounted to a 'human rights border' in the Irish sea (Hansard, 2018b: 142; 2018c: 368), a reference to, and knowing subversion of, the fear of some DUP politicians that Northern Ireland could end up subject to a different regulatory regime than the rest of the UK after Brexit.

By using a human rights framing and appealing to Supreme Court and UN proclamations, pro-repeal MPs were able to suggest that it would be acceptable, both morally and technically, to override normal concerns relating to devolution; 'while abortion law may be devolved to Stormont, human rights are not' (Hansard, 2018a: 237). As Johnson put it: 'We can't just say, "oh well, human rights are being breached"'.[15] The failure of the Northern Ireland Assembly to reconvene brought calls to action a sense of urgency. Crucially, many pointed out that to repeal sections of OAPA would be to repeal legislation made at Westminster rather than to interfere with Northern Irish law itself. Decriminalization in this account would therefore relax Westminster's hold on Northern Ireland rather than extend it; as Creasy noted, even if the Assembly was currently sitting, any conversation it could have about extending abortion rights would be defined within OAPA's parameters (Hansard, 2018a: 209).

Government legislation intended to set in place contingency plans for Northern Ireland in Stormont's absence therefore provided a perfect opportunity to act on abortion. Creasy had attempted to insert an amendment repealing sections 58 and 59 of OAPA into the Northern Ireland Act 2018 but was told by the parliamentary clerks that this was outside the scope of the legislation and would not be debated.[16] Instead, the amendment required the Secretary of State for Northern Ireland to issue guidelines about human rights in Northern Ireland, specifically in relation to abortion and same-sex marriage, and report to Parliament on her progress every 12 weeks. This amendment was limited in scope, but its victory served to further erode the assumption that Northern Irish abortion law is 'nothing to do' with Westminster. The continued failure of Northern Irish parties to come to a new power-sharing agreement forced the UK government to introduce a new Northern Ireland Bill in 2019. This time, Creasy was able to attach a new amendment. The original text of this amendment simply required the UK government to implement CEDAW's recommendations in full if Stormont did not reconvene by 21 October 2019. As CEDAW proposed repealing OAPA, this would have had the effect of decriminalizing abortion in England and Wales as well as in Northern Ireland. However, the clause was revised in the Lords to restrict this change to Northern Ireland alone, curtailing its potential impact on the rest of the UK. The Lords also set a deadline of 31 March 2020 for the new abortion regulations to come into effect, fearing that the 21 October deadline might prove technically unfeasible. This, however, would not prevent OAPA itself being repealed in Northern Ireland on 22 October – a change that has rendered Northern Ireland's abortion law the most liberal in the UK.

This development reflects the turmoil in UK politics at the time; namely, the government's increasing inability to control Parliament as the UK headed towards Brexit, and the cracks that had appeared at the senior levels of government during the process. On abortion, there were already signs of dissent: in spite of the government's agreement with the DUP, several senior Conservative MPs backed change in Northern Ireland and had put pressure on Prime Minister Theresa May to bring about reform (Perkins, 2018). The cabinet minister Penny Mordaunt even voted for Johnson's second Bill when she could easily have abstained. Facing further upheaval due to May's pending departure, the government dramatically lost control of the Northern Ireland Act 2019. As well as passing key amendments on abortion and marriage equality, MPs were also able to pass a measure intended to prevent a future prime minister from proroguing (suspending) Parliament to facilitate a no-deal Brexit.

Creasy's amendment was, nonetheless, made possible by the CEDAW report and its judgement that the lack of access to abortion in Northern Ireland constituted a violation of human rights, requiring Westminster to act where Stormont could not. What is striking throughout all of these debates is that opponents of reform were generally unable to defend the law from the allegation of human rights abuse, instead relying on technicalities to deflect calls for change. Responding to MPs who cited CEDAW, the Conservative MP Fiona Bruce asserted repeatedly that CEDAW was only a 'minor UN sub-committee' (Hansard, 2018b: 146; 2019a: 184–5) and therefore could not force the UK to act (2018a: 233–4; 2018c: 369). Bruce also argued the amendments to both Northern Ireland Acts were 'inappropriate' as they went beyond the government's intentions in tabling the Bills (2018c: 367). This was a popular assessment in the Lords, where peers decried the amended Bill as a 'Christmas tree Bill' hung with the 'baubles' of abortion and marriage equality (Hansard, 2019b).

New battlegrounds: sex selection

While MPs who are anti-abortion, or at least in favour of more restrictive legislation, may have recently found themselves on unsteady footing in relation to the decriminalization campaign, they have evolved new messaging to undermine the pro-choice cause. This group has used the tactic of representing the foetus as female since at least the 1980s in the hope that it will subvert messaging about abortion as a women's rights issue. However, this tactic has recently become central to anti-abortion campaigning. After a 2012 *Daily Telegraph* sting found a handful of doctors willing to perform abortions on the ground of foetal sex, some parliamentarians began to depict the female foetus as particularly threatened by abortion (for example Amess in Hansard, 2012: 85; Dorries in Hansard, 2012: 74). These interventions also saw the belated entry of race into parliamentary debates on abortion, as 'young Asian girls' were alleged to be vulnerable to pressure to undergo sex-selective abortions (Dorries in Hansard, 2012: 75).

The *Daily Telegraph*'s reports portrayed doctors as unconstrained by legislation, failing to carry out their role as abortion gatekeepers responsibly and potentially engaging in criminal activity (Watt et al, 2012), and quoted David (now Lord) Alton as saying that sex-selective abortions were a product of abortion becoming 'routine' (Mason, 2012). These anxieties were exacerbated by an *Independent* story alleging that there were between 1,400 and 4,700 'lost girls' in the national census records of England and Wales, which it claimed was caused by the widespread practice of sex-selective abortion among 'some ethnic groups' (Connor, 2014). Sex-selective abortion is known to be common in parts of India (Arnold et al, 2004; Sarkaria, 2009), and it was claimed that the practice was being imported by Indian migrants. Statistics subsequently produced by the Department of Health suggested on the contrary that sex selection was not taking place on a large enough scale to skew the ratio of baby boys to baby girls born in any ethnic group. The Department's analysis noted that the *Independent* article had been based on an assessment of numbers of boys and girls living in certain households, rather than an analysis of sex ratios at birth, meaning it could be influenced by factors such as the extent to which male and female children accompany their parents when emigrating and the proportions of boys and girls leaving the family home to live elsewhere or staying on in education after the age of sixteen (Department of Health, 2014).

The doctors caught in the *Telegraph* sting had mostly worked for private for-profit abortion clinics, as opposed to the charitable abortion providers who provide the vast majority of abortions in Britain. According to BPAS, the undercover reporters had approached several other clinics and been 'sent packing right away'.[17] One BPAS counsellor was caught up in the controversy after *Daily Telegraph* reporters claimed that she had offered to arrange an abortion for an undercover reporter who told her she did not want to have a girl, and to obscure this on official paperwork (Newell, 2012). The report alleged that the termination had only been cancelled after a BPAS manager intervened. In the accounts of BPAS's campaigns team, however, the counsellor in question had actually approached the manager herself due to discomfort with the request and the appointment was cancelled before the reporters left the premises.[18] Allegations about sex selection were nonetheless used to stoke perceptions of abortion clinics' non-compliance with the law, although it is not altogether clear whether sex-selective abortion is always illegal. Foetal sex is not one of the legal grounds for abortion but doctors could make a legal case that they had acted to preserve a woman's mental health by authorizing an abortion if, for example, she had claimed she would be at risk of violence were she to continue the pregnancy (Sheldon, 2012).

The Stop Gendercide campaign

In response to the allegations, the Stop Gendercide campaign was launched by Fiona Bruce MP, a staunch anti-abortionist, alongside a coalition of groups and individuals, including anti-abortion actors such as Bruce herself but also groups working to combat violence against South Asian women such as Karma Nirvana and Jeena International. The campaign framed sex-selective abortion as a form of violence against women, as exemplified in its use of the word 'gendercide', a term more typically associated with female infanticide and the murder of women and girls. Its key claim was that the abortion of female foetuses is happening in UK within South Asian communities, and that women are often forced or pressured to have such abortions. As the previous discussion suggests, the reality of this is difficult to determine; while there is little statistical evidence that sex selection is widespread, it may still be occurring on a small scale. Jeena International claim to know of several specific cases (Haque, 2018). This accords with a 2007 study which found an increase in the ratio of boys born to girls among Indian-born women in England and Wales (Dubuc and Coleman, 2007); however, if this ratio is caused by sex-selective abortion it only suggests that a small minority of Indian-born women have had such abortions, and there is no statistical evidence for the practice being undertaken by South Asian women born in the UK.

The campaign supported multiple attempts by Bruce to address sex-selective abortion in legislation. In 2013, Bruce introduced a Ten Minute Rule Bill that would have required the Secretary of State to compile statistics on the gender ratios of foetuses aborted, and impose harsher penalties on those found to have assisted such an abortion (Hansard, 2013a). Bruce situated her Bill as an attempt to combat the 'gender discrimination', already taking place in 'some countries' and now threatening the UK:

> Here in the United Kingdom, a country that prides itself on striving for gender equality and tackling discrimination in all its forms, any indication of this most fundamental form of gender discrimination and violence against women must surely be investigated further. (Bruce in Hansard, 2013a: 170)

As well as expressing concern for the female foetus, Bruce depicted doctors as at best irresponsible, at worst 'committing a criminal offence' (Hansard, 2013a: 170). The Bill gained considerable support, but as a Ten Minute Rule Bill did not progress. Bruce went on to introduce another Bill through the Ten Minute Rule in 2014, which aimed to 'clarify the law relating to abortion', presumably through the explicit criminalization of sex selection (Hansard, 2014). At First Reading Bruce spoke at length about the connection between sex-selective abortion and abuse and read out the stories of South Asian women who had faced pressure to abort or violence due to son preference in their families. The Bill passed by 181 votes to 1 but also did not progress.

Support for the two Bills galvanized Bruce to table an amendment to the Serious Crime Bill in 2015 that would have explicitly criminalized sex selection by stating that 'nothing in section 1 of the Abortion Act 1967 is to be interpreted as allowing a pregnancy to be terminated on the grounds of the sex of the unborn child' (Hansard, 2015). The debate on this amendment contained similar tropes: the portrayal of such abortions as violence against women and girls, and fears that abortion providers were ignoring the law. The amendment was defeated following campaigning by a coalition of abortion rights advocates and women's groups, but for a while seemed likely to become law. Instead, an amendment was passed committing the government to monitor population data for evidence of sex-selective abortions taking place.

A key concern here is how such interventions tie into anti-abortion strategy more broadly. As noted, the depiction of the foetus as female has long been a pro-life tactic, with American anti-abortion handbooks advising activists to borrow feminist language and apply it to the foetus. Seen in this context, claims about the threatened female foetus seem to be yet another permutation of the claim that abortion harms women, with the implication that access to abortion should not be considered a legitimate women's right. The claims made about doctors' role in sex selection are also congruent with past anti-abortion strategy. The depiction of doctors as irresponsible, even criminal, is very familiar (Lee, 2017).

MPs' claims about the vulnerability of 'young Asian women' also require extra examination. Angela McRobbie has described the process of the 'disarticulation' of feminism since the mid-1990s. Disarticulation refers to how the networks tying together social movements are unpicked, 'forcing apart and dispersing subordinate social groups who might have possibly found some common cause' (McRobbie, 2009: 26). The result is a narrative that pitches Western women, seen as 'the fortunate beneficiaries of Western sexual freedoms', against women in non-Western societies, and 'interrupts whatever chances there may be for feminism to speak again to a wider constituency of women' (2009: 26). Narratives that posit non-white women, and Asian women in particular, as 'passively waiting to be rescued from cultural norms that mysteriously impose no restraints on Western feminists' (Volpp, 2000: 111; see also Kalantry, 2017: 56–7), are popular. Consider for example this extract from a speech made by Nadine Dorries:

> I was staggered to hear what one MP who came up to me the other day said. Her actual words were, 'Every woman who wants an abortion knows exactly what she is doing.' Well, in her rather slick, well-educated Oxbridge world and her leafy shires I am sure they do, but what about the young Asian girl who was recently marched into a clinic in floods of tears by two family members? … Not every woman makes the decision because she went to university and marched up and down streets in Oxford and chanted about women's rights. (Hansard, 2012: 74–5)

Disarticulatory claims are thus at once turned outwards, at activity in countries such as India that 'we' as enlightened British people must resist, and inwards, at South Asian communities in the UK. In these claims, the young South Asian women thought to be victims of such practices are pitched against the (presumably white) Western women thought capable of exercising true freedom of choice. This has the effect of foreclosing the possibility of a pro-choice politics that encompasses these women's concerns (as might be realized within a reproductive justice movement), instead representing South Asians as a problem community that must be 'acted on' rather than 'acted for' (Amery, 2015b). Narratives such as these present a significant threat to pro-choice coalition building.

Defeating the campaign

The initial parliamentary response to the campaign worried abortion rights groups. A debate in Westminster Hall (used for parliamentary debates that do not end in a vote) following the *Daily Telegraph* report saw many otherwise pro-choice MPs seeking to qualify their support for legal abortion. The Labour MP Diane Abbott stated that she found 'the notion of gender-selective abortion impossible to support' as it 'reinforces patriarchal and oppressive ideas' (Hansard, 2013b: 101). Her colleague Emily Thornberry similarly advanced a feminist argument against sex selection and condemned the decision of the Crown Prosecution Service not to pursue a case against the doctors caught in the sting (2013b: 102–3). Bruce's two Bills both passed their First Reading without MPs speaking to oppose them.

Sex-selection allegations may well perturb feminists (Cherry, 1995; Oomman and Ganatra, 2002; Widdows, 2009; Mahalingam and Wachman, 2012; Gupta, 2014; Kalantry, 2017: 47–73). UK pro-choice groups were however concerned that explicit criminalization of sex-selective abortions would serve to penalize the women it was supposed to protect and undermine abortion rights more generally. They also objected to the amendment's use of the term 'unborn child' – language not otherwise used in abortion legislation – in Bruce's amendment to the Serious Crime Bill, as defining a foetus as a 'child' in statute might bring child-protection laws to bear on abortion and allow 'a woman's right to life to become secondary' (Abortion Rights, 2015a). These groups thus framed the Bruce amendment as a 'Trojan horse' (Abortion Rights, 2015b) aimed at undermining confidence in abortion providers and at opening the door for further legal restrictions on abortion.

In their early responses to the allegations, abortion rights advocates relied heavily on individualistic narratives of personal choice. Abortion Rights, for instance, asserted its belief 'that all women have the right to make their own reproductive choices. Pro-choice means women are best placed to make their own pregnancy choices, for only they know their personal situation' (2014). The statement went on to describe pressure to bear male children as 'terrible', but did not examine how such pressure might in itself complicate or undermine the exercise of 'choice' (Amery, 2015b: 518). BPAS's first statement on sex selection similarly presented 'choice' in legalistic terms, arguing that gender inequality 'will not be improved by further curbing women's ability to make decisions about their own bodies and lives' (2014b).

While concerns about the negative potential impact of criminalization are not unwarranted (Oomman and Ganatra, 2002: 186–7), these early statements from pro-choice groups were somewhat wanting in that they did not engage with South Asian women's voices, nor with the realities of son preference for some of these women. This is partially because providers such as BPAS knew that women attending their clinics were not requesting abortions on the basis of foetal sex, so had reason to be sceptical of Stop Gendercide's claims.[19] However, there are broader issues to address here. Some feminists have drawn attention to the difficulties inherent in exercising 'choice' in contexts where boys are heavily favoured over girls, particularly if violence against women is commonplace (Cherry, 1995; Moazam, 2004; Sarkaria, 2009; Mahalingam and Wachman, 2012; Gupta, 2014). Most of us would not argue that a woman who was coerced into having an abortion under threat of violence had engaged in a free exercise of choice. The US reproductive justice movement has frequently made the point that restrictions on reproductive choice are not always legal and bureaucratic in nature, but this perspective has sometimes been absent from British pro-choice discourse.

While remaining opposed to outright criminalization, many abortion rights advocates did ultimately shift their public line on sex selection. This shift was heavily dependent on the initiative of an individual, Shaheen Hashmat, who was working for BPAS as an executive assistant. Hashmat, an experienced campaigner against 'honour' violence and forced marriage, approached BPAS's campaigns team to express concerns about the lack of consideration of these issues in their public statements.[20] This conversation became a turning point in BPAS's campaigning on the issue and it began to engage in more outreach work around sex selection, particularly with South Asian women's groups. This initiative was assisted by a broader strategy BPAS had been undertaking since 2011 to 'embed the reproductive rights movement in this country as part of the broader women's movement' and in doing so draw support from a wider base.[21]

Drawing on Hashmat's wide network of activist contacts, BPAS mobilized a coalition of organizations from across the women's sector, including Southall Black Sisters, the Iranian and Kurdish Women's Rights Organisation (IKWRO) and EVAW. Some of these groups subsequently produced statements opposing the amendment and arguing that criminalization was the wrong way to tackle son preference (IKWRO, 2015; Southall Black Sisters, 2015). This change in tactic appears to have been instrumental in defeating the Bruce amendment. Given the success of Bruce's previous Bills, abortion rights advocates expected that they would lose, and the amendment would pass.[22] Yet the parliamentary debate demonstrated that the message had got across to pro-choice MPs (Hansard, 2015). Their speeches cited a lack of evidence that sex-selective abortions were taking place on a large scale and expressed the concern that criminalization might have a negative impact on the women it aimed to protect as well as about the 'unborn child' phrasing within the amendment. Some cited lobbying from groups such as Southall Black Sisters and EVAW as having helped to solidify their position. One MP, Fiona Mactaggart, who had sponsored the earlier Bruce Bill said she regretted doing so, and further identified the focus on sex selection as a pro-life tactic aimed at causing turmoil within the pro-choice movement (Hansard, 2015: 130). The amendment was defeated by 292 votes to 201, with 52 MPs who had voted for Bruce's second Bill now voting against her.

Following the vote, women's sector groups led by BPAS came together to draft a new statement on sex-selective abortion and ensure there were 'some concrete lessons learned'.[23] While still calling into question the claims made by Stop Gendercide, their statement focused squarely on abuse resulting from son preference and misogyny. It articulated a shared position on safeguarding within abortion care, insisting that this is already done to a high standard within clinics and pointing out that if women are discouraged from accessing services this may prevent them from getting help. The statement also articulated a shared opposition to austerity, condemning its impact on women's services, especially those used by BAME women (BPAS, 2015a). In contributing to this statement, BPAS took cues from US organizations such as the National Asian Pacific American Women's Forum, which has drawn on a politics of reproductive justice in order to fight against sex-selective abortion bans.[24]

Pursuing their goals through the means of broad coalition-building was clearly highly effective for BPAS in this case. However, interviews with those involved in the campaign suggest that there are significant impediments in the way of sustaining these coalitions, and the groups involved have not always continued to work together. Some of these impediments are structural: abortion rights advocates are restricted due to the constant need to fend off anti-abortion attacks, but the women's sector is time-pressured in general.[25] One interviewee, however, felt that in spite of the short-term success of the campaign, it ultimately failed to address 'the issue at stake': namely, an attempt by the colluding agendas of right-wing neoliberal, austerity-driving conservatism and the Christian Right to divide feminists against one another, which she connected to a broader anti-immigration agenda[26] (see also Purewal and Eklund, 2018). All of this matters, because claims about sex selection have not gone away. The spectre of sex selection has haunted recent debates on abortion, with opponents of decriminalization arguing that, without criminal sanctions on abortion, there would be no way to prevent it (for example Caulfield in Hansard, 2017: 30). These claims have emerged again recently following a BBC investigation that reported that 'thousands' of British Asian women were discussing using genetic testing during early pregnancy to find out the sex of the foetus, with the intention of aborting depending on the outcome (Haque, 2018). They are likely to remain a feature of abortion debates going forward.

New battlegrounds: disability

Another attempt to place further legal restrictions on abortion, albeit a less sustained attack than that concerning sex selection, revolved around section 1(1)(d) of the Abortion Act 1967, which provides for abortion right up to birth if there is a 'substantial risk' that the child would be 'seriously handicapped'. In 2013, a parliamentary inquiry chaired by Bruce recommended repealing this clause, or at least bringing the time limit for such abortions in line with the 24-week limit applied elsewhere (Parliamentary Inquiry into Abortion on the Grounds of Disability, 2013). In 2016, the Conservative peer Lord Shinkwin, himself born with brittle bone disease, introduced a Bill in the House of Lords that would have introduced a 24-week limit for abortions performed on the grounds of disability. Shinkwin argued that the disability clause represented 'a stark anomaly' that enshrined discrimination on the grounds of disability in law, despite it being prohibited elsewhere (Hansard, 2016: 2545). Opponents, on the other hand, warned that many severe disabilities might not be diagnosed until after the 24th week of pregnancy. Shinkwin's concerns were not new (see Shakespeare, 1998). However, it is rare for a bill on abortion to directly address disability in this way.

Shinkwin and his supporters (including Lord Alton) decried the foetal anomaly clause as 'eugenic' in character and as implying that people with disabilities would be 'better off dead' (Hansard, 2016: 2545). Some feminists would agree; Sheelagh McGuinness, for example, argues that if the aim is simply to protect pregnant women's interests, it is discriminatory to allow these abortions and not other abortions post-24 weeks where a woman might have a profound interest in not having a child (2013). Similarly, Deborah Steinberg has argued that the clause has long been justified on eugenic terms rather than woman-centred terms via arguments that do not refer to bodily autonomy or freedom of choice, but rather treat disability as though it exempts pregnant women from their usual moral obligations towards the foetus (1991: 187). However, the arguments of Shinkwin and his supporters could hardly themselves be described as 'woman-centred'. Indeed, Shinkwin's speech at Second Reading rendered the people *choosing* to have abortions entirely invisible, and instead portrayed the abortion decision as an impersonal governmental exercise in wiping out people with disabilities:

> By rights I should not be here. I should be dead. Indeed, more than that, according to the eugenic screening programme of our Department of Health, I would be better off dead because of serious handicap, to use the outdated terminology of the Act. (Hansard, 2016: 2545)

The realities of the abortion decision-making process – the personal situations of the people who decide, and the time they need to make this decision – are missing, both here and in other supporting speeches. The only participant in the debate to mention this reality was the Independent peer Baroness Tonge, who stressed that '[women's] voice must be heard too':

> It is untrue and cruel to suggest that women who, in the later stages of pregnancy, undergo abortion because of foetal abnormality are doing it simply because they want a 'perfect baby' and that they want to discriminate against disabled people. They have to take into consideration the effect on themselves and their ability to cope, as well as the

ability and tolerance of their partner and family to cope in the future. ... These women have to make the decision, which is theirs alone, and I say that they have the right to decide. (Hansard, 2016: 2556–7)

Tonge's speech drew on the trope of maternal faultlessness, emphasizing that late diagnoses of severe disability occur 'through no fault of the mother' (Hansard, 2016: 2556). Nonetheless, it was the only speech to even mention women and their experiences. The Bill made it to Report stage but could not progress as a general election was called in 2017. Lord Shinkwin introduced a similar Bill after the election but this never made it past First Reading.

The Shinkwin Bill was supported by the We're All Equal campaign, which described itself as a 'campaign for disability equality', despite its exclusive focus on promoting a more restrictive abortion law. This campaign bore a striking resemblance to Stop Gendercide. The campaigns used similar language, used the 'equals' sign prominently in their campaign material, and had clearly procured the services of the same web designer. As someone involved in disability rights advocacy beyond the scope of this Bill, Lord Shinkwin is clearly genuine in his desire to end disability discrimination. However, the similarities between the two campaigns suggest that they may also form part of a broader effort to undermine the abortion rights movement by detaching it from its association with liberation and equality. The similarity was certainly not lost on BPAS's campaigns team, who took the lessons learned fighting the Bruce amendment into outreach work with disabled women's groups,[27] which ultimately produced a brief report on disabled women's reproductive rights (BPAS, 2017).

A reinvigorated pro-choice politics

That a campaign to decriminalize abortion would have garnered such widespread parliamentary support would have been almost unthinkable just a few years ago. For BPAS, it represented a 'phenomenal progression'.[28] Lesley Regan, president of the RCOG, has described Johnson's efforts as having 'lit a touch paper among like-minded MPs, with abortion being discussed in Parliament more frequently than I can remember in my time as a practicing clinician' (Regan, 2018). What has changed to allow this to happen? Johnson suggested that the greater numbers of women elected to the House of Commons in the last two general elections had made a difference.[29] This makes sense, as women MPs are more likely to be active on issues relating to abortion, vote in a more liberal manner in abortion divisions, and are more likely to centre women's concerns in their speeches (Childs et al, 2013). However, this alone does not explain the shift towards decriminalization; as Johnson herself noted, it was primarily pro-choice women MPs who warned her away from introducing a liberalizing Bill early on. BPAS campaigns staff further intimated that, in the upheaval following the election of Jeremy Corbyn as leader of the Labour Party in 2015 – particularly during the internal party turmoil between then and the 2017 general election – some Labour backbenchers may have felt they had less to lose in backing more radical Bills.[30]

The political moment for decriminalization extends far beyond Parliament, however. The campaign has knowingly tapped into the resurgent feminism of the last few years, spurred on by the viral success of the Me Too movement in late 2017, but in evidence well before this. Resurgent feminism is likely also a factor in the medical profession's support for reform. A key figure in driving RCOG support for decriminalization, for example, was Regan herself – the organization's first woman president since 1952 and a longstanding advocate of reproductive rights. All of these things came together to allow a decriminalization movement to flourish across the UK.

That such a stunning change could be made to Northern Irish abortion law is also a sign of the times. This change required the collision of several events. First, the Irish abortion referendum and the subsequent turning of public consciousness towards Northern Ireland, which is so often overlooked in the rest of the UK. Second, the continued failure of Stormont – which had been blocking abortion reform for some time – to reconvene. Third, CEDAW's denouncement of the UK as violating the human rights of women in Northern Ireland, which made it possible for abortion rights advocates at Westminster to argue that devolution could be superseded. Finally, the increasing inability of the government to control Parliament in the context of the UK's impending exit from the European Union, which opened an opportunity to use the government's own legislation to enact change.

Does the success of this wing of the decriminalization campaign mean that the issue of abortion law in Northern Ireland has again been decoupled from that of abortion law in the rest of the UK? There is a risk that, now that the most pressing matter of reproductive injustice in the UK has seemingly been solved, the rest of the campaign may lose steam. Clearly aware of this, Diana Johnson took the opportunity following the passage of the Northern Ireland Act 2019 to call for 'a new Abortion Act for England and Wales' which would fully repeal OAPA (Johnson, 2019). Her article pointed to the 'anomaly' that, following the changes, those seeking abortion in England and Wales would still be subject to criminal law, while in Northern Ireland they would not. This 'anomaly' will surely become the focus of future abortion rights campaigning. Supporters of decriminalization have cause to be optimistic: Johnson's drafted Bill is 'ready to go' and she may well be able to pass the torch to a like-minded MP who has success in the private members' ballot.

Far from opening up the Abortion Act 1967 to further attack, the decriminalization campaign appears to have wrongfooted opponents – at least temporarily. The campaign thrust anti-abortion groups into the difficult position of defending the existing abortion regime in England and Wales, resulting in contradictions in their messaging: abortion doctors are portrayed as at once the putative saviours of women (who would, the narrative goes, otherwise be preyed upon by abusive partners and families) and at the same time irresponsible, money-grubbing and potentially criminal (Lowe, 2018: 11). This is quite a reversal of fortune. Anti-abortion campaigners are now in the position of defending the Abortion Act 1967 and its flaws, while pro-choice campaigners have finally been able to move on.

Abortion rights advocates must not grow complacent. Allegations about sex selection (and, to a lesser extent, disability) may not represent an entirely new anti-abortion tactic. Indeed, a direct line can be drawn between these and Nadine Dorries's earlier attempts to impose new counselling requirements on abortion care; both seem designed to undermine public confidence in abortion providers while swathing this in pro-women and pro-equality rhetoric. In the past, such strategies have not been successful in shifting the terms of the debate in the UK (Lee, 2003; Lowe, 2018: 5). But in adding a racialized element that hinged on fears about 'patriarchal' migrant groups and their behaviours, sex selection was almost successful. As an issue, it sucked in groups beyond the 'usual suspects' on either side of the abortion debate, including BAME women's groups and others campaigning against violence against women. As Hashmat observed, 'it really divided the whole feminist community as well, in that anyone who called themselves a feminist, well how could they not get on board with this issue?'[31] These divisions have certainly not gone away. The final chapter asks how they might be overcome.

8

Conclusion

The parliamentary politics of abortion cannot now be neatly arranged around the twin poles of 'pro-life' and 'pro-choice' – but they never could. The Abortion Act 1967 did not, and was never meant to, establish a 'right to choose' in law. Instead, it was meant as a partial fix to social problems including poverty, poor housing, and 'overlarge' families with tired mothers, but also 'problem' families, 'unfit' mothers, and 'delinquent' children. This was to be achieved not by liberating women to exercise their reproductive rights, but by engaging medical professionals as social agents and delivering (especially working-class) women into their care and control. The passage of the Act relied heavily on the dual image of doctors as socially responsible and of women seeking abortions as vulnerable and in need of paternal guidance.

This has funnelled discussions in a particular way, ultimately producing debates on abortion that are not about 'life' versus 'choice'. Debates have instead hinged on questions of the meaning of 'health', the appropriate role of doctors in the governance of 'social' concerns, and the correct way to 'protect' women often conceived of as vulnerable. Attempts to further restrict abortion rights have rarely been made on the basis of the 'right to life' of the unborn, but rather on the basis that abortions are somehow harming women, while doctors are being corrupted by their role in performing them. In the wake of allegations that some women are selectively aborting female foetuses, some have asked questions about the appropriateness of 'choice' as a model for making sense of abortion.

Abortion rights advocacy in context

British abortion law is something of an anomaly in requiring such a great level of medical control over abortion (Cooper, 2016: 50–5). Many European countries allow abortion on request; that is, without the need for medical grounds to be met. On the other hand, in countries where this is the case, it is usually much harder to access abortion after a certain point in pregnancy (usually 12 weeks' gestation). This has allowed participants in the abortion debate to claim, variously, that the UK has some of the most restrictive abortion laws in Europe *and* that it has some of the most permissive. As around 90 per cent of abortions in England and Wales[1] are carried out in the first 12 weeks of pregnancy (Department of Health and Social Care, 2018b: 12), the need for two doctors' signatures and medical grounds to be met are clearly the more pressing barriers for most women seeking abortion, perhaps explaining why increasing numbers have turned to services such as Women on Web.

The Abortion Act 1967 was never straightforwardly a victory for 'choice', nor a 'feminist' achievement. Yet it was still a significant step forward, and the need to defend it from anti-abortion attack has had a significant impact on pro-choice and feminist arguments in Parliament. These arguments have tended to adopt a similar protective and medicalized frame to the Act itself, emphasizing the supposed vulnerability of women seeking abortion and playing heavily on trauma narratives. When overtly feminist arguments did enter parliamentary debates on abortion in the 1970s, these accepted and promoted the image of women seeking abortion as essentially vulnerable and tended to assume a natural alignment between the interests of women and doctors, even as feminists outside Parliament grew increasingly critical of medicine as an institution.

Initially, this merely involved the representation of such women as traumatized by their situation and in need of paternal guidance. But by the 1980s, feminist parliamentarians were routinely constructing narratives of 'acceptable' abortion and representations of women as virtuous, needing abortions 'through no fault of their own'. In the face of mounting delays in accessing abortion in the 1980s, feminist politicians began to criticize the system of abortion provision. Ultimately, though, such attacks were levelled at failings in the NHS rather than at the medicalization encoded in the Act. Meanwhile, 'women's rights' were discursively transformed into 'patients' rights': a clever framing that on the one hand allowed pro-choice feminists to justify the demands they made of the state in a way that had broad resonance, but on the other hand eclipsed questions of reproductive freedom and bodily autonomy.

Pro-choice MPs have tended to default to statements about the 'medical necessity' of abortion, which tacitly reinforce the Abortion Act 1967's requirement for medical grounds to be met. In doing so, their arguments have often closely resembled arguments made by supporters of legal abortion in the US, and can be subjected to the same critiques. US feminists have also tended to prioritize the health impact of illegal abortion and unwanted pregnancy in their arguments. This has meant that 'the central political battle – arguing that women's access to abortion is necessary for the kind of self-determination men take for granted – remains unfought' (Purdy, 2001: 256). Daniel Skinner has developed this argument, advancing a critique of the pro-choice focus on medical necessity:

> However well intended, pro-choice advocates who evoke these kinds of arguments unintentionally suggest that abortion rights are substantively necessary only in relation to the social conditions they address, rather than to the existence of a self-authorizing, self-standing right to determine what one does with one's body. (2012: 12)

As Skinner notes, the focus on medical necessity has had unintended consequences. In the US, it has underlined the withholding of federal funding for abortions deemed unnecessary for physical survival, and the recent extension of such restrictions to private healthcare providers who participate in government programmes (2012: 3–10). The use of medical necessity arguments has also opened up the debate to attempts to demonstrate that abortion is *not* necessary to health or is in fact harmful (2012: 13–14). Similar claims have been made in debates in the UK. These have generally not made the same impact on either media or political discourse as they have in the US and have largely been ignored by the medical profession (Lee, 2003). However, the reliance on narratives of medically necessary and 'acceptable' abortions has also made it difficult to make the case for abortion law that does not require certain medical grounds to be met. It is still extremely rare in political arenas to hear the argument that a woman should be able to have an abortion simply because she wants one.

Until recently, pro-choice actors in the UK Parliament have been unable to set the frame of the debate, having instead to respond to the assumptions about female vulnerability encoded in the Abortion Act 1967 as well as to anti-abortion arguments. Representing women seeking abortions as virtuous-yet-traumatized victims is an understandable response to the claim that women abort for 'frivolous' reasons, but risks reinforcing a divide between 'deserving' and 'undeserving' aborters and distracting from abortion's importance to the social status of *all* women. This hinders the normalization of abortion as a relatively common procedure undergone by women from all walks of life. Moreover, it has gone hand in hand with the portrayal of doctors as necessary mediators in the decision to abort. It is only now – since two decriminalization Bills have been introduced in Parliament and decriminalization has successfully been enacted in Northern Ireland – that pro-choice MPs have tentatively begun to change the script.

In assessing the prospects of decriminalization, lessons might be learned from other countries. The most obvious of these are Canada, the only country to have fully decriminalized abortion, and Australia (often cited by decriminalization campaigners in the UK), where many states have decriminalized or partially decriminalized abortion. Canada first legalized abortion in certain circumstances in 1969 via a law that required abortions to be performed in hospitals and approved by three-doctor 'therapeutic abortion committees'. Massive variations in how these committees operated resulted in inequalities in access around the country. The *R v Morgentaler* decision of the Supreme Court removed abortion from the criminal code due to the 'unworkable' nature of the law, although it did not grant a right to access abortion (Studlar and Tatalovich, 1996: 79–80).

In Canada, abortion is now recognized as a matter of public health rather than of criminal law. From a UK pro-choice perspective this may seem like the ideal outcome. However, public policy researcher Rachael Johnstone cautions against too celebratory a reading: the framing of abortion as 'healthcare' rather than a human right has in reality had mixed effects. In some cases, this framing has allowed advocates to make the case for more funding for abortion as part of the provision of adequate healthcare. However, it has also allowed individual Canadian provinces to use their authority over healthcare to erect barriers to access, while the federal government and Parliament have evaded responsibility for abortion. The result has been large disparities in access of the kind that *Morgentaler* was supposed to prevent (Johnstone, 2017). While the UK lacks a federal government, similar evasions at the centre have been observed in both the process of devolving abortion law (Moon et al, 2019) and the activity of commissioning services (APPGSRH, 2015). The UK government is now committed to introducing liberal provisions for abortion in Northern Ireland by 31 March 2020, but Stormont, when it reconvenes, could still introduce regulations that make it difficult for clinics to operate in practice.

A similarly mixed picture emerges from Australia, where abortion was decriminalized as early as 2002 in the Australian Capital Territory and as recently as 2018 in Queensland and 2019 in New South Wales. Barbara

Baird finds that in states that have decriminalized abortion, improved access has not necessarily resulted. In fact, in some cases access to abortion has been reduced, due to clinics closing or withdrawing certain services. These closures result from pressure due to the increasingly privatized model of provision in these states, and cannot be directly blamed on decriminalization itself. However, Baird also suggests that there is no evidence that decriminalization has had the hoped-for effect of destigmatization, either for women or providers (2017).

The UK differs from Australia and Canada in important ways. The extensive network of charitable provision in Britain supported by NHS funding is well-placed to take advantage of decriminalization to improve access by, for example, introducing more nurse-led care, and clinics are extremely unlikely to close due to pressures from the private sector. Also, with the exception of the Australian Capital Territory, the states surveyed by Baird had only decriminalized abortions administered by medical practitioners (Queensland and New South Wales changed their own laws too recently to be included in Baird's assessment), obstructing their ability to improve access for women who might struggle to attend a clinic (Baird, 2017: 204–5). This kind of partial decriminalization is clearly not the intent of campaigners in the UK; women's access to abortion pills has been high on their agenda.

Framing abortion as 'just like any other medical procedure', as decriminalization advocates often have, may however have other drawbacks. It risks decoupling the issue of abortion from broader questions of women's social status: their access to jobs and education, for starters, as well as the ability to be considered as more than just a reproductive body. Without a *right* to abortion enshrined in law, the 'health' framing is also left open to attempts to prove that abortion is not 'necessary' to health or is harmful. Johnstone suggests that an expansive definition of health, such as the World Health Organisation's well-known statement that it is 'a state of complete physical, mental, and social well-being' (quoted in Johnstone, 2017: 111–12) always justifies liberal abortion access, as it is necessary for 'social well-being'. This is true; however, this broad definition has not necessarily always informed government action on reproductive and sexual health (Evans, 2006). None of this ought to discourage advocates: most importantly, decriminalization will remove a huge barrier to abortion provision in Northern Ireland, and has the potential to facilitate improvements to access and services in England and Wales. And crucially, it is socially and culturally symbolic. As suggested by a feminist commentator in Victoria: 'for the first time women will be recognised as the authors of our own lives. With that comes our full citizenship' (Wainer, 2008).

Anti-abortion politics in context

The Abortion Act 1967 also channelled anti-abortion arguments along a particular path. Early parliamentary opposition to the Act focused not on the question of preserving 'life' – indeed, conventional 'pro-life' arguments regarding the moral status of the foetus are notable by their near absence – but about whether it was appropriate to expect doctors to intervene in 'social' issues. Subsequent anti-abortion challenges have attacked the image of the 'socially responsible' doctor on which the Act rests. From the 1970s, these challenges have mainly involved claims about the occurrence of 'racketeering' and other abuses in the private sector, with the addition of gory images of medical butchery in the allegations about 'partial-birth' abortion in the 1990s. In recent years, this has been accompanied by sustained harassment of abortion providers by anti-abortion activists (McGuinness, 2015). Yet the need to respond to calls for decriminalization has resulted in contradictions in anti-abortion arguments, in which doctors now figure both as irresponsible, untrustworthy butchers *and* as necessary gatekeepers to abortion (Lowe, 2018: 11).

The Act also introduced a 'woman problem' for anti-abortion actors in that it positioned them 'against' helping vulnerable women, and since 1967 anti-abortion politics has been characterized by attempts to solve this problem. Primarily, this has been attempted by portraying women who have abortions as victims of unscrupulous doctors and the trauma of abortion itself. However, the portrayal of women as victims has occasionally clashed with depictions of female vice and abortion for 'frivolous' reasons. Anti-abortion MPs and peers have nonetheless attempted to deploy feminist language and concepts, complaining, for example, about women's sexual treatment at the hands of men and arguing that legal abortion lets men 'get away with it'. Yet this has not been blamed on a history of male societal dominance but on the sexual revolution and loss of traditional values: some even lamented that a 'sense of responsibility' had been lost in the uncoupling of sex from the context of the traditional heterosexual marriage. In this way, the appropriation of feminism paradoxically coincided with a backlash politics that identified feminism and social change as the *cause* of women's problems rather than the solution.

Claims about the supposed harms of abortion are part of a broader shift towards 'woman-centred' (Cannold, 2002) arguments in anti-abortion strategy. As Paul Saurette and Kelly Gordon put it, 'contemporary "conservative" political discourse is increasingly colonizing and employing explicit arguments, principles and narratives that have traditionally been associated with progressive feminist, pro-women and pro-choice movements' (2013: 158). This trend is certainly not confined to the UK; it has been observed across the Anglosphere in the US (Cannold, 2002; Rose, 2011), Canada (Saurette and Gordon, 2013; Duerksen and Lawson, 2017), Australia (Cannold, 2002; Baird, 2013) and New Zealand (Leask, 2013). Leslie Cannold (2002) suggests that this trend came about due to the failure of strategies centring the foetus and its 'right to life'. As even the belief that life begins at conception does not necessarily deter people from supporting liberal abortion laws (Cannold, 2002: 172), a change of tack was required. The core arguments are familiar: that women's mental (and sometimes physical) health is harmed by abortion, that the decision to abort is often coerced, and that organizations claiming to support women's rights are actually undermining them. Proponents believe the 'woman-centred' strategy to be stronger than older strategies as it reverses the script on abortion, placing anti-abortion actors in the position of defending, rather than attacking, women considering abortion. However, both this and foetus-centred arguments 'seek to undermine women's decision-making agency' (Cannold, 2002: 172). Foetus-centred arguments do this by implying that women are morally deficient for choosing to abort. Woman-centred arguments, on the other hand, suggest that women are incapable of making a free and informed choice.

Analyses of anti-abortion movements in other countries generally suggest that woman-centred arguments became popular in the 1980s or later (Cannold, 2002; Rose, 2011; Saurette and Gordon, 2013), and this is certainly when anti-abortion actors in the UK began to borrow explicitly *feminist*-sounding arguments. However, this book's analysis has found that a rudimentary woman-centred frame was present in UK parliamentary debates as early as 1970. Recall, for example, Godman Irvine's accounts of vulnerable 'girls' attending poorly-managed abortion clinics and becoming 'desperately ill' (Hansard, 1970: 1664–5), or the various narratives of vulnerability and exploitation that drove support for the White Bill (Hansard, 1975). While this did not necessarily reflect the views of anti-abortion activists outside Parliament (Clarke, 1987), it is interesting that arguments used in the UK Parliament may have pre-dated those of other countries. It is sometimes alleged that anti-abortion actors in the UK have 'imported' American tactics (Bates, 2016; Braithwaite, 2017). Specific claims regarding the relationship between abortion and women's mental health do appear to have spread from the US to the UK, although they have found more purchase in the former (Lee, 2003). Nonetheless, 'woman-centred' frames were a feature of UK abortion debates years before abortion was even legalized in the US.

As stated previously, these strategies have not generally been successful in shifting the legislative agenda in the UK. Claims about sex-selective abortion therefore require extra attention, as legislation that would have criminalized the practice was, unusually, very nearly passed. These claims were also apparently modelled on US anti-abortion campaigns: since 2009, multiple states have banned or considered banning sex-selective abortion, despite a lack of evidence for such abortions taking place among the targeted group, Asian Americans (Kalantry, 2015; 2017). Claims about sex-selective abortion are structured along the lines of older 'woman-centred' tropes. Accordingly, in these claims it is women (not only, or even primarily, foetuses) who are framed as the victims of abortion, while abortion doctors are persistently villainized (Lee, 2017). This framing has again spread from the US to the UK.

What sex selection claims add is an explicit racialization of abortion debates. It is not that abortion was not already a racialized issue. However, awareness of race has typically been lacking from abortion debates in the UK Parliament (whereas in the US, for example, the allegation that 'abortion is black genocide' has been around for years). Sex-selection claims brought race hurtling into (white) political and public consciousness. Quoting Gayatri Spivak, Sundari Anitha and Aisha Gill characterize recent attempts to amend the law as 'an example of what feminist postcolonial critiques would describe as an impulse to "save brown women from brown men"' (2018: 9). Debates on sex selection also refer to the nation and the place of feminism and gender equality within it. As Jennifer Musial has observed, debates in the US have played heavily on 'the notion that the American Empire is a benevolent, rights-upholding, progressive nation by which others are oppositely cast as coercive, violent, rights-denying and regressive' (2014: 271). Debates in the UK, as we have seen, similarly rely on the mythologized image of the UK as a haven of gender equality that must be defended from the 'oppressive' practices of racial minorities. I suggest that these constructions of race and nation are what propelled the sex-selection ban to near-success where previous 'woman-centred' attacks on UK abortion law failed to land.

Interrogating 'choice'

Narratives of vulnerability and trauma have featured heavily on all sides of the abortion debate. The Abortion Act 1967 is grounded in the idea that women need protecting, and this claim has been made over and over in Parliament by those defending the Act. Of course, it is imperative to speak up about trauma, especially in cases of burning injustice such as the criminalization of rape survivors in Northern Ireland. Yet what is lacking in parliamentary abortion debates is any defence of women who are not victims, are not 'faultless', but simply do not want to be pregnant. If this is not yet considered permissible speech, we are still a long way from realizing the radical potential of abortion access to liberate women from norms about motherhood.

Feminist politics that focus on appealing to the law to protect women have always come at a price. As Wendy Brown has argued:

> Historically, the argument that women require protection by and from men has been critical in legitimating women's exclusion from some spheres of human endeavor and confinement within others. ... Whether one is dealing with the state, the Mafia, parents, pimps, police, or husbands, the heavy, dual price of institutionalized protection is always a measure of dependence and agreement to abide by the protector's rules. (1992: 8–9)

In the case of abortion law, the price of protection has been that those seeking abortion have had to submit to medical surveillance and control and assessment of them as 'deserving' or 'undeserving' aborters. But the tone of debate is now shifting, as MPs and even medical bodies have become increasingly critical of criminalization and the strictures of the Abortion Act 1967. Outside Parliament, advocates call for liberation rather than protection, and frame decriminalization as the next step for gender equality.

Yet demands for action on reproductive injustice still often draw upon a politics of protection that clashes with these more liberatory frames. Recent calls for a ban on foetal sex testing in early pregnancy serve well to illustrate these more protective frames and the response they have garnered. The issue was thrown into the spotlight in 2018 when the BBC's *Victoria Derbyshire* programme alleged that 'thousands' of British South Asian women were discussing using non-invasive prenatal testing (NIPT), a DNA test more commonly used to test for genetic conditions, to screen for female foetuses and potentially abort based on the results. The Labour Party frontbencher Naz Shah subsequently called for a ban on using NIPT for foetal sex, stating that son preference in some South Asian families forced women to use it 'to live up to expectations of family members' (Haque, 2018). This drew angry responses from other quarters, with one commentator noting that 'if there is something knowable, particularly about my body, I want to know it' (Ramaswamy, 2018). BPAS's Director of External Affairs, Clare Murphy, characterized the proposed ban as an effort to 'deny every pregnant woman the right to find out information about her own pregnancy' (BPAS, 2018), and the Voice for Choice coalition of pro-choice organizations has previously resisted calls for a ban (Alliance for Choice, 2017).

Shah herself was clearly motivated by the perception of a need to protect vulnerable women, a perspective that underpins many responses to sex-selective abortion. This clashed with many abortion rights advocates' emphasis on the need for reproductive choice as a key component of women's liberation. The fault lines emerging here recall the broader debate about the appropriateness of 'choice' as a framework for understanding abortion. The writer and Southall Black Sisters activist Rahila Gupta, for example, has argued that conversations about 'choice' in the context of sex selection are 'a red herring' (2014: 86) as these may be forced abortions, and called to ban foetal sex testing (an outright sex-selective abortion ban being in her view unworkable).

Gupta's position on 'choice' is reminiscent of other feminist critiques often associated with the reproductive justice movement. Reproductive justice activists have criticized what they see as the mainstream US pro-choice movement's narrow conceptualization of reproductive rights as *legal* rights concerning the protection of women from state interference. As the US scholar Zakiya Luna has observed, conceptualizing reproductive rights as a matter of choice may seem to make sense to those women 'who have evidence that, but for their gender, they could participate fully in society' (2011: 224). Yet the portrayal of abortion as solely an exercise in legal, individual choice has been questioned by Luna and other feminists, who point out that choices are not made in a vacuum. Susan Himmelweit has noted that women rarely make the choice to abort or keep a pregnancy in ideal physical, material, and emotional circumstances and would often choose differently in different circumstances, meaning that their choice cannot be separated from the context in which it was made (1988: 42). Similarly, for Rhonda Copelon, choices are shaped by social conditions, and 'cannot be fully free' in a world of poverty, inequality and discrimination (1990: 28). Choices may be most restricted for those facing intersecting systems of oppression.

These ideas have met with some resistance. Perhaps most forcefully, BPAS chief executive Ann Furedi has condemned them as belonging to a 'new anti-choice movement' (2013b). Furedi wrote in response to both the claims of the reproductive justice movement and the news that the Planned Parenthood Federation of America (along with other US organizations) was to drop the language of 'choice', in response to data that the organization claimed showed that the labels of 'pro-life' and 'pro-choice' do not accurately represent the views of most US citizens (Holpuch, 2013). Rightly, Furedi pointed out that the data do not in fact support such a shift: a key finding is that while some people avoid labelling themselves 'pro-choice', closer examination of their beliefs reveals that they do in fact support the right of individuals to decide according to their circumstances (Marcotte, 2013).

Furedi's article also criticized the subsequent decision of the US group Physicians for Reproductive Choice and Health (PRCH) to drop the word 'choice' from its name and become Physicians for Reproductive Health (PRH). As she noted, reproductive choice and health are not always the same:

> Where will the doctors in PRH stand when faced with the controversies about women who base their reproductive decisions on issues that are nothing to do with reproductive health at all? I know what a doctor in PRCH will say about a 35-year-old woman who chooses to have an abortion because she prefers to delay starting her family. That doctor will support her patient's choice. But if the doctor is only interested in her patient's reproductive *health*? Given the increase in risks with maternal age, I'm not so sure what she'll say in the above situations. (2013, emphasis in original)

So far, I am sympathetic to Furedi's concerns; this book and chapter have argued that conceptualizing abortion solely as a matter of health has severe limitations. Yet her article muddies the water in associating these particular anti-'choice' moves with reproductive justice critiques. 'Health' and 'justice' are very different concepts: the former depoliticizes reproduction, while the latter *politicizes* it. The contribution of the reproductive justice movement has not simply been to critique the concept of 'choice' in the abstract, but to highlight what they see as important issues missing from mainstream US 'pro-choice' politics in practice. This includes the question of access to abortion in practice as well as on statute (the latter, they argue, being the sole focus of much pro-choice activism). It also includes access to contraception, sex education, sexual health services, adequate pre- and post-natal care, sexual and domestic violence services, and social justice more broadly. Advocates argue that these issues can only be adequately addressed by a movement that analyses power systems and centres the most marginalized (SisterSong, undated). This is a far cry from the vague and apolitical notion of 'reproductive health' that Furedi critiques. It is also not a call for a return to a politics of protection, which relies on the legal system to defend the vulnerable; as indigenous and anti-racist activists, US reproductive justice advocates have been sceptical of any such move. The reproductive justice movement should not be described as 'anti-choice' but more 'beyond choice' or 'choice plus'; as SisterSong put it, individual choice is 'necessary, but not enough' (SisterSong, undated).

Furedi's article ends by citing in full the London Declaration of Pro-Choice Principles – developed by BPAS with the group Catholics for Choice and a coalition of activists, practitioners and academics in September 2012 – along with the challenge, 'To those who wish to drop the C-word: with what, in this declaration, do you disagree?' The Declaration in fact reads similarly to many reproductive justice movement demands, citing the need for *access* in addition to the legal right to abortion, as well as the need for access to a broader range of services alongside 'legal, social, political and economic changes'. It can therefore be argued that there is a fair amount of overlap between reproductive justice movement norms and those of the UK pro-choice movement, at least on paper. This was underlined by discussions at a recent Abortion Rights public meeting.[2] For those at the meeting, 'choice' clearly stood for more than statutory rights, narrowly conceived: it also stood for the ability to access better and non-judgemental healthcare and for measures to end women's suffering.

The future of abortion politics

The key question is not whether a movement based on 'choice' *can* speak to a broader set of concerns than simply the legal right to access abortion, but *whether it does in practice*. What has historically been lacking in UK pro-choice politics is the reproductive justice movement's explicitly intersectional awareness, broad critique of power structures, and situation of abortion as part of a wider reproductive rights and social justice agenda (Evans, 2015: 183–4). I argue that such an agenda is vital. There is a clear moral case for it, in that, as Crenshaw argues, a movement that does not address intersecting power structures cannot hope to speak for all women (1989; 1991). But there is also a practical case, in that those seeking to restrict access to abortion are already aware of and exploiting differences between women. Without broad, intersectional coalitions, the pro-choice movement will remain vulnerable to the charge that it does not care about the rights of South Asian women, for example, or those of disabled people.

There are clear signs of a shift towards such an approach from segments of the movement. The collaborative statement on sex selection produced by BPAS, IKWRO, Southall Black Sisters, EVAW and others is a good example of this. Since 2011, BPAS has made a sustained effort to reframe the organization's activity as part of a broader social justice movement and collaborate with activist groups beyond the pro-choice sphere.[3] Documents produced during this time include reports on disabled women's reproductive rights (BPAS, 2017), young deaf people's sexual and reproductive health needs (BPAS, 2014c), pregnancy and maternity discrimination (BPAS, 2016), and support for improved childcare services and affordable housing to make it easier for women to choose to have children (BPAS, 2015b).

Other leading advocacy groups, such as Abortion Rights and the Voice for Choice coalition, have been narrower in their focus. Due to its historical ties with the trade union movement, Abortion Rights has always stressed that abortion is an economic issue and has campaigned against austerity (Jackson, 2011; Abortion Rights, 2015c). However, many in the movement have been reluctant to explicitly organize under a broader reproductive rights or reproductive justice banner. This is in part due to the perception that there is less inequality in access to healthcare services in the UK than there is in the US, and therefore less need for such a movement (Jackson, 2011; Evans, 2015: 183–4). As Chapter 2 suggested, however, there is still plenty of inequality, both in access to services and in health outcomes, and migrant women's fertility is particularly stigmatized.

There are also structural barriers to doing this kind of work. Building broad, intersectional coalitions takes time, and this is something that can prevent those working and campaigning in the pressured women's sector from doing as much outreach work as they might like. Campaigners interviewed by the feminist blogger Sarah Jackson also suggested that the movement's specific aim of defending the Abortion Act 1967 naturally resulted in a narrower focus (Jackson, 2011). Indeed, constant attempts to chip away at the Act have often placed abortion rights advocates on the back foot. But does this mean that, if abortion is decriminalized, the movement might be able to reformulate and broaden its scope? In the wake of the decriminalization campaign and the watershed moment for abortion rights in Northern Ireland, it certainly seems as if the movement has gained agenda-setting power. If time constraints allow, perhaps this can be capitalized upon.

What might a reproductive justice movement look like in the UK? It might, for example, seek to tackle the vast discrepancies in maternal health and wellbeing between white and minority women. It might in particular campaign against policies that aim 'to dissuade "undesirable" migrants from having children' (Lonergan, 2015: 124) via a combination of strict spousal visa rules and limits on access to maternity services. It might also address the far right and its ongoing mainstreaming (Mondon and Winter, 2018), including scare stories about immigration and fertility amongst migrant groups. As Jackson (2011) notes, it is not that there are not groups already doing this work. However, they have not formulated together as a movement under the same banner.

A UK reproductive justice movement might also revisit arguments about abortion and disability. Abortion rights advocates have tended to defend the Abortion Act 1967's exemption to the normal 24-week limit to legal abortion for cases of severe foetal disability. However, as Sheelagh McGuinness has argued, this exemption is discriminatory as 'some foetuses are being stripped of a layer of legal protection they would otherwise have: disability is being used to differentiate legal protections between foetuses' (2013: 237). For McGuinness, the argument that the clause exists to protect 'choice' or pregnant women's interests, given the need for extra time after discovery of the disability, does not hold. The law does not protect other abortion choices after 24 weeks' gestation, even when 'extra time' is clearly needed to protect the pregnant person's interests and ability to choose (McGuinness recounts a scenario in which a distraught young woman learned she was 28 weeks pregnant, not 14 weeks as she believed, and therefore would be denied an abortion [2013: 235]). The answer is not necessarily to scrap the relevant clause altogether, as proposed by Lord Shinkwin. The discriminatory element of the law lies in its protection of some choices and not others. McGuinness suggests that an alternative solution would be to reject the requirements of the Abortion Act 1967 entirely (2013: 238). Decriminalization would obviously make a start in this direction. However, as the decriminalization campaign currently aims to preserve the 24-week upper limit in law for abortion on grounds other than disability (and thereby preserve good relations with the medical bodies, which insist on this limit), this discrepancy is not close to being tackled.

Key to reproductive justice organizing is not just *what* is being addressed, but *how* and *who by*. Kimberlé Crenshaw's famous account of intersectionality suggests that it is not simply about how identities (such as womanhood or blackness) intersect, but about how movements (women's movements, civil rights movements) may be made to speak to one another (1991). We should be wary of the assumption that 'natural' coalitions exist among marginalized groups (Cole, 2008). There may be differences between groups that cannot easily be transcended, if at all. Examples are the question of whether foetal sex testing should be banned or whether this is an infringement on the right to know about one's own pregnancy, and that of whether late-term abortions for disability are discriminatory or necessary to protect pregnant women's interests. The experience of US activists suggests that the way forward is not to gloss over or attempt to transcend these differences but rather to confront them 'openly and honestly' (Roberts and Jesudason, 2013: 315), through a process of coalition-building that involves learning about one another's movements and developing solidarity. This requires sustained engagement that goes beyond an immediate single issue such as a Bill before Congress or Parliament; it means, for example, 'co-sponsoring and attending each other's events' (Roberts and Jesudason, 2013: 319). This generates long-term shared goals and values even where there is disagreement on individual issues. While UK reproductive rights activism will naturally have different goals and involve different actors, there might be useful lessons here for building a broader movement.

Notes

Chapter 1

1. Ten Minute Rule Bills allow a backbench MP to make the case for a new bill in a ten-minute speech, with the opportunity for an opponent also to make a speech. In theory they should be allowed to progress into full bills if MPs vote to allow them to do so, but in practice even successful bills are rarely prioritized in the parliamentary timetable, so tend to be dropped.

Chapter 2

1. Bordo cites the case of *McFall v Shimp*, in which it was ruled that David Shimp could not legally be forced to donate bone marrow to his cousin, Robert McFall, despite the unlikelihood that the latter would find another compatible donor. The court decision stated that to infringe upon Shimp's 'absolute right to his "bodily security"' would 'change every concept and principle upon which our society is founded' (Bordo, 2003: 73; *McFall v Shimp*, 1978).
2. I use the male pronoun because, as the failure of liberal theory to accommodate the pregnant body demonstrates, this individual is implicitly male (Pateman, 1988; Brown, 1992).
3. The importance of accessibility should not be underestimated. As Petchesky has forcefully argued, legal abortion makes little difference for many women without the ability to access abortion in practice (1980; 1986).
4. Peter Conrad defines medicalization as 'a process by which nonmedical problems become defined and treated as medical problems' (1992: 209). This definition is shared by much of the literature, but is problematic in that it assumes that there is a clear-cut distinction between those issues that are 'genuinely' medical and those that are not. The dividing line is more blurred than this, as my discussion of the medicalization of pregnancy and abortion should indicate.
5. These authors are referring to the power of medicine as a 'system' (Ehrenreich and English, 2011 [1973]: 31) or 'institution' (Zola, 1972: 487), rather than simply the status of individual doctors.

Chapter 3

1. Private Members' ballots are a means through which backbench MPs can propose new legislation.
2. It is ironic that the medical body with the most explicitly feminist aims should also have been the most explicitly in favour of the medicalization of pregnancy, given

the feminist critiques discussed in Chapter 2. However, it should also be noted that the MWF's report includes an appendix written by a dissenting member of the committee, which states in unequivocal terms her belief that the right to decide whether a pregnancy should continue 'belongs to the pregnant woman herself and no-one else' (MWF, 1966: 1514).

3   The euphemism 'the other place' or 'another place' is, by tradition, used by members of one House of Parliament to refer to business conducted in the other.
4   Higginson's syringes were used to inject fluids into the uterus to induce abortion – a particularly dangerous method, but achievable to those without access to medical tools or training.
5   As Keown notes, 'abortion on demand' may be distinguished from 'abortion on request' in that the former refers to a woman's right to access abortion independently of the decision of a doctor, whereas the latter refers to a doctor's decision to abort on no other grounds than the patient's request. However, in practice they are often used interchangeably to mean the latter (1988: 111).
6   In making this comment I do not mean to suggest that self-abortion is always preferable to abortion carried out by medical professionals; however, it would entail a right to bodily integrity that is lacking in the 1967 Act (see Purdy, 2001: 255–7 for a discussion of self-abortion in relation to US law).

Chapter 4
1   By the time of the Benyon Bill, the issue had abated slightly as figures reported a decrease in women travelling to the UK for abortion. Anxieties over 'foreign' women were not even mentioned during the Corrie debate.

Chapter 5
1   A 24-week limit in practice means that abortions can be carried out at 23 weeks and 6 days at the latest.
2   Interview with Alice Mahon, 11 April 2013.
3   Interview with Alice Mahon, 11 April 2013.
4   Interview with Alice Mahon, 11 April 2013.
5   Interview with Alice Mahon, 11 April 2013.
6   Interview with Alice Mahon, 11 April 2013.
7   'Specialing' refers to the nursing practice of giving special care to an individual patient with significant needs.
8   Interview with Alice Mahon, 11 April 2013.
9   Claims that abortion damages women's mental health are made frequently in abortion debates; however, there is no conclusive evidence for this (see Chapter 6).
10 Interview with Brian Iddon, 24 May 2013.

Chapter 6
1   Interview with Julie Morgan AM, 17 May 2013.
2   Whether abortion presents a risk to women's mental health remains contested. MPs tasked with investigating evidence related to abortion in 2007 described the evidence as inconclusive (Science and Technology Committee, 2007; interview with Brian Iddon, 24 May 2013; interview with Des Turner MP, 28 May 2013).
3   Crisis pregnancy centres are non-profit organizations offering counselling and help to women with unplanned pregnancies. According to a mystery shopping

exercise conducted by the Education for Choice project, the counsellors in these organizations often operate with an anti-abortion agenda, and many do not provide impartial advice (Education for Choice, 2011).
4. Interview with Brian Iddon, 24 May 2013.
5. A programme motion is used by the government to timetable a bill's progress through the House of Commons, and can be used to curtail time for debate.
6. Interview with Brian Iddon, 24 May 2013; interview with Des Turner, 28 May 2013.
7. Interview with Brian Iddon, 24 May 2013.
8. The Committee's support for home abortion was not unanimous, even among pro-choice members. One former member expressed concern that complications might set in for some women, and that the process might be difficult to deal with (interview with Brian Iddon, 24 May 2013).
9. Interview with Julie Morgan AM, 17 May 2013.
10. Interview with Brian Iddon, 24 May 2013; interview with Des Turner, 28 May 2013.
11. Interview with Kate Green MP, 10 July 2013.
12. See Pierson and Bloomer (2017; 2018) and Thomson (2018a; 2018b) for accounts of debates on abortion in the Northern Ireland Assembly since its creation.
13. Interview with Kate Green MP, 10 July 2013.
14. Interview with Kate Green MP, 10 July 2013.
15. Interview with Kate Green MP, 10 July 2013.
16. Interview with Kate Green MP, 10 July 2013.
17. Interview with Julie Morgan AM, 17 May 2013.
18. Interview with Brian Iddon, 24 May 2013.
19. Interview with Des Turner, 28 May 2013.
20. Interview with Brian Iddon, 24 May 2013.
21. Interview with Kate Green MP, 10 July 2013.
22. Interview with Des Turner, 28 May 2013.

Chapter 7

1. www.notinmyname.org.uk/
2. The Queen's Speech sets out the UK government's agenda for the coming parliamentary session.
3. Interview with Cara Sanquest, 25 January 2019.
4. Interview with Cara Sanquest, 25 January 2019.
5. Interview with Clare Murphy and Abigail Fitzgibbon, 27 February 2017.
6. The Windrush scandal, which broke in 2018, concerned the wrongful deportation, detention or denial of rights to UK citizens. Many of these were members of the 'Windrush generation' (named for the ship that brought one of the first groups of West Indian migrants to the UK) who migrated from the Caribbean to the UK between 1948 and 1970, having been granted citizen status and the right to settle in the UK.
7. Interview with Diana Johnson MP, 19 November 2018.
8. Abortion Rights was formed in 2003 as a merger of ALRA and the National Abortion Campaign.
9. Interview with Diana Johnson MP, 19 November 2018.
10. Interview with Diana Johnson MP, 19 November 2018.

11 https://www.youtube.com/watch?v=IflD1dHN2S0
12 Abortion Rights public meeting, Portcullis House, 10 October 2018.
13 Abortion Rights public meeting, Portcullis House, 10 October 2018.
14 The 'cattle market' quote refers a Care Quality Commission inspection of a Marie Stopes clinic, which found that staff felt under pressure to treat patients quickly and in a way that worked against patient choice, and that safeguarding measures were not in line with national guidance (CQC, 2017). The most recent inspection of this clinic, however, returned scores of 'good' across all aspects of the service (CQC, 2018).
15 Interview with Diana Johnson MP, 19 November 2018.
16 Interview with Cara Sanquest, 25 January 2019.
17 Interview with Clare Murphy and Abigail Fitzgibbon, 27 February 2017.
18 Interview with Clare Murphy and Abigail Fitzgibbon, 27 February 2017.
19 Abigail Fitzgibbon, personal correspondence, 7 February 2019.
20 Interview with Clare Murphy and Abigail Fitzgibbon, 27 February 2017; interview with Abigail Fitzgibbon, 28 June 2018; interview with Shaheen Hashmat, 12 July 2018.
21 Interview with Clare Murphy and Abigail Fitzgibbon, 27 February 2017; Abigail Fitzgibbon, personal correspondence, 7 February 2019.
22 Interview with Abigail Fitzgibbon, 28 June 2018; Kerry Abel at Abortion Rights public meeting, Portcullis House, 10 October 2018; Abigail Fitzgibbon, personal correspondence, 7 February 2019.
23 Abigail Fitzgibbon, personal correspondence, 7 February 2019.
24 Interview with Clare Murphy and Abigail Fitzgibbon, 27 February 2017.
25 Interview with Clare Murphy and Abigail Fitzgibbon, 27 February 2017; Abigail Fitzgibbon, personal correspondence, 7 February 2019.
26 Interview with Dr Navtej Purewal, 18 July 2018.
27 Interview with Clare Murphy and Abigail Fitzgibbon, 27 February 2017.
28 Interview with Clare Murphy and Abigail Fitzgibbon, 27 February 2017.
29 Interview with Diana Johnson MP, 19 November 2018.
30 Interview with Clare Murphy and Abigail Fitzgibbon, 27 February 2017.
31 Interview with Shaheen Hashmat, 12 July 2018.

Chapter 8

1 As abortion statistics are calculated differently in Scotland, it was not possible to obtain comparable figures. However, the overwhelming majority of abortions in Scotland are carried out at an early stage of pregnancy.
2 Abortion Rights public meeting, Portcullis House, 10 October 2018.
3 Abigail Fitzgibbon, personal correspondence, 7 February 2019.

References

Abortion Rights (2011) 'Women's and Equalities groups speak out on abortion counselling', 1 September, www.abortionrights.org.uk/index.php/media-and-resource-centre/news/261.

Abortion Rights (2012) 'Inaccuracy and anecdote: Dorries' time limit debate', 1 November, www.abortionrights.org.uk/index.php/media-and-resource-centre/news/467-inaccuracy-and-anecdote-dorries-time-limit-debate.

Abortion Rights (2014) 'Statement on sex-selective abortion', January 2014, http://test.abortionrights.org.uk/wp-content/uploads/2014/09/Statement%20on%20sex-selection%20abortion.pdf.

Abortion Rights (2015a) 'AR Letter to MPs RE: Bruce amendment to the Serious Crime Bill on 23.02.15', 4 February, www.abortionrights.org.uk/abortion-rights-letter-to-re-bruce-amendment-to-the-serious-crime-bill-on-9-2-15/.

Abortion Rights (2015b) 'Say no to Big Bad Bruce's sex-selection amendment', 3 February, www.abortionrights.org.uk/say-no-to-big-bad-bruces-sex-selection-amendment/.

Abortion Rights (2015c) 'Austerity is forcing more women into unintended pregnancy – defend women's access to abortion!', 18 June, www.abortionrights.org.uk/austerity-is-forcing-more-women-into-unintended-pregnancy-defend-womens-access-to-abortion/.

Abortion Rights (2018) 'Ten minute rule bill – act before 23 October', 20 October, www.abortionrights.org.uk/ten-minute-rule-bill-act-before-23-october/.

Addelson, K.P. (1999) 'The emergence of the fetus' in L.M. Morgan and M.W. Michaels (eds), *Fetal Subjects, Feminist Positions*, Philadelphia: University of Pennsylvania Press, pp 26–42.

Aiken, A., Guthrie, K.A., Schellekens, M., Trussell, J. and Gomperts, R. (2018) 'Barriers to accessing abortion services and perspectives on using mifepristone and misoprostol at home in Great Britain', *Contraception*, 97(2): 177–83.

Allen, J. (1990) 'Does feminism need a theory of the state?' in S. Watson (ed.), *Playing the State: Australian Feminist Interventions*, London: Verso, pp 21–37.

Alliance for Choice (2017) 'Voice for Choice response to Nuffield Council on Bioethics Report: Non-invasive prenatal testing: Ethical issues', Alliance for Choice news, 3 January, www.alliance4choice.com/news/2017/3/voice-for-choice-response-to-nuffield-council-on-bioethics-report-non-invasive-prenatal-testing-ethical-issues.

Ameh, C.A. and van den Broek, N. (2008) 'Increased risk of maternal death among ethnic minority women in the UK', *The Obstetrician & Gynaecologist*, 10: 177–82.

Amery, F. (2014) 'Social questions, medical answers: Contesting British abortion law', *Social Politics*, 21(1): 26–49.

Amery, F. (2015a) 'Solving the "woman problem" in British abortion politics: A contextualised account', *British Journal of Politics and International Relations*, 17(4): 551–67.

Amery, F. (2015b) 'Intersectionality as disarticulatory practice: Sex-selective abortion and reproductive politics in the United Kingdom', *New Political Science*, 37(4): 509–24.

Anitha, S. and Gill, A.K. (2018) 'Making politics visible: Discourses on gender and race in the problematisation of sex-selective abortion', *Feminist Review*, 120(1): 1–19.

Annesley, C. (2010) 'Gender, politics and policy change: The case of welfare reform under New Labour', *Government and Opposition*, 45(1): 50–72.

Annesley, C., Gains, F. and Rummery, K. (eds) (2007) *Women and New Labour: Engendering Politics and Policy?* Bristol: Policy Press.

APPGSRH (2015) *Breaking Down the Barriers: The Need for Accountability and Integration in Sexual Health, Reproductive Health and HIV Services in England*, report of the All Party Parliamentary Group on Sexual and Reproductive Health in the UK.

Arnold, F., Kishor, S. and Roy, T.K. (2004) 'Sex-selective abortions in India', *Population and Development Review*, 28(4): 759–85.

Baird, B. (2013) 'Abortion politics during the Howard years: Beyond liberalisation', *Australian Historical Studies*, 44(2): 245–61.

Baird, B. (2017) 'Decriminalization and women's access to abortion in Australia', *Health and Human Rights Journal*, 19(1): 197–208.

Baird, D. (1966) 'Experience at Aberdeen' in *Abortion in Britain: Proceedings of a conference held by the Family Planning Association at the University of London Union on 22 April 1966*, London: Pitman Medical, pp 15–21.

Bates, L. (2016) 'Reproductive rights are under attack – and not just in the US', *The Guardian*, 7 April.

Battersby, C. (1998) *The Phenomenal Woman: Feminist Metaphysics and the Patterns of Identity*, New York: Routledge.

Bayley, P. (2004) 'Introduction: The whys and wherefores of analysing parliamentary discourse' in P. Bayley (ed.), *Cross-Cultural Perspectives on Parliamentary Discourse*, Philadelphia: John Benjamins, pp 1–44.

BBC (2018) 'Judge throws out challenge to Scots abortion pill move', *BBC News*, 15 August, https://www.bbc.co.uk/news/uk-scotland-45196213.

de Beauvoir, S. (2011 [1949]) *The Second Sex*, trans. C. Borde and S. Malovany-Chevallier, London: Vintage.

Beynon-Jones, S.M. (2012) 'Timing is everything: The demarcation of "later" abortions in Scotland', *Social Studies of Science*, 42(1): 53–74.

Beynon-Jones, S.M. (2013) 'Expecting motherhood? Stratifying reproduction in 21st-century Scottish abortion practice', *Sociology*, 47(3): 509–25.

Bhavnani, K. and Coulson, M. (1986) 'Transforming socialist-feminism: The challenge of racism', *Feminist Review*, 23: 81–92.

Bloomer, F. and Fegan, E. (2014) 'Critiquing recent abortion law and policy in Northern Ireland', *Critical Social Policy*, 34(1): 109–20.

BMA (1966) 'Therapeutic abortion: Report by BMA special committee', *British Medical Journal*, 2(5502): 40–4.

BMA (2007) *The Law and Ethics of Abortion: BMA Views*, London: BMA.

BMA (2017a) *Decriminalisation of Abortion: A Discussion Paper from the BMA*, London: BMA MEC.

BMA (2017b) 'Doctors back decriminalisation of abortion', 27 June, https://www.bma.org.uk/news/2017/june/doctors-back-decriminalisation-of-abortion.

BMJ (1966) 'Abortion law', *British Medical Journal*, 2: 1607–8.

BMJ (1971) 'Abortion or contraception?' *British Medical Journal*, 3: 261–2.

Bordo, S. (2003) *Unbearable Weight: Feminism, Western Culture, and the Body*, Berkeley: University of California Press.

Boryczka, J.M. (2012) *Suspect Citizens: Women, Virtue and Vice in Backlash Politics*, Philadelphia: Temple University Press.

BPAS (undated) 'Consent, decision-making and safeguarding: A briefing on the frameworks to protect and support women and girls seeking pregnancy advice and abortion care in the UK today', BPAS briefing, https://www.bpas.org/media/2080/consent-and-decision-making.pdf.

BPAS (2014a) 'Abortion clinics need buffer zones', BPAS press release, 28 November, https://www.bpas.org/about-our-charity/press-office/press-releases/bpas-release-abortion-clinics-need-buffer-zones/.

BPAS (2014b) 'BPAS statement on 10 Minute Rule Bill on sex selective abortion', BPAS press release, 4 November, https://www.bpas.org/about-our-charity/press-office/press-releases/bpas-statement-on-10-minute-rule-bill-on-sex-selec/.

BPAS (2014c) 'No sign of support: Understanding young deaf people's sexual and reproductive health needs', https://www.bpas.org/media/1895/no-sign-of-support.pdf.

BPAS (2015a) 'Sex selection', https://www.bpas.org/get-involved/campaigns/briefings/sex-selection/.

BPAS (2015b) 'Becoming a mother: Understanding women's choices today', https://www.bpas.org/media/1698/becoming-a-mother-understanding-womens-choices-today.pdf.

BPAS (2016) 'BPAS submission to Pregnancy and Maternity Discrimination inquiry by Women and Equalities Committee, April 2016', https://www.bpas.org/media/1864/bpas-submission-to-pregnancy-and-maternity-discrimination-inquiry-by-women-and-equalities-committee.pdf.

BPAS (2017) 'Reproductive rights: What do they mean for disabled women?', https://www.bpas.org/media/2030/reproductive-rights-and-disability-event-write-up-final.pdf.

BPAS (2018) 'BPAS comment on calls to ban NIPT gender test', BPAS press release, 17 September, https://www.bpas.org/about-our-charity/press-office/press-releases/bpas-comment-on-calls-to-ban-nipt-gender-test/.

Braidwood, E. (2018) 'LGBTQ campaigners say trans men in Ireland "will be denied abortion access"', *Pink News*, 31 May, https://www.pinknews.co.uk/2018/05/31/transgender-activists-call-for-gender-neutral-language-in-irelands-abortion-law-2/.

Brain, R. (1966) 'Medical issues in abortion law reform', *British Medical Journal*, 1(5489): 727–9.

Braithwaite, P. (2017) 'How UK anti-abortion activists use American tactics to shock and shame women', *OpenDemocracy*, 19 December, https://www.opendemocracy.net/5050/phoebe-braithwaite/uk-anti-abortion-american-tactics-shock-shame.

Brookes, B. (2013) *Abortion in England 1900–1967*, vol 7, Oxon: Routledge.

Brown, W. (1992) 'Finding the man in the state', *Feminist Studies,* 18(1): 7–34.

Cameron, S., Glasier, A., Dewart, H. and Johnstone, A. (2010) 'Women's experiences of the final stage of early medical abortion at home: Results of a pilot survey', *Journal of Family Planning and Reproductive Health Care,* 36(1): 213–16.

Campaign Against Corrie (undated) 'Abortion: Who decides?' CAC poster, Wellcome Archives, reference SA/ALR/H66 box 112, Wellcome Library.

Cannold, L. (2002) 'Understanding and responding to anti-choice woman-centred strategies', *Reproductive Health Matters,* 10(19): 171–9.

Carne, S. (1966) 'The general practitioner' in *Abortion in Britain: Proceedings of a Conference Held by the Family Planning Association at the University of London Union on 22 April 1966,* London: Pitman Medical, pp 75–9.

Catholic Herald (1967) 'A licence to kill', *Catholic Herald,* 3 February.

CEDAW (2018) *Report of the inquiry concerning the United Kingdom of Great Britain and Northern Ireland under article 8 of the Optional Protocol to the Convention on the Elimination of All Forms of Discrimination against Women,* C/OP.8/GBR/1. New York: UN.

Celis, K. (2009) 'Substantive representation of women (and improving it): What it is and should be about?' *Comparative European Politics,* 7(1): 95–113.

Cherry, A. (1995) 'A feminist understanding of sex-selective abortion: Solely a matter of choice?' *Wisconsin Women's Law Journal,* 10(2): 161–223.

Chesler, E. (2007) *Woman of Valor: Margaret Sanger and the Birth Control Movement in America,* New York: Simon and Schuster.

Childs, S. (2000) 'The New Labour women MPs in the 1997 British Parliament: Issues of recruitment and representation', *Women's History Review,* 9(1): 55–73.

Childs, S. (2002) 'Hitting the target: Are Labour women MPs "acting for" women?' *Parliamentary Affairs,* 55(1): 143–53.

Childs, S., Evans, E. and Webb, P. (2013) '"Quicker than a consultation at the hairdressers": Abortion and the Human Fertilisation and Embryology Act 2008', *New Genetics and Society,* 32(2): 119–34.

Clarke, A. (1987) 'Moral reform and the anti-abortion movement', *Sociological Review,* 35(1): 123–49.

Clyne, D.G.W. (1966) 'Correspondence: Abortion law reform', *British Medical Journal,* 4: 1482–3.

Coates, P.W. (2008) *Margaret Sanger and the Origin of the Birth Control Movement, 1910–1930: The Concept of Women's Sexual Autonomy*, New York: Edwin Mellen.

Cole, E.R. (2008) 'Coalitions as a model for intersectionality: From practice to theory', *Sex Roles*, 59(5–6): 443–53.

Collins, P.H. (1990) *Black Feminist Thought: Knowledge, Consciousness and the Politics of Empowerment*, Boston: Unwin Hyman.

Collins, P.H. (2007) 'Shifting the center: Race, class, and feminist theorizing about motherhood' in A. O'Reilly (ed.), *Maternal Theory: Essential Readings*, Ontario: Demeter Press, pp 274–89.

Colthart, G. (2009) 'Abortion law', House of Commons Library, Standard Note SN/SES/4309.

Connell, R.W. (1994) 'The state, gender and sexual politics: Theory and appraisal' in H.L. Radtke and H.J. Stam (eds), *Power/gender: Social relations in theory and practice*, London: Sage, pp 136–73.

Connor, S. (2014) 'The lost girls: Illegal abortion widely used by some UK ethnic groups to avoid daughters "has reduced female population by between 1,500 and 4,700"', *The Independent*, 15 January.

Conrad, P. (1992) 'Medicalisation and social control', *Annual Review of Sociology*, 18: 209–32.

Cooper, S. (2016) *Regulating Women: Policymaking and Practice in the UK*, London; New York: Rowman and Littlefield.

Copelon, R. (1990) 'From privacy to autonomy: The conditions for sexual and reproductive freedom' in M. Gerber Fried (ed.), *From Abortion to Reproductive Freedom: Transforming a Movement*, Boston, MA: South End Press, pp 27–43.

Cowley, P. and Stuart, M. (2010) 'Party rules, OK: Voting in the House of Commons on the Human Fertilisation and Embryology Bill', *Parliamentary Affairs*, 63(1): 173–81.

CQC (2017) *Marie Stopes International Maidstone Centre quality report*, 2 October.

CQC (2018) *Marie Stopes International Maidstone Centre quality report*, 9 October.

Crenshaw, K.W. (1989) 'Demarginalizing the intersection of race and sex: A black feminist critique of antidiscrimination doctrine, feminist theory and antiracist politics', *University of Chicago Legal Forum*, 1: 139–67.

Crenshaw, K.W. (1991) 'Mapping the margins: Intersectionality, identity politics, and violence against women of color', *Stanford Law Review*, 43(6): 1249–99.

Davis, A.Y. (1981) *Women, Race & Class*, New York: Random House.

Daviss, B. (2001) 'Reforming birth and (re)making midwifery in North America' in R. De Vries, S. Wrede, E. van Teijlingen and C. Benoit (eds), *Birth by Design: Pregnancy, Maternity Care and Midwifery in North America and Europe*, New York: Routledge, pp 74–86.

Dean, J. (2010) *Rethinking Contemporary Feminist Politics*, Basingstoke: Palgrave.

Department of Health (2005) *Partial Regulatory Impact Assessment: The Prohibition of Abortion (England & Wales) Bill*, London: HMSO.

Department of Health (2007) *Partial Regulatory Impact Assessment: Termination of Pregnancy Bill*, London: HMSO.

Department of Health (2012) 'Written ministerial statement: Enforcement of the Abortion Act 1967', www.parliament.uk/documents/commons-vote-office/March_2012/23-03-12/7-Health-AbortionAct1967.pdf.

Department of Health (2014) *Birth Ratios in England and Wales: A Report on Gender Ratios at Birth in England and Wales*, London: Williams Lea.

Department of Health (2015) *Assessment of Termination of Pregnancy on Grounds of the Sex of the Foetus – Response to Serious Crime Act 2015*, London: TSO.

Department of Health (2016) *Birth Ratios in Great Britain, 2010–14: A Report on Gender Ratios at Birth in Great Britain*, London: TSO.

Department of Health and Social Care (2018a) 'The Abortion Act 1967 – Approval of a class of place', Government guidance, https://assets.publishing.service.gov.uk/government/uploads/system/uploads/attachment_data/file/768059/Approval_of_home_use_for_the_second_stage_of_early_medical_abortion.pdf.

Department of Health and Social Care (2018b) *Abortion Statistics, England and Wales: 2017*, London: Williams Lea.

Department of Information Services (2008) 'Abortion Bills: Parliamentary information list', House of Commons Library, Standard Note SN/PC/03657.

Dewan, S. (2010) 'Anti-abortion ads split Atlanta', *New York Times*, 5 February.

Donchin, A. (1986) 'The future of mothering: Reproductive technology and feminist theory', *Hypatia*, 1(2): 121–38.

Dubuc, S. and Coleman, D. (2007) 'An increase in the sex ratio of births to India-born mothers in England and Wales: Evidence for sex-selective abortion', *Population and Development Review*, 33(2): 383–400.

Duden, B. (1999) 'The fetus on the "farther shore": Toward a history of the unborn' in L.M. Morgan and M.W. Michaels (eds), *Fetal Subjects, Feminist Positions*, Philadelphia: University of Pennsylvania Press, pp 13–25.

Dudley-Brown, M. (1969) 'The duties of the general practitioner under the Abortion Act' in *The Abortion Act 1967: Proceedings of a Symposium Held by the Medical Protection Society, in Collaboration with the Royal College of General Practitioners, at the Royal College of Obstetricians and Gynaecologists*, London, 7 February 1969, London: Pitman Medical, pp 1–8.

Duerksen, K.N. and Lawson, K.L. (2017) ' "Not brain-washed, but heart-washed": A qualitative analysis of benevolent sexism in the anti-choice stance', *International Journal of Behavioural Medicine*, 24(6): 864–70.

Education for Choice (2011) 'Snapshot of crisis pregnancy centres operating in England', www.efc.org.uk/PDFs/CPC%20report%20 executive%20summary%20EFC%202011.pdf.

Ehrenreich, B. and English, D. (2011 [1973]) *Complaints & Disorders: The Sexual Politics of Sickness*, New York: The Feminist Press.

Elgot, J. (2017) 'Northern Irish women offered free abortion services in England', *The Guardian*, 23 October.

Evans, D. (2006) ' "We do not use the word 'crisis' lightly..." Sexual health policy in the United Kingdom', *Policy Studies* 27(3): 235–52.

Evans, E. (2015) *The Politics of Third Wave Feminisms: Neoliberalism, Intersectionality and the State in Britain and the US*, London: Palgrave.

EVAW (2018) 'Abortion law in need of reform – the negative impact on women', https://www.endviolenceagainstwomen.org.uk/wp-content/uploads/Briefing-from-Women-Organisations-Abortion-Bill.pdf.

Faludi, S. (2006 [1991]) *Backlash: The Undeclared War Against American Women*, New York: Three Rivers.

Ferree, M.M., Gamson, W.A., Gerhards, J. and Rucht, D. (2002) *Shaping Abortion Discourse: Democracy and the Public Sphere in Germany and the United States*, Cambridge: Cambridge University Press.

Ferree, M.M. (2003) 'Resonance and radicalism: Feminist framing in the abortion debates of the United States and Germany', *The American Journal of Sociology*, 109(2): 304–44.

Firestone, S. (1971) *The Dialectic of Sex: The Case for Feminist Revolution*, London: Jonathan Cape.

Flatseth, M. and Madsen, O.J. (2013) 'The mind is a brittle object: The abortion law and therapeutic legitimation', *History of the Human Sciences*, 26(1): 111–27.

Flavins, J. and Paltrow, L.M. (2010) 'Punishing pregnant drug-using women: Defying law, medicine and common sense', *Journal of Addictive Diseases*, 29(2): 231–44.

Foucault, M. (1981) *The History of Sexuality* vol.1, London: Penguin.

Fox, B. and Worts, D. (1999) 'Revisiting the critique of medicalized childbirth: A contribution to the sociology of birth', *Gender & Society*, 13(3): 326–46.

Francome, C. (1984), *Abortion Freedom: A Worldwide Movement*, London: George Allen & Unwin.

Franklin, S. (1991) 'Fetal fascinations: New dimensions to the medical-scientific construction of fetal personhood' in S. Franklin, C. Lury and J. Stacey (eds), *Off-Centre: Feminism and Cultural Studies*, Lancaster: HarperCollins, pp 190–205.

FSRH (2017) 'FSRH position statement on abortion including decriminalisation', 20 March, https://www.fsrh.org/policy-and-media/fsrh-position-statements/fsrh-position-statement-on-abortion/.

Furedi, A. (2008) 'A shocking betrayal of women's rights', *spiked*, 23 October, www.spiked-online.com/newsite/article/5845#.UfoII9LVAo4.

Furedi, A. (2013a) 'You can't be pro-choice only when you like the choice', *spiked*, 16 September, https://www.spiked-online.com/2013/09/16/you-cant-be-pro-choice-only-when-you-like-the-choice/.

Furedi, A. (2013b) 'Remaking the case for a woman's right to choose', *spiked*, 24 April, https://www.spiked-online.com/2013/04/24/remaking-the-case-for-a-womans-right-to-choose/.

Furedi, A. and Hume, M. (eds) (2007 [1997]) *Abortion Law Reformers: Pioneers of Change*, Stratford-upon-Avon: British Pregnancy Advisory Service.

Fyfe, W. (1991) 'Abortion Acts: 1803 to 1967' in S. Franklin, C. Lury and J. Stacey (eds), *Off-Centre: Feminism and Cultural Studies*, Lancaster: HarperCollins, pp 160–74.

Gerber Fried, M. (1990) 'Transforming the reproductive rights movement: The post-*Webster* agenda' in M. Gerber Fried (ed.), *From Abortion to Reproductive Freedom: Transforming a Movement*, Boston, MA: South End Press, pp 1–14.

Gill, R. and Orgad, S. (2015) 'The confidence cult(ure)', *Australian Feminist Studies*, 30(86): 324–44.

Gleeson, K. (2007) 'Persuading parliament: Abortion law reform in the UK', *Australasian Parliamentary Review*, 22(2): 23–42.

Goldbeck-Wood, S., Aiken, A., Horwell, D., Heikenhimo, O. and Acharya, G. (2018) 'Criminalised abortion in UK obstructs reflective choice and best care', *British Medical Journal*, 362.

Gordon, L. (1986) 'Who is frightened of reproductive freedom for women and why? Some historical answers', *Frontiers: A Journal of Women Studies*, 9(1): 22–6.

Greasley, K. (2011) 'Medical abortion and the "golden rule" of statutory interpretation', *Medical Law Review*, 19 Spring 2011: 314–25.

Greenwood, V. and Young, J. (1976) *Abortion in Demand*, London: Pluto Press.

Gupta, R. (2014) 'Pro-choice: All the way to the sex-selection gallows', *Feminist Review*, 107(1): 84–9.

Hadley, J. (1997) *Abortion: Between Freedom and Necessity*, London: Virago.

Halfmann, D. (2011) *Doctors and Demonstrators: How Political Institutions Shape Abortion Law in the United States, Britain, and Canada*, Chicago: University of Chicago Press.

Hansard (1966) HC Deb 22 July 1966 vol 732 cc 1067–165.

Hansard (1967a) SC Deb (F) 1 Feb 1967 vol X cc 108–58.

Hansard (1967b) SC Deb (F) 8 Feb 1967 vol X cc 159–210.

Hansard (1967c) HC Deb 29 June 1967 vol 749 cc 895–1102.

Hansard (1967d) HC Deb 13 July 1967 vol 750 cc 1239–92.

Hansard (1967e) HL Deb 19 July 1967 vol 285 cc 258–355.

Hansard (1967f) HL Deb 26 July 1967 vol 285 cc 981–1103.

Hansard (1969) HC Deb 15 July 1969 vol 787 cc 411–24.

Hansard (1970) HC Deb 13 February 1970 vol 795 cc 1653–703.

Hansard (1975) HC Deb 7 February 1975 vol 885 cc 1757–868.

Hansard (1977) HC Deb 25 February 1977 vol 926 cc 1783–895.

Hansard (1979) HC Deb 13 July 1979 vol 970 cc 891–983.

Hansard (1981) HC Deb 1 July 1981 vol 7 cc 877–82.

Hansard (1982) HL Deb 6 December 1982 vol 437 cc 55–106.

Hansard (1987) HL Deb 28 January 1987 vol 483 cc 1406–51.

Hansard (1988) HC Deb 22 January 1988 vol 125 cc 1228–96.

Hansard (1989a) HC Deb 3 March 1989 vol 148 c 570.

Hansard (1989b) HC Deb 14 December 1989 vol 513 cc 1461–502.

Hansard (1990a) HC Deb 21 June 1990 vol 174 cc 1136–69.

Hansard (1990b) HC Deb 24 April 1990a vol 171 cc 166–304.

Hansard (1991) HC Deb 22 July 1991 vol 195 cc 884–902.

Hansard (1993) HC Deb 23 February 1993 vol 219 cc 769–72.

Hansard (1996a) HC Deb 4 December 1996 vol 286 cc 1041–4.

Hansard (1996b) HC Deb 17 December 1996 vol 287 cc 776–80.

Hansard (2003) HL Written Answers 12 May 2003 vol 648 c 16.

Hansard (2006) HC Deb 21 October 2006 vol 451 cc 155–8.

Hansard (2007) HC Deb 5 June 2007 vol 461 cc 138–42.

Hansard (2008) HC Deb 20 May 2008 vol 476 cc 222–71.

Hansard (2010) HC Deb 2 November 2010 vol 517 cc 896–902.

Hansard (2011a) HC Deb 7 September 2011 vol 532 cc 362–88.
Hansard (2011b) HC Deb 12 December 2011 vol 537 cc 629–36.
Hansard (2012) HC Deb 31 October 2012 vol 552 cc 69–93WH.
Hansard (2013a) HC Deb 16 April 2013 vol 561 cc 169–71.
Hansard (2013b) Westminster Hall Deb 9 October 2013 vol 568 cc 87–111.
Hansard (2014) HC Deb 4 November 2014 vol 587 cc 677–82.
Hansard (2015) HC Deb 23 February 2015 vol 593 cc 113–34.
Hansard (2016) HL Deb 21 October 2016 vol 774 cc 2545–562.
Hansard (2017) HC Deb 13 March 2017 vol 623 cc 26–33.
Hansard (2018a) HC Deb 5 June 2018 vol 642 cc 205–57.
Hansard (2018b) HC Deb 23 October 2018 vol 688 cc 141–9.
Hansard (2018c) HC Deb 24 Oct 2018 vol 648 cc 355–99.
Hansard (2019a) HC Deb 9 July 2019 vol 663 cc 161–282.
Hansard (2019b) HL Deb 15 July 2019 vol 799 cc 95–138.
Haque, A. (2018) 'Labour calls for ban on early foetus sex test', 17 September, https://www.bbc.co.uk/news/health-45497454.
Hart, S. (2016) 'Late, gruesome abortions should be relegated to history – the Royal College of Midwives has a duty to make sure they are', *The Daily Telegraph*, 18 May.
Hartouni, V. (1991) 'Containing women: Reproductive discourse in the 1980s' in C. Penley and A. Ross (eds), *Technoculture*, Minneapolis: University of Minnesota Press, pp 27–56.
Heffer, S. (2018) 'DUP warns of "consequences" over Northern Ireland abortion calls', *Sky News*, 29 May, https://news.sky.com/story/dup-warns-of-consequences-over-northern-ireland-abortion-calls-11389271.
Heinämaa, S. (1997) 'What is a woman? Butler and Beauvoir on the foundations of the sexual difference', *Hypatia,* 21(1): 20–39.
Henebury M. (undated) 'Comment: Thoughts on the "Dorries debate"', *Abortion Rights*, www.abortionrights.org.uk/index.php/media-and-resource-centre/news/139.
Himmelweit, S. (1988) 'More than "a woman's right to choose"?' *Feminist Review*, 29: 38–56.
Hindell, K. and Simms, M. (1968) 'How the abortion lobby worked', *The Political Quarterly*, 39(3): 269–82.
Hindell, K. and Simms, M. (1971) *Abortion Law Reformed*, London: Peter Owen.
Hoggart, L. (undated) 'Feminist principles meet political reality: The case of the National Abortion Campaign', *Pro Choice Forum*, www.prochoiceforum.org.uk/al6.php.

Hoggart, L. (2012) '"I'm pregnant... what am I going to do?" An examination of value judgements and moral frameworks in teenage pregnancy decision making', *Health, Risk & Society*, 14(6): 533–49.

Hohmeyer, A. (1995) 'The National Abortion Campaign: Changing the law and fighting for a real choice' in G. Griffin (ed.), *Feminist Activism in the 1990s*, London; New York: Taylor & Francis, pp 39–45.

Holpuch, A. (2013) 'Planned parenthood moves away from "pro-choice" label amid abortion debate', *The Guardian*, 14 January.

Houghton, V. (2007) 'Interview with Lady Vera Houghton' in Furedi, A. and Hume, M. (eds) *Abortion Law Reformers: Pioneers of Change*, Stratford-upon-Avon: British Pregnancy Advisory Service, pp 29-32.

Howard, S. (2017) 'After 50 years of legal abortion in Great Britain, calls grow for further liberalisation', *British Medical Journal*, 359.

IKWRO (2015) 'Why IKWRO oppose the proposed amendments to the Serious Crime Bill to criminalise sex selective abortion', IKWRO blog, 18 February, http://ikwro.org.uk/2015/02/amendments-criminalise-selective/.

Jackson, S. (2011) 'Reproductive justice in the UK: Part 2', *Bad Reputation* blog, 3 March, https://badreputation.org.uk/2011/03/03/reproductive-justice-in-the-uk-part-2/.

Javid, S. (2018) 'Outcome of the abortion clinic protest review: Written statement – HCWS958', Parliament UK, 13 September, https://www.parliament.uk/business/publications/written-questions-answers-statements/written-statement/Commons/2018-09-13/HCWS958.

Johnson, D. (2019) 'As we celebrate votes on decriminalising abortion in Northern Ireland, it's time for a new Abortion Act for England and Wales too', *The House Magazine*, 18 July, https://www.politicshome.com/news/uk/health-and-care/house/house-magazine/105399/diana-johnson-we-celebrate-votes-decriminalising.

Johnson, J. (1966) 'Correspondence: Abortion on psychiatric grounds', *British Medical Journal*, 2: 646.

Johnstone, R. (2017) *After Morgentaler: The Politics of Abortion in Canada*, Vancouver; Toronto: UBCPress.

Jones, C. (2013) '"Human weeds, not fit to breed?" African Caribbean women and reproductive disparities in Britain', *Critical Public Health*, 23(1): 49–61.

Kalantry, S. (2015) 'Sex-selective abortion bans: Anti-immigration or anti-abortion?', *Georgetown Journal of International Affairs*, 16(1): 140–58.

Kalantry, S. (2017) *Women's Human Rights and Migration: Sex-Selective Abortion Laws in the United States and India*, Philadelphia: University of Pennsylvania Press.

Kallianes, V. and Rubenfeld, P. (1997) 'Disabled women and reproductive rights', *Disability & Society*, 12(2): 203–22.

Kaplan, L. (1997), *The Story of Jane: The Legendary Underground Feminist Abortion Service*, Chicago: University of Chicago Press.

Keown, J. (1988) *Abortion, Doctors and the Law*, Cambridge: Cambridge University Press.

Lane Committee (1974) *Report of the Committee on the Working of the Abortion Act*, London: HMSO.

Lay, K. (2018) 'Let women take abortion pill at home, Hunt told', *The Times*, 27 April.

Leask, M. (2013) 'From bad woman to mad woman: A genealogical analysis of abortion discourses in Aotearoa New Zealand', *New Zealand Sociology*, 28(2): 104–19.

Lee, E. (2003) *Abortion, Motherhood, and Mental Health: Medicalizing Reproduction in the United States and Great Britain*, Hawthorne, NY: Walter de Gruyter.

Lee, E. (2013) 'Whither abortion policy in Britain?', *Journal of Family Planning and Reproductive Health Care*, 39(1): 5–8.

Lee, E. (2017) 'Constructing abortion as a social problem: "Sex-selection" and the British abortion debate', *Feminism & Psychology*, 27(1): 15–33.

Lee, E., Sheldon, S., Macvarish, J. (2018) 'The 1967 Abortion Act fifty years on: Abortion, medical authority and the law revisited', *Social Science & Medicine*, 212: 26–32.

Lentin, R. (2013) 'A woman died: Abortion and the politics of birth in Ireland', *Feminist Review*, 105: 130–6.

Life (2016) 'Royal College of Midwives radical support for abortion up to birth', Life blog, 15 May, https://lifecharity.org.uk/news-and-views/royal-college-midwives-radical-support-abortion-birth/.

Life (2017) 'Life disappointed MPs narrowly vote in favour of motion of abortion for any reason', Life blog, 13 March, https://lifecharity.org.uk/news-and-views/life-disappointed-abortion-bill-continuing-parliament/.

Life (2018a) 'Diana Johnson's extreme abortion bill fails to move ahead', Life press release, 23 November.

Life (2018b) 'Diana Johnson's morally repugnant abortion bill', Life press release, 23 October.

Life (2018c) 'Protect women by rejecting Diana Johnson's Bill', Life press release, 10 October.

Litchfield, M. and Kentish, S. (1974) *Babies for Burning: The Abortion Business in Britain*, London: Serpentine.

Lloyd, L. (1988) 'Fighting Alton', *Spare Rib*, 188: 22–3.

Lohr, P., Wade, J., Riley, L., Fitzgibbon, A. and Furedi, A. (2010) 'Women's opinions on the home management of early medical abortion in the UK', *BMJ Sexual and Reproductive Health*, 36(1): 21–5.

Lonergan, G. (2012) 'Reproductive justice and migrant women in Great Britain', *Women: A Cultural Review*, 23(1): 26–45.

Lonergan, G. (2015) 'Migrant women and social reproduction under austerity', *Feminist Review*, 109(1): 124–45.

Lovenduski, J. (2007), 'Unfinished business: Equality policy and the changing context of state feminism in Great Britain' in J. Outshoorn and J. Kantola (eds), *Changing State Feminism*, Basingstoke: Palgrave Macmillan, pp 144–63.

Lowe, P. (2018) '(Re)imagining the "backstreet": Anti-abortion campaigning against decriminalisation in the UK', *Sociological Research Online*, https://journals.sagepub.com/doi/10.1177/1360780418811973.

Lowe, P. and Hayes, G. (2018) 'Anti-abortion clinic activism, civil inattention and the problem of gendered harassment', *Sociology*, https://journals.sagepub.com/doi/abs/10.1177/0038038518762075.

Ludlow, J. (2008) 'The things we cannot say: Witnessing the traumatization of abortion in the United States', *Women's Studies Quarterly*, 38(1&2) 28–41.

Luker, K. (1984) *Abortion and the Politics of Motherhood*, Berkeley: University of California Press.

Luna, Z. (2009) 'From rights to justice: Women of color changing the face of US reproductive rights organising', *Societies Without Borders*, 4(3): 343–65.

Luna, Z. (2011) '"The phrase of the day": Examining contexts and co-optation of reproductive justice activism in the women's movement' in Anna C. Snyder and Stephanie P. Stobbe (eds), *Critical Aspects of Gender in Conflict Resolution, Peacebuilding, and Social Movements*, Bingley: Emerald Group Publishing, pp 219–46.

Lundquist, C. (2008) 'Being torn: Toward a phenomenology of unwanted pregnancy', *Hypatia*, 23(3): 136–55.

Lupton, D. (1997) 'Foucault and the medicalisation critique' in A. Petersen and R. Bunton (eds), *Foucault, Health and Medicine*, London; New York: Routledge, pp 94–110.

Lupton, D. (2012) '"Precious cargo": Foetal subjects, risk and reproductive citizenship', *Critical Public Health*, 22(3): 329–40.

Lupton, D. (2013) *The Social Worlds of the Unborn*, Basingstoke: Palgrave.

MacGillivray, I. (1965), 'Correspondence: Abortion law reform', *British Medical Journal*, 1: 1433.

MacIntyre, S.J. (1973) 'The medical profession and the 1967 Abortion Act in Britain', *Social Science and Medicine*, 7(2): 121–34.

Mackenzie, C. (1986) 'Simone de Beauvoir: Philosophy and/or the female body' in C. Pateman and E. Gross (eds), *Feminist Challenges: Social and Political Theory*, Boston: Northeastern University Press, pp 144–56.

MacKinnon, C.A. (2005), *Women's Lives, Men's Laws*, Cambridge, MA: Harvard University Press.

MacLeavy, J. (2011) 'A "new politics" of austerity, workfare and gender? The UK coalition government's welfare reform proposals', *Cambridge Journal of Regions, Economy and Society*, 4(3): 355–67.

Mahalingam, R. and Wachman, M. (2012) 'Female feticide and infanticide: Implications for reproductive justice' in J.C. Chrisler (ed.), *Reproductive Justice: A Global Concern*, Santa Barbara, CA: ABC-CLIO, pp 251–68.

Marcotte, A. (2013) 'Planned parenthood wants to abandon the "pro-choice" label', *Slate*, 11 January, https://slate.com/human-interest/2013/01/planned-parenthood-to-move-away-from-pro-choice-label-abortion-rights-will-suffer.html.

Marsh, D. and Chambers, J. (1981) *Abortion Politics*, London: Junction Books.

Mason, R. (2013) 'The abortion of unwanted girls taking place in the UK', *The Daily Telegraph*, 10 January.

McBride Stetson, D. (1996) 'Abortion policy triads and women's rights in Russia, the United States, and France' in M. Githens and D.M. Stetson (eds), *Abortion Politics: Public Policy in Cross-Cultural Perspective*, New York; London: Routledge, pp 97–117.

McBride Stetson, D. (2001a), 'Introduction' in D.M. Stetson (ed.), *Abortion Politics, Women's Movements and the Democratic State: A Comparative Study of State Feminism*, Oxford: Oxford University Press, pp 1–16.

McBride Stetson, D. (2001b) 'Women's movements' defence of legal abortion in Great Britain' in D.M. Stetson (ed.), *Abortion Politics, Women's Movements and the Democratic State: A Comparative Study of State Feminism*, Oxford: Oxford University Press, pp 135–56.

McBride Stetson, D. ed. (2001c) *Abortion Politics, Women's Movements and the Democratic State: A Comparative Study of State Feminism*, Oxford: Oxford University Press.

McCann, C.R. (1994) *Birth Control Politics in the United States, 1916–1945*, New York: Cornell University Press.

McFall v Shimp (1978), 10 Pa. D. & C. 3d 90.

McFerran, F. (2018) 'Progress in Northern Ireland is well overdue', Stonewall blog, 23 October, https://www.stonewall.org.uk/our-work/blog/progress-northern-ireland-well-overdue.

McGrane, F. and Nicholls, J. (1977) 'Tribunal on abortion rights', *Spare Rib*, 56.

McGuinness, S. (2013) 'Law, reproduction, and disability: Fatally "handicapped"?', *Medical Law Review*, 21(2): 213–42.

McGuinness, S. (2015) 'A guerrilla strategy for a pro-life England', *Law, Innovation and Technology*, 7(2): 283–314.

McGuinness, S. and Thomson, M. (2015) 'Medicine and abortion law: Complicating the reforming profession', *Medical Law Review*, 23(2): 177–99.

McNeil, M. (1991) 'Putting the Alton Bill in context' in S. Franklin, C. Lury and J. Stacey (eds), *Off-Centre: Feminism and Cultural Studies*, Lancaster: HarperCollins, pp 149–59.

McRobbie, A. (2000) 'Feminism and the Third Way', *Feminist Review*, 64: 97–112.

McRobbie, A. (2009) *The Aftermath of Feminism: Gender, Culture and Social Change*, LA: Sage.

Michaels, M.W. and Morgan, L.M. (1999) 'Introduction: The fetal imperative' in L.M. Morgan and M.W. Michaels (eds), *Fetal Subjects, Feminist Positions*, Philadelphia: University of Pennsylvania Press, pp 1–9.

Moazam, F. (2004) 'Feminist discourse on sex screening and selective abortion of female foetuses', *Bioethics*, 18(3): 205–20.

Mondon, A. and Winter, A. (2018) 'Whiteness, populism and the racialisation of the working class in the United Kingdom and the United States', *Identities*, advance online access, https://www.tandfonline.com/doi/abs/10.1080/1070289X.2018.1552440.

Moon, D., Thomson, J. and Whiting, S. (2019) 'Lost in the process: The impact of devolution on abortion law in the United Kingdom', *British Journal of Politics and International Relations*, https://journals.sagepub.com/doi/10.1177/1369148119857591.

Morgan, K.P. (1998) 'Contested bodies, contested knowledges: Women, health, and the politics of medicalization' in S. Sherwin (ed.), *The Politics of Women's Health: Exploring Agency and Autonomy*, Philadelphia: Temple University Press, pp 83–121.

Munday, D. (2007) 'Interview with Diane Munday' in Furedi, A. and Hume, M. (eds) *Abortion Law Reformers: Pioneers of Change*, Stratford-upon-Avon: British Pregnancy Advisory Service, pp8-13.

Munk-Olsen, T., Munk Laursen, T., Pedersen, C.B., Lidegaard, Ø. and Mortensen, P.B. (2011) 'Induced first-trimester abortion and risk of mental disorder', *New England Journal of Medicine*, 364: 332–9.

Musial, J. (2014) 'Fetal citizenship in the borderlands: Arizona's house bill 2443 and state logics of racism and orientalism', *Social Identities*, 20(4–5): 262–78.

MWF (1966) 'Abortion law reform: Memorandum prepared by a subcommittee of the Medical Women's Federation', *British Medical Journal*, 2(5528): 1512–14.

Nair, M., Kurinczuk, J.J. and Knight, M. (2014) 'Ethnic variations in severe maternal morbidity in the UK: A case control study', PLOS One, 9(4): e95086.

Newell, C. (2012) 'Abortion investigation: Forgery that was prevented by a manager', *The Daily Telegraph*, 24 February.

Newell, C. and Watt, H. (2012) 'Abortion investigation: Doctors filmed agreeing illegal abortions "no questions asked"', *The Daily Telegraph*, 22 February.

Newman, C. (2012) 'How the agony of my abortion made me see both sides', *The Daily Telegraph*, 2 October.

Norton, P. (2005) *Parliament in British Politics*, Basingstoke: Palgrave.

Nossiff, R. (2007) 'Gendered citizenship: Women, equality, and abortion policy', *New Political Science*, 29(1): 61–76.

O'Connor, J.S., Orloff, A.S. and Shaver, S. (1999) *States, Markets, Families: Gender, Liberalism and Social Policy in Australia, Canada, Great Britain and the United States*, Cambridge: Cambridge University Press.

Oakley, A. (1980) *Women Confined: Towards a Sociology of Childbirth*, Oxford: Martin Robertson.

Oakley, A. (1984) *The Captured Womb: A History of the Medical Care of Pregnant Women*, Oxford: Blackwell.

Oliver, K. (2010) 'Motherhood, sexuality, and pregnant embodiment: Twenty-five years of gestation', *Hypatia*, 25(4): 60–777.

Oomman, N. and Ganatra, B. (2002) 'Sex selection: The systematic elimination of girls', *Reproductive Health Matters*, 10(19): 184–8.

Orr, J. (2017) *Abortion Wars: The Fight for Reproductive Rights*, Bristol: Policy Press.

Parliamentary Inquiry into Abortion on the Grounds of Disability (2013) *Report of the Inquiry into Abortion on the Grounds of Disability*, www.abortionanddisability.org/resources/Abortion-and-Disability-Report-17-7-13.pdf.

Parsons, W. (2002) 'From muddling through to muddling up: Evidence based policy making and the modernisation of British government', *Public Policy*, 17(3): 43–60.

Pateman, C. (1988) *The Sexual Contract*, Stanford, CA: Stanford University Press.

Pells Cocks, D. (1966) 'Correspondence: Abortion law reform', *British Medical Journal,* 1: 539.

Perkins, A. (2018) 'Theresa May enters Northern Ireland abortion debate', *The Guardian*, 8 June.

Petchesky, R.P. (1980) 'Reproductive freedom: Beyond "a woman's right to choose"', *Signs,* 5(4): 661–85.

Petchesky, R.P. (1986) *Abortion and Woman's Choice: The State, Sexuality and Reproductive Freedom*, London: Verso.

Petchesky, R.P. (1987) 'Fetal images: The power of visual culture in the politics of reproduction', *Feminist Studies,* 13(2): 263–92.

Petersen, K.A. (1993) *Abortion Regimes*, Aldershot: Dartmouth Publishing.

Pierson, C. and Bloomer, F. (2017) 'Macro- and micro-political vernaculizations of rights: Human rights and abortion discourses in Northern Ireland', *Health and Human Rights Journal*, 19(1): 173–86.

Pierson, C. and Bloomer, F. (2018) 'Anti-abortion myths in political discourse' in C. MacQuarrie, C. Pierson, S. Strettner and F. Bloomer (eds), *Crossing Troubled Waters: Abortion in Ireland, Northern Ireland, and Prince Edward Island*, Charlottetown: Island Studies Press, pp 184–203.

Press Association (2012) 'Home births cheaper than hospital, study suggests', *The Guardian,* 20 April.

Purdy, L. (2001) 'Medicalization, medical necessity, and feminist medicine', *Bioethics,* 15(3): 248–61.

Purewal, N. and Eklund, L. (2018) '"Gendercide", abortion policy, and the disciplining of prenatal sex-selection in neoliberal Europe', *Global Public Health*, 13(6): 724–41.

Ramaswamy, C. (2018) 'The state has no right to stop me learning the sex of my unborn child', *The Guardian*, 17 September.

Rawlinson, K. (2018) 'Varadkar: Northern Irish women may be able to have abortions in republic', *The Guardian*, 29 May.

RCGP (2019) 'RCGP to support decriminalisation of abortion', Royal College of General Practitioners news, 22 February, https://www.rcgp.org.uk/about-us/news/2019/february/rcgp-to-support-decriminalisation-of-abortion.aspx.

RCN (2018a) 'Decriminalisation of termination of pregnancy: RCN membership response', Royal College of Nursing 007 005.

RCN (2018b) 'Decriminalisation of termination of pregnancy: Position statement (December 2018)', Royal College of Nursing 007 401.

RCOG (1966) 'Legalized abortion: Report by the Council of the Royal College of Obstetricians and Gynaecologists', *British Medical Journal,* 1(5491): 850–4.

RCOG (2008) 'Q&A: Approving abortions', https://www.rcog.org.uk/en/news/campaigns-and-opinions/human-fertilisation-and-embryology-bill/qa-approving-abortions.

RCOG (2017) 'RCOG backs decriminalisation of abortion', RCOG news, 22 September, https://www.rcog.org.uk/en/news/rcog-backs-decriminalisation-of-abortion/.

RCOG and FSRH (2018) 'Submission to the Home Office abortion clinic protest review', https://www.fsrh.org/news/rcog-fsrh-evidence-home-office-review-harassment-abortion-clinic/.

Regan, L. (2018) 'Abortion: View from Westminster', *International Journal of Gynecology & Obstetrics,* 143(2): 133–6.

Rich, A. (1986) *Of Woman Born: Motherhood as Experience and Institution,* London: Virago.

Rickman, D. (2012) 'Abortion: Marie Stopes director asks whether it's time to change the law on terminations', *Huffington Post,* 23 June, www.huffingtonpost.co.uk/2012/05/23/abortion-marie-stopes-director-tracey-mcneill-bbc-5-live-victoria-derbyshire_n_1539079.html.

Right to Life (2018) 'Radical abortion bill fails to pass at second reading', Right to Life press release, 23 November.

Riley, D. (1981) 'Feminist thought and reproductive control: The State and the "right to choose"' in Cambridge Women's Studies Group (eds), *Women in Society: Interdisciplinary Essays,* London: Virago, pp 185–99.

Rimmer, A. and Coombes, R. (2017) 'BMA annual meeting: Doctors who carry out abortions should not face criminal sanctions, says BMA', *British Medical Journal,* 357: j3116.

RMPA (1967 [1966]) 'British policy on therapeutic abortion: Report of the Royal Medico-Psychological Association, June 1966', *Journal of the American Medical Association,* 199(3): 167–8.

Roberts, D. (2017) *Killing the Black Body: Race, Reproduction and the Meaning of Liberty,* 2nd ed., New York: Vintage.

Roberts, S. and Jesudason, S. (2013) 'Movement intersectionality: The case of race, gender, disability and genetic technologies', *Du Bois Review,* 10(2): 313–28.

Robinson, G.E., Stotland, N.L., Russo, N.F., Lang, J.A. and Occhiogrosso, M. (2009) 'Is there an "Abortion Trauma Syndrome"? Critiquing the evidence', *Harvard Review of Psychiatry,* 17(4): 268–90.

Rose, M. (2011) 'Pro-life, pro-woman? Frame extension in the American antiabortion movement', *Journal of Women, Politics & Policy*, 31(1): 1–27.

Rose, N. (1999) *Powers of Freedom: Reframing Political Thought*, Cambridge: Cambridge University Press.

Rowlands, S. and Amy, J. (2018) 'Preserving the reproductive potential of transgender and intersex people', *European Journal of Contraception and Reproductive Health Care*, 23(1): 58–63.

Rudgard, O. (2018) 'Abortion clinic buffer zones set "dangerous precedent" for freedom of speech, campaigners say', *The Daily Telegraph*, 28 May.

Ruhl, L. (1999) 'Liberal governance and prenatal care: Risk and regulation in pregnancy', *Economy and Society*, 28(1): 95–117.

Ruhl, L. (2002) 'Disarticulating liberal subjectivities: Abortion and fetal protection', *Feminist Studies*, 28(1): 37–60.

Salmon, A. (2011) 'Aboriginal mothering, FASD prevention and the contestations of neoliberal citizenship', *Critical Public Health*, 21(2): 165–78.

Sanderson, I. (2003) 'Is "what works" what matters? Evaluation and evidence-based policy-making', *Research Papers in Education* 18(4): 331–45.

Sanger, M. (1920) *Woman and the New Race*, New York: Brentano's.

Sarkaria, M.K. (2009) 'Lessons from Punjab's missing girls: Toward a global feminist perspective on choice in abortion', *California Law Review*, 97(3): 905–42.

Saurette, P. and Gordon, K. (2013) 'Arguing abortion: The new anti-abortion discourse in Canada', *Canadian Journal of Political Science*, 46(1): 157–85.

Science and Technology Committee (2005) *Inquiry into Human Reproductive Technologies and the Law*, London: HMSO.

Science and Technology Committee (2007a) *Government Proposals for the Regulation of Hybrid and Chimera Embryos*, London: HMSO.

Science and Technology Committee (2007b) *Scientific Developments Relating to the Abortion Act 1967*, London: HMSO.

Select Committee on Abortion (1976) *First Report from the Select Committee on Abortion*, London: HMSO.

Shackleton Bailey, J. (1967) 'Correspondence: Abortion Act', *BMJ*, 4: 352.

Shakespeare, T. (1998) 'Choices and rights: Eugenics, genetics and disability equality', *Disability & Society*, 13(5): 665–81.

Sheldon, S. (1997) *Beyond Control: Medical Power and Abortion Law*, London; Ann Arbor, MI: Pluto.

Sheldon, S. (2009) 'A missed opportunity to reform an outdated law', *Clinical Ethics,* 4(3): 3–5.

Sheldon, S. (2012) 'Abortion for reasons of sex: Correcting some basic misunderstandings of the law', *Abortion Review,* 1 March, www.abortionreview.org/index.php/site/article/1143/.

Sheldon, S. (2016a) 'The decriminalisation of abortion: An argument for modernisation', *Oxford Journal of Legal Studies,* 36(2): 334–65.

Sheldon, S. (2016b) 'British abortion law: Speaking from the past to govern the future', *The Modern Law Review,* 79(2): 283–316.

Side, K. (2006) 'Contract, charity, and honorable entitlement: Social citizenship and the 1967 Abortion Act in Northern Ireland after the Good Friday Agreement', *Social Politics,* 1(1): 89–116.

Silliman, J., Gerber Fried, M., Ross, L. and Gutiérrez, E.R. (2004) *Undivided Rights: Women of Color Organize for Reproductive Justice,* Cambridge, MA: South End Press.

Sim, M. (1963) 'Abortion and the psychiatrist', *British Medical Journal,* 2(5454): 145–8.

Simpson, C. (2019) 'Women from north "will be charged €450 for an abortion" at Dublin family planning clinic', *Irish News,* 4 January.

SisterSong (undated) 'What is reproductive justice?' SisterSong website, https://www.sistersong.net/reproductive-justice.

Skinner, D. (2012) 'The politics of medical necessity in American abortion debates', *Politics & Gender* 8(1): 1–24.

Soldenhoff, R. de (1966) 'Correspondence: Abortion law reform', *British Medical Journal,* 1: 1168.

Southall Black Sisters (2015) 'SBS urges a no vote to the amendment on sex selective abortion on the Serious Crime bill', https://www.southallblacksisters.org.uk/news/sbs-urges-no-vote-amendment-sex-selective-abortion-serious-crime-bill.

Spallone, P. (1989) *Beyond Conception: The New Politics of Reproduction,* Basingstoke: Macmillan.

SPUC (2018) *We Care About Women: Why Abortion Should Not Be Decriminalised,* London: Society for the Protection of Unborn Children.

Squier, S. (1996) 'Fetal subjects and maternal objects: Reproductive technology and the new fetal/maternal relation', *The Journal of Medicine and Philosophy,* 21(5): 515–35.

Steel, D. (1971) 'Foreword' in K. Hindell and M. Simms, *Abortion Law Reformed,* London: Peter Owen, pp 7–8.

Steinberg, D. (1991) 'Adversarial politics: The legal construction of abortion' in S. Franklin, C. Lury and J. Stacey (eds), *Off-Centre: Feminism and Cultural Studies*, Lancaster: HarperCollins, pp 175–89.

Studlar, D.T. and Tatalovich, R. (1996) 'Abortion policy in the United States and Canada: Do institutions matter?' in M. Githens and D. McBride Stetson (eds), *Abortion Politics: Public policy in Cross-Cultural Perspective*, New York: Routledge, pp 75–95.

Theobald, G.W. (1966) 'Correspondence: Abortion law reform', *British Medical Journal*, 1: 977–8.

Thomas, T.A. (2012) 'Misappropriating women's history in the law and politics of abortion', *Seattle University Law Review*, 36(1): 1–68.

Thomson, M. (1998) *Reproducing Narrative: Gender, Reproduction and Law*, Aldershot: Ashgate.

Thomson, J. (2016) 'Explaining gender equality difference in a devolved system: The case of abortion law in Northern Ireland', *British Politics*, 11(3): 371–88.

Thomson, J. (2018a) *Abortion Law and Political Institutions: Explaining Policy Resistance*, London: Palgrave.

Thomson, J. (2018b) 'A "United Kingdom?": The 1967 Abortion Act and Northern Ireland' in C. MacQuarrie, C. Pierson, S. Strettner and F. Bloomer (eds), *Crossing Troubled Waters: Abortion in Ireland, Northern Ireland, and Prince Edward Island*, Charlottetown: Island Studies Press, pp 161–83.

Tilley, E., Walmsley, J., Earle, S. and Atkinson, D. (2012) '"The silence is roaring": Sterilization, reproductive rights and women with intellectual disabilities', *Disability & Society*, 27(3): 413–26.

Tooley, P.H. (1969) 'If all abortions are legal, which are desirable?' in *The Abortion Act 1967: Proceedings of a Symposium Held by the Medical Protection Society, in Collaboration with the Royal College of General Practitioners, at the Royal College of Obstetricians and Gynaecologists, London, 7 February 1969*, London: Pitman Medical, pp 8–14.

Tyler, I. (2000) 'Reframing pregnant embodiment' in S. Ahmed, J. Kilby, C. Lury, M. McNeil and B. Skeggs (eds), *Transformations: Thinking Through Feminism*, London: Routledge, pp 288–302.

Vallance, E. (1979) *Women in the House: A Study of Women Members of Parliament*, London: Athlone Press.

Volpp, L. (2000) 'Blaming culture for bad behavior', *Yale Journal of Law and the Humanities*, 12: 89–116.

Wainer, J. (2008) 'Celebrate sisters, the battle is won', *New Matilda*, 25 November, https://newmatilda.com/2008/11/25/celebrate-sisters-battle-won/.

Waterfield, B. (2013) 'Irish abortion law key factor in death of Savita Halappanavar, official report finds', *The Daily Telegraph,* 13 June.

Watt, H., Newell, C. and Khimji, Z. (2012) 'Abortion investigation: Available on demand – an abortion if it's a boy you wanted', *The Daily Telegraph,* 23 February.

We Trust Women (2018) 'About the campaign', https://www.wetrustwomen.org.uk/about-the-campaign/.

West, R. (2009) 'From choice to reproductive justice: De-constitutionalizing abortion rights', *The Yale Law Journal,* 118(7): 1394–432.

Widdows, H. (2009) 'Persons and their parts: New reproductive technologies and risks of commodification', *Health Care Analysis,* 17(1): 36–46.

Wintour, P. (2008) 'NHS review to push for more nurse-led care', *The Guardian,* 27 June.

Wise, J. (2016) 'Reform UK abortion law, say health organisations', *British Medical Journal* 355: i6841.

Woolf, R. (1966) 'Changes' in *Abortion in Britain: Proceedings of a Conference Held by the Family Planning Association at the University of London Union on 22 April 1966,* London: Pitman Medical, pp 70–2.

Yeatman, A. (1997) 'Feminism and power' in M.L. Shanley and V. Narayan (eds), *Reconstructing Political Theory: Feminist Perspectives,* Cambridge: Polity, pp 144–57.

Young, I.M. (1984) 'Pregnant embodiment: Subjectivity and alienation', *Journal of Medicine and Philosophy,* 9(1): 45–62.

Yuval-Davis, N. (1997) *Gender and Nation,* London: Sage.

Zerilli, L. (1992) 'A process without a subject: Simone de Beauvoir and Julia Kristeva on maternity', *Signs,* 18(1): 11–135.

Zerilli, L. (2005) '"We feel our freedom": Imagination and judgment in the thought of Hannah Arendt', *Political Theory,* 33(2): 158–88.

Zola, I.K. (1972) 'Medicine as an institution of social control', *The Sociological Review,* 20(4): 487–504.

Index

Note: page numbers in *italic* type refer to tables.

A

Abbott, Diane 138, 140, 141, 168
Abortion Act (1967)
   challenges to 5–6, 67–8, 70, 93–4, 182
    see also anti-abortion position
   defence of 70–5, 102–3, 143, 175
    by pro-choice position 6, 68, 75–82, 93, 120, 178
   historical context 26–8
   and inequality 34–5
   and medicalization 29, 31–3, 58, 60, 64–5
   Northern Ireland excluded 40, 98, 138
   notification requirement 43, 44–5, 49, 60–1
   passage of 39–41, *51–2*, 63–5
    gendered discourses 58–60, 62
    medical opinion 44–9, 54
    origins 41–4
    social role of doctor 50–8
   paternalistic ideology of 5, 6, 36–7, 58, 62, 64, 184–5
   provisions 2
   social purpose of 177
abortion bills (1969–80) 71
   1969 St John-Stevas Bill 68–9, *71*
   1969–70 Irvine Bill *71*, 83–4
   1974–5 White Bill *71*, 84–6, 92–3
   1976–7 Benyon Bill *71*, 86–8
   1979–80 Corrie Bill *71*, 76–7, 88–9, 94
abortion bills (1981–89) 96–7
   1981 Richardson Bill *96*, 99–100
   1982 Robertson Bill *96*, 100–2
abortion bills (1990s) 97, 118–19
abortion bills (2005–12) 124
   2006/7 Dorries Bills (2006) *124*, 125–9
   2007 Winterton Bill *124*, 125–9
   2008 HFE Bill *124*, 129–38
   Department of Health impact assessments 128–9
abortion bills (2013–19) 146

2013/2014 Bruce Bills *146*, 166, 168
2015 Serious crime Bill *146*, 166–7, 168, 170
2016/2017 Johnson Bills *146*, 153, 154, 155, 159, 160
2016/2017 Shinkwin Bills *146*, 171–3
2018/2019 Northern Ireland Acts *146*, 154–5, 162–4
abortion clinics
   buffer zones 152–3
   CQC inspection of 124, 139
   see also charitable providers; private (for profit) providers
abortion debates
   changing context of 147–53
   overview 3–4, 27–8
abortion on demand/request 62–3, 74–5, 88, 100, 119, 177–8
abortion law
   current context 5–8
   global context 177–8, 180–1
   history of 25–8, 41
   legislative process 8–9, 33
Abortion Law Reform Association (ALRA) 25, 41, 42, 55
abortion pills *see* home abortions; mifepristone; misoprostol
abortion providers *see* charitable providers; illegal abortion/abortionists; medical profession/doctors; private (for profit) providers
Abortion Rights (organization) 189
abusive relationships 157–8, 159, 168
'acceptable' abortion discourse 75–7, 107–10, 137, 161, 178
access to abortion 4, 5, 123, 131–2
   impact of decriminalization on 180–1
   impact of devolution on 150–2
   'two-doctor' rule 4, 7, 43, 131–2, 142–3, 149
   and women's status 20–5

alliances *see* coalitions
Alton, David 114, 115
Alton Bill (1988) 27, 96, 110, 114
Amess Bill (1989) 96
Amess Bill (1993) 118
Amess Bill (1996) 97, 119
Ancram, Michael 89
antenatal care 31
anti-abortion position
 1969–80 amendment attempts 5–6, 67–8, 71, 93–4, 182
  1969 St John-Stevas Bill 68–9, 71
  1969–70 Irvine Bill 71, 83–4
  1974–5 White Bill 71, 84–6, 92–3
  1976–7 Benyon Bill 71, 86–8
  1979–80 Corrie Bill 71, 88–9, 94
 1980s discourse 100–2, 110–15, 120–1
 1990s discourse 115–19
 2000s discourse 124–7, 129, 132–5, 138–41
 appropriation of feminist discourse 86, 101–2, 114, 120, 126–7, 134, 139–40, 167, 182–3
 defence of 1967 Act 175
 overview 182–4
 portrayals of doctors *see* medical profession/doctors
 portrayals of women 58, 69, 70, 82–9, 93–4
  see also female vice; female vulnerability
 recent debates 147
  decriminalization 158–60, 161, 175
  disability 171–3
  sex-selection 164–8
 on risks of abortion 110, 126, 132, 134, 158, 182–3
anti-abortion protests 152–3
anti-feminist backlash 95–7, 102, 105–6, 114–15, 120–1, 127, 182
Australia 180–1

B

Babies for Burning (Kentish and Litchfield) 67, 85
backlash *see* anti-feminist backlash
backstreet abortions *see* illegal abortion/abortionists
Baird, Barbara 181
Baird, Dugald 45
Barrington, Patrick (Viscount) 56–7
Bennett Bill (1989) 96
Benyon Bill (1976–7) 71, 86–8
biopolitics 31–2
Bishop of Birmingham Bill (1986–7) 96
black feminist theory 18–19
BMA *see* British Medical Association

BMJ *see* British Medical Journal
Bordo, Susan 16–17, 18
Bourne case (1938) 25–6
BPAS *see* British Pregnancy Advisory Service
Brain, R. 48–9
Braine, Bernard 53, 55, 87, 89
Braine Bill (1978) 171
Braine Bill (1989) 96
Braine Bill (1995) 97, 118
Brentford Bill (1996) 97, 118
Brexit 161–2
British Medical Association (BMA) 7, 44, 148, 150
British Medical Journal (BMJ) 48–9, 62, 148–9
British Pregnancy Advisory Service (BPAS)
 buffer zones 152
 coalitions 169–70, 171, 188, 189
 disability debate 173
 home abortion 28
 NIPT 186
 sex-selection debate 2, 165, 169–71
 We Trust Women campaign 148, 155–7
Brown, Wendy 185
Browne, Stella 22–3
Bruce, Fiona 163, 165, 166
Bruce Bill (2013) 146, 166, 168
Bruce Bill (2014) 146, 166, 168
Bruinvels Bill (1987) 96
buffer zones 152–3

C

Campaign Against Corrie 76–7
Canada 180
Carder, Angela 17
Care Quality Commission (CQC) 124, 139
Carne, Stuart 46
charitable providers 1–2, 5, 85, 139, 165, 181
 see also British Pregnancy Advisory Service
choice, and reproductive justice 35, 184–8
Chorley, Robert (Lord) 57
coalitions 75–7, 165, 170–1, 188–9, 190–1
Colquhoun, Maureen 79, 81
Committee on the Elimination of all forms of Discrimination Against Women (CEDAW) 154, 155, 163
conscientious objection 85–6, 87, 110
contraception 24, 128, 136
'cooling off' period 125, 127
Copelon, Rhonda 186
Cormack, Patrick 115

Corrie Bill (1979–80) 71, 76–7, 88–9, 94
counselling 3, 28, 125, 127, 137, 138, 139–40
CQC (Care Quality Commission) 124, 139
Creasy, Stella 151, 154–5, 161, 162
Crenshaw, Kimberlé 18, 190–1
Cronin, John 72
Curtis-Thomas, Claire 134

D

Daily Telegraph 1–2, 138, 164, 165
Davis, Angela 24
de Beauvoir, Simone 14–16, 21
decriminalization 153–5
  campaigning against 158–60
  campaigning for 155–8
  international examples 180–1
  medical profession opposition to 149–50
  medical profession support for 7, 148–9
  in Northern Ireland 3–4, 28, 153–5, 161–3
  parliamentary debates 160–4
  shift towards 4, 7, 173–5, 180–1, 185
  and time limits 190
Deedes, Bill 54, 55
delinquency 59
Department of Health 128–9
  see also notification
devolution 150–2, 161–3
dilation and extraction (D&X) 118–19
disability/foetal abnormality
  in abortion bills 41, 42, 44
  in debates 3, 102–3, 111, 137, 171–3, 190
  in Science and Technology Committee report 131
doctors *see* medical profession/doctors
Dorries, Nadine 125, 132–3, 134, 138, 139–40, 167
Dorries Bill (2006) 124, 125–6
Dorries Bill (2007) 124, 125, 128–9
Draeger, Eleanor 149
Dunwoody, John 59

E

early abortion, statistical argument for 62, 85, 88, 100
early medical abortion 28, 116–18, 123–4, 142, 147, 150–1
Ehrenreich, Barbara 30–1
End Violence Against Women (EVAW) 157–8
England, home abortions in 151
English, Deirdre 30–1
Ennals, David 73
ethnicity *see* race and ethnicity

eugenics 24, 42, 94, 172
EVAW (End Violence Against Women) 157–8

F

Faculty of Sexual and Reproductive Healthcare (FSRH) 148
Faludi, Susan 95, 97
Family Planning Association conference (1966) 45–6
fathers' rights 89
female vice 90, 91, 92–3, 111–12, 119, 133–4, 182
female virtue/faultlessness 90–1
  in anti-abortion discourse 111–12
  in decriminalization debate 160
  in disability debate 173
  in pro-choice discourse 108–9, 120, 127–8, 160, 178, 179
female vulnerability
  in anti-abortion discourse 69, 83–4, 87–8, 110–11, 126, 139–40, 158, 167, 182
  in decriminalization discourse 157–8, 160
  in discourse of 1967 Act 58–60
  in evidence-based policy-making 128–9
  of foetal subject 113, 164, 167
  and medicalization 32, 149
  in pro-choice discourse 93, 102, 107–8, 120, 136–7, 141–2, 178, 184–5
  in sex-selection debate 167, 186
  see also paternalism/protection discourse
feminism
  backlash against 95–7, 102, 105–6, 114–15, 120–1, 127, 182
  deradicalization of 75–7
  disarticulation of 167–8
  resurgent 174
  see also pro-choice position
feminist analyses 9
  of abortion 20–4
  of medicalization 30–3
  of pregnancy and motherhood 14–20, 36
feminist demands/objectives 33–4, 77–80, 103–6, 128, 140–1
feminist discourse
  anti-abortion appropriation of 86, 101–2, 114, 120, 126–7, 134, 139–40, 167, 182–3
  in 'We Trust Women' campaign 156
Field, Frank 138, 139
Firestone, Shulamith 15
foetal abnormality *see* disability/foetal abnormality

foetal subject
  in anti-abortion discourse 101, 112–14, 119, 133, 164, 167
  as female 113, 164, 167
  in feminist analyses 17–18, 19
  in Science and Technology Committee Report 131
foetal viability 25, 107, 130–1, 132, 135
  see also time limits for abortion
foreign women 91–3
Foucault, Michel 31
FSRH (Faculty of Sexual and Reproductive Healthcare) 148
funding, for Northern Irish women 150, 151
Furedi, Ann 2, 186–8
Fyfe, Wendy 28–9

G

gender-selective abortion *see* sex-selective abortion
Gordon, Kelly 182–3
Gordon, Linda 22
Gordon, Mildred 105
Gorman, Teresa 107
governmentality 8
Green, Kate 136, 142
Grylls Bill (1974) 171
Gupta, Rahila 186
Guthrie, Kate 153

H

Hadley, Janet 120
Halappanavar, Savita 142, 153
Hargreaves Bill (1989) 96
Hashmat, Shaheen 169–70, 175
health
  abortion as risk to mothers' 110–11, 126, 131, 132, 134, 158, 182–3
  conceptualizations of 45–6, 53–4, 56, 57, 64, 181
  continued pregnancy as risk to 41, 43, 58–9, 73, 74
  as grounds for abortion 25–6, 41, 43
Health and Social Care Bill (2011) 124
healthcare, abortion framed as 180, 181
Heinämaa, Sara 16
Himmelweit, Susan 186
Hobson, John 54
Hoggart, Leslie 75–7
home abortions 28, 117, 123–4, 131, 132–3, 142, 147, 150–1
Houghton, Arthur 72
Houghton Bill (1989) 97
Human Fertilisation and Embryology (HFE) Act (1990) 27, 34, 97–8
Human Fertilisation and Embryology (HFE) Bill (1990) 97, 104, 106

Human Fertilisation and Embryology (HFE) Bill (2008) 124, 129–30
  anti-abortion arguments 132–5
  Northern Ireland 137–8
  pro-choice arguments 135–7
  Science and Technology Committee report 130–2
human rights law 154, 155, 162–3
Hunt Bill (1971) 171

I

Iddon, Brian 132
illegal abortion/abortionists 26, 53, 59–60, 73, 82, 102
Independent 164–5
inequalities
  and 1967 Act 34–5
  intersecting *see* intersectionality
Infant Life (Preservation) Act (1929) 25, 29, 98
informed consent 126–7
intersectionality 7–8, 18–19, 34–5, 186, 188–91
Ireland *see* Northern Ireland; Republic of Ireland
irresponsible doctors (in anti-abortion discourse) 110, 118–19, 133
  amendments to tackle 68–9, 83–4, 85–6, 100
  responsible doctors and 6, 83–4, 85–6, 126, 134–5, 158–9, 175, 182
  sex selection debate 138–9, 164, 166, 167
Irvine, Bryant Godman 83–4, 183
Irvine Bill (1969–70) 71, 83–4

J

Jackson, Sarah 189
Javid, Sajid 153
Jeena International 165–6
Jeger, Lena 78, 80, 81
Johnson, Diana 7, 153, 154, 173–5
Johnson Bill (2016) 146, 153
Johnson Bill (2017) 146, 154, 155, 159, 160
Johnstone, Rachael 180

K

Kentish, Susan 67, 85
Keown, John 39, 61
Knight, Jill 56, 100, 111
knowledge 126–7, 134

L

labour force participation 22, 26
labour movement 76, 78–9

INDEX

Lane Committee (1971–74) 70, 73–5, 91, 92
late abortions
  anti-abortion discourse of 110, 113, 133–4
  and disability 102–3, 137
  and morality 108–9
  political context of 95
  Science and Technology Committee report 131
legislative process 8–9, 33
Leigh Bill (1987) 96
LGBTQ activists 10
liberal legal tradition 16–18
life of mother
  as grounds for abortion 25–6, 41, 43
  see also health
Life (organization) 158–9
Litchfield, Michael 67, 85
Lockwood, Betty (Baroness) 108–9
London-Irish Abortion Rights Campaign 151
Lowe, Pam 159
Ludlow, Jeannie 77
Luker, Kristin 21–2
Luna, Zakiya 186

M

McBride Stetson, Dorothy 33–4
McCafferty, Christine 127–8, 136
McGinn, Connor 154–5
McGuinness, Sheelagh 172, 190
Mackenzie, Catriona 15
MacKinnon, Catharine 20
McLaren, Hugh 48
McRobbie, Angela 167
Mactaggart, Fiona 170
Mahon, Alice 103, 104, 106, 109–10
Mahon, Peter 54
Malhotra, Seema 140–1
Mallaber, Judy 136, 137
media articles 1–2, 67, 92, 138, 164–5
medical profession/doctors
  in anti-abortion discourse
    as irresponsible *see* irresponsible doctors
    qualification categorization 68, 70, 72, 74, 83, 85, 87
    responsible/irresponsible split 6, 83–4, 85–6, 126, 134–5, 158–9, 175, 182
  control of reproduction by 6, 28–33
  'joint interests' argument 80, 107, 116–17, 141, 156, 178
  medical purist opinion 47–9
  opinion after 1967 Act 62–3
  opinion before 1967 Act 44–9, 54
  opposition to decriminalization 149–50
  social role of 5, 50–8, 62–4
  and state *see* state–medical profession relationship
  support for decriminalization 7, 148–9
  support for law reform 7, 34, 44–6, 132, 141, 147–9, 174
  'two doctor' rule 4, 7, 43, 131–2, 142–3, 149
  see also charitable providers; private (for profit) providers
medical purity 47–9, 132
Medical Termination of Pregnancy Bill *see* Steel Bill
Medical Women's Federation (MWF) 45
medicalization 27, 28–33
  and 1967 Act 29, 31–3, 58, 60, 64–5
  challenges to 68–9, 70, 116–17, 120, 131–2
  complicating factors 33–6
  and defence of 1967 Act 74–5, 81–2, 120
  pro-choice reinforcement of 81–2, 98, 99, 107, 120, 135–6, 141, 178–9
  professional support for 44, 45
men's behaviour 114, 115
mental health
  abortion as risk to 110, 126, 131, 134, 158, 182–3
  'post-abortion syndrome' 110, 126
  unwanted pregnancy as risk to 47–8, 58–9, 73, 74
mifepristone (RU486) 116–18, 123
migrants 1, 2, 164, 190
Milton, Anne 138
misoprostol 123
Moffatt, Laura 127, 128
moral arguments 68–9, 95
Morgan, Julie 136
motherhood
  and 1967 Act 58–9
  in disability debates 103
  feminist analyses of 14–20, 36
Murphy, Clare 186
Musial, Jennifer 184
MWF (Medical Women's Federation) 45

N

nation 90, 91–3, 184
National Abortion Campaign (NAC) 76–7
National Health Service Act (Amendment) Bill (1981) 99–100
New Right ideology 97, 105
News of the World 67
Nicholson, Emma 106, 107
non-invasive prenatal testing (NIPT) 185–6

non-resident women 91–3
Northern Ireland
  and decriminalization debate 3–4, 28, 153–5, 161–3, 174
  excluded from Abortion Act (1967) 40, 98, 138
  funding for women from 150, 151
  and HFE Bill (2008) debate 137–8
Northern Ireland Act (1998) 137–8
Northern Ireland Assembly 151–2, 162
Northern Ireland (Executive Formation and Exercise of Functions) Bill (2018) 146, 154–5
Northern Ireland (Executive Formation and Exercise of Functions) Bill (2019) 146, 155, 162–4
Northern Ireland Human Rights Commission 154
'Not in Our Name'/'Not in My Name' campaigns 149–50
notification 43, 44–5, 49, 60–1

O

Oakley, Ann 31
Offences Against the Person Act (1837) 25
Offences Against the Person Act (OAPA) (1861) 25, 137
  repeal of 148, 153, 154, 155–6, 160–2
Owen, David 53–4, 58–9

P

Paintin, David 40
Parliament 8–9, 33
paternalism/protection discourse 5, 6, 36–7, 58, 62, 64, 75, 84, 184–5, 186
patients, women as 64, 81, 107, 120, 136, 178
Peacock Bill (1996) 97, 118–19
Penning, Mike 134–5
Petchesky, Rosalind 24, 26, 112–13
Petersen, Kerry 29
Physicians for Reproductive Choice and Health (PRCH) 187
Planned Parenthood Federation of America 187
Platt, Robert (Lord) 57
'post-abortion syndrome' 110, 126
pregnancy
  feminist analyses of 14–20, 36
  as risk to health 41, 43, 58–9, 73, 74
Primarolo, Dawn 104, 107, 135
Pritchard, Mark 133
private (for profit) providers
  anti-abortion discourse of 6, 140, 158–9, 182
  amendments to tackle 68–9, 83–4, 85–6, 88
  sex-selection debate 1–2, 164, 165
pro-choice position
  1980s discourse 98–100, 102–10
  1990s discourse 116–17, 119–20
  2000s discourse 127–8, 130, 135–7, 140–3
  'acceptable' abortion discourse 75–7, 107–10, 137, 161, 178
  choice and reproductive justice 184–8
  coalitions 75–7, 170, 188–91
  critique of 1967 Act 106
  defence of 1967 Act 6, 68, 75–82, 93, 120, 178
  deradicalization of 75–7
  feminist demands 33–4, 77–80, 103–6, 128, 140–1
  'joint interests' discourse 80, 107, 116–17, 141, 156, 178
  medical framework in 81–2, 98, 99, 107, 120, 135–6, 141, 178–9
  overview 178–80
  recent debates 145–7
    decriminalization 155–8, 160–1
    disability 171–3
    sex-selection 168–71
  recent progress of 173–5, 180
  and status of women 21–2
  virtue/faultlessness discourse 108–9, 120, 127–8, 160, 178, 179
  vulnerability discourse 93, 102, 107–8, 120, 136–7, 141–2, 178, 184–5
  women's rights eclipsed in 81, 99, 107, 109, 120, 135–6, 161, 178–9
pro-life activists 21–2
psychiatric discourses 47–8, 58–9
  see also mental health
Pugh, John 133–4

R

race and ethnicity
  absent from 1967 debates 94
  in feminist analyses 18–19
  and reproductive justice 7–8, 24, 34–5, 185–6, 190
  in sex-selection debates 1, 2–3, 164–71, 184
rape 25, 41–2, 43, 44, 161
RCGP (Royal College of General Practitioners) 148
RCN (Royal College of Nursing) 148, 150
RCOG *see* Royal College of Obstetricians and Gynaecologists
Regan, Lesley 173, 174

INDEX

'Repeal of the Eighth' campaign 153
reproductive justice 7–8, 34–6, 184–91
reproductive rights 22–4
  see also women's rights
Republic of Ireland 153
Rich, Adrienne 16, 18
Richardson, Jo 108, 117
Richardson Bill (1981) 96, 99–100
'right to life' terminology 5
rights *see* women's rights
RMPA (Royal Medico-Psychological Association) 44, 45
Roberts, Dorothy 19, 23–4
Robertson Bill (1982) 96, 100–2
Robertson Bill (2005) 124, 125, 128–9
Roe v Wade (US) 26
Rose, Nikolas 8
Royal College of General Practitioners (RCGP) 148
Royal College of Midwives 148, 149–50
Royal College of Nursing (RCN) 148, 150
Royal College of Obstetricians and Gynaecologists (RCOG) 7, 47, 148, 173, 174
Royal Medico-Psychological Association (RMPA) 44, 45
RU486 (mifepristone) 116–18, 123
Rudd, Amber 152–3
Ruhl, Lealle 17

S

St John-Stevas, Norman 84
St John-Stevas Bill (1969) 68–9, 71
Sanger, Margaret 20, 24
Saurette, Paul 182–3
Scanlan, Anne 158–9
Science and Technology Committee report (2007) 130–2
Scotland 150, 151
Serious Crime Bill (2015) 146, 166–7, 168, 170
sex education 128, 136
sex-selective abortion 1–3, 28, 175, 184
  and foetal subjectivity 113
  media articles 1–2, 138, 164–5
  and NIPT 185–6
  'Stop Gendercide' campaign 1, 2, 165–71, 173
Shah, Naz 185, 186
Sheldon, Sally 31–2, 115–16, 117
Shinkwin Bill (2016) 146, 171–3
Shinkwin Bill (2017) 146, 173
Short, Clare 105, 109
Short, Renée 59, 78, 80, 84
Shuker, Gavin 140

The Silent Scream (film) 112, 113
Silkin, Lewis (Lord) 56
Silkin Bill (1965–6) 39–40, 41–2, 51
Sim, Myre 48
Skinner, Daniel 179
social class 23, 26, 59–60, 65, 79
social clause 39–40
  in Silkin Bill 41, 42–3, *51*
  in Steel Bill 44, 50, 52–3, 56
social grounds for abortion
  medical opinion on 44, 45–6, 48–9, 54, 63
  and passage of 1967 Act 50–8
social problems
  abortion law as solution to 4, 177
  and defence of 1967 Act 72–3, 74
social role of doctor 5, 50–8, 62–4
Society for the Protection of Unborn Children (SPUC) 132, 150, 158, 159, 160
Soubry, Anna 139, 161
Spink, Bob 132–3
state–medical profession relationship
  in anti-abortion amendments 88–9
  and defence of 1967 Act 70, 72, 74
  doctors wary of 44, 47, 48–9, 60–1
statistical argument 62, 85, 88, 100
Steel, David 43, 50, 60
Steel Bill (1966) 43–4, 50–8, 90–1
  see also Abortion Act (1967)
Steinberg, Deborah 110, 137, 172
sterilization 24
'Stop Gendercide' campaign 1, 2, 165–71, 173
Stopes, M. 24
subjectivity
  of foetus *see* foetal subject
  of women 15–18, 19, 21

T

technological advances 95, 112, 125, 133
thalidomide tragedy 42
Thornberry, Emily 168
time limits for abortion
  amendment attempts 70, 98, 129
  in anti-abortion discourse 70, 110, 129
  and decriminalization 155, 158
  disability and 171–3, 190
  in Infant Life (Preservation) Act 25
  Lane Committee on 74
  lowered to 24 weeks 98
  Science and Technology Committee report 130–1, 132
Tonge, Jenny (Baroness) 172–3
trade union activists 76
transgender people 10, 23, 24

trauma narratives
  anti-abortion 86, 93, 139, 161
  pro-choice 73, 77, 81–2, 102, 161, 178, 184–5
Turner, Des 132
'two-doctor' rule 4, 7, 43, 131–2, 142–3, 149

U

UN Committee on the Elimination of all forms of Discrimination Against Women (CEDAW) 154, 155, 163
United States 97, 112, 113, 179, 183–4, 188

V

Vallance, Elizabeth 78
Vickers, Joan 60
violence against women 165–8, 169
vulnerability *see* female vulnerability

W

Wales 150, 151
'We Care About Women' campaign 158
'We Trust Women' campaign 148, 155–7
Wells, William 54, 55
'We're All Equal' campaign 173
White Bill (1974–5) 71, 84–6, 92–3
Widdecombe, Ann 111
Widdecombe Bills (1989) 96
Williams, Glanville 41
Winterbourne Bill (2017) 146
Winterton Bill (1987) 96
Winterton Bill (2007) 124, 125–9
Wise, Audrey 104
women
  in anti-abortion discourse *see* anti-abortion position
  constructed in 1967 Act 40, 53, 58–60, 62, 65
  constructed as competent 127, 137
  constructed as incapable 32–3, 75
  constructed as patients 64, 81, 107, 120, 136, 178
  constructions in defence of 1967 Act 74–5, 102–3
  'joint interests' with doctors 80, 107, 116–17, 141, 156, 178
  and 'maternal instinct' 47–8
  medical control of 6, 28–33
  medicalization and constructions of 32–3
  paternalistic approach to *see* paternalism/protection discourse
  see also female vice; female virtue/faultlessness; female vulnerability
women MPs
  feminist demands/objectives 33–4, 77–80, 103–6, 128, 140–1
  position in Parliament 104, 109, 123, 173–4
Women on Web 147
women's rights
  centred in pro-choice arguments 136
  demands of women MPs 77–80, 103–6, 140–1
  discourse appropriated *see* anti-abortion position
  eclipsed in pro-choice arguments 81, 99, 107, 109, 120, 135–6, 161, 178–9
  reproductive rights 22–4
  in sex-selection discourse 166, 169
  'We Trust Women' campaign 155–6
women's status
  significance of abortion for 20–5, 36
  in social/legal tradition 16–20
Woolf, Rowena 46

Y

Young, Iris Marion 18

Z

Zerilli, Linda 16
Zola, I.L. 30

www.ingramcontent.com/pod-product-compliance
Lightning Source LLC
Chambersburg PA
CBHW070923030426
42336CB00014BA/2513